The New American Dream

Finding Lifestyle Freedom
on the Road

Stories & Secrets From
Those Who Live It

K Shawtree

HOW TO FIND WHAT YOU ARE LOOKING FOR

A "THANK YOU" TO OTHERS

Living on the road full-time and not working a formal job means that funds can be tight. In anticipation of the expenses involved in writing and publishing this book, I ran a Kickstarter campaign to raise a portion of the funds, at least to offset the expenditures. I received significant support in the form of pledges, as well as kind words. I'd like to take a moment to recognize some of these behind-the-scenes Kickstarter contributors: Karen Selsor and Michael McCrae, Jennifer Brown and Mary Chapman, Sue, Jennifer Dinh, and Michelle Allison and family.

In addition, there are no words to express my gratitude and love for my wife. If it wasn't for her, these travels would be so boring, and my book, without a line editor. Additionally, I'd like to recognize my mother, who was a financial contributor as well as a copy editor, and who has always encouraged me, in every crazy thing I do.

Finally, I'd like to thank all of the Road Travelers who took time out of their adventures to share their stories, secrets, strategies, and wisdom. Without you, this book would have been just another recounting from one traveler, and not the multi-dimensional tale that it is now.

To all these people, I'd like to say "thank you," for it is with your support that this book has become a reality.

A WORD TO YOU

My wife and I have always loved travel and would fantasize about setting out in an RV. We would dream about the places we would go....someday. At the time, though, I was focused on my career, making money, buying the latest and greatest products, and pursuing "things" rather than "experiences." Then a neighbor our age died suddenly, and a younger friend got a catastrophic illness. These two tragedies made us re-examine our priorities. Chasing the traditional American Dream was becoming less and less meaningful, and we made the decision to live our dreams now.

I wrote this book with the hope of helping *you* get out of your chair and on with your dream. If your desire is to travel on the road, full-time, for pleasure and life, then you need this book. Within its pages are answers to the fears that are limiting you. It is my hope that you will find inspiration, secrets, tips, strategies, suggestions, and insights. The people offering their stories range in age from 24 to 70+ and live on the road *full-time*. People of all generations are living this life; therefore I know you can too!

Let me first define "full-time," because I learned while researching the topic that people have different understandings of that term. I use "full-time" to refer to people who are living in a recreational vehicle of some sort for 365 consecutive days or more. Some have only been at it for six months, but their *intention* is to do it for at least one year. I also specify that my stories are from "full-time *travelers*." I am using this phrase to differentiate from the person who lives in an RV full time, but who doesn't move their RV out of its parked spot. While these stationary RVers have chosen a unique lifestyle as well, they are not the focus of this book.

I must also explain the unusual names used in this book. I came in contact with many of these travelers by following them on Instagram. I have chosen to use their Instagram names, when it applies. If I was introduced to them some other way, then I've opted to use whatever name they have requested.

As you will learn, travelers come in many forms: those who move daily or almost daily (see **HotSauceHippo** and the **TheAmericanFieldTrip**), those who move once every four to seven days (see **TravelExploreUncover** and **LivingLifeInBetween**) or those who move only once or twice a month — or even less (see **RVWanderlust**, **Jeff and Coffee** and **Jax733**). Some live in vans or small RVs (see the **Vagabroads**, **Wandrly**, **HotSauceHippo**, and **HappyCamperWives**) and others live in large "Class As" (see **Michael and Brenda** and **Steve K**) — and everything in between. What's interesting to me, though, is that despite the differences, these traveling RVers have very similar goals (freedom, seeing the U.S.'s wonders, escaping the grind, enjoying constant newness, etc.). Even the ones that work full-time on the road (see **Heath and Alyssa**, **LivingLifeInBetween** and **WanderlandTravelers**) have the objective of a freer life. That is what being a *traveling RVer* is all about. That is what I'm calling "The New American Dream." America has always been about freedom; for these people, freedom is a new expression of their lives.

You can read this book a variety of ways, but I do suggest you read it from page one through to the end, in order. I structured it this way so you could meet the people you are learning from first, and then read the lessons from their commonalities and differences. The third section of the book allows you to delve deeper into a Road Story by reading an interview in its entirety. If you connect with a particular person or family, go there to read more. If, however, you are short on time, then simply read the second section, which will give you the nitty gritty. If you solely want to be entertained and enthralled, then just read the Road Stories at the beginning and the interviews at the end.

How to Find a Traveler With Similarities To You

I'm assuming you bought this book because you want to live this lifestyle, but something may be stopping you. Knowing this, I've created a chart to help you find a particular Road Story that addresses your fears, concerns or questions. Find your particular issues in the list below and look to see which road stories address them.

I Want to Live this Lifestyle But...

A. ...I want to have a baby.

B. ...I have young children.

C. ...I have school-aged children.

D. ...I just got married.

E. ...I have never lived with the person with whom I want to travel.

F. ...I don't have someone with whom to travel.

G. ...A big RV isn't my style.

H. ...I don't know how I would make money on the road.

I. ...I have to work but don't have a job in the tech field.

J. ...I don't know if I can afford it without working full-time.

K. ...I don't want to travel in the U.S.

L. ...I have one (or more) dogs.

M. ...I have one (or more) cats.

N. ...I have a non-traditional pet (bird, lizard, snake, etc.).

O. ...I have an elderly parent/grandparent.

P. ...I don't want to be away from my church congregation/community.

Q. ...I am gay and concerned about safety or prejudice.

R. ...I have grandkids.

S. ...People may think I'm too young.

T. ...I just recently graduated from college.

ROAD STORY																									
ISSUE	1	2	3	4	5	6	7	8	9	10	11	12	13	14	15	16	17	18	19	20	21	22	23	24	25
A			X		X				X					X				X							
B			X		X			X						X				X							
C					X									X				X							
D				X																				X	
E			X		X									X										X	
F		X													X									X	
G			X				X	X	X		X			X	X				X		X				
H		X	X	X	X	X		X	X	X	X			X				X	X	X		X			
I			X				X		X		X								X	X					
J							X	X	X		X	X	X		X				X	X			X	X	X
K				X			X							X					X						
L	X				X	X	X	X		X		X	X		X	X	X		X		X				
M			X													X		X							
N																		X							
O					X												X							X	
P																	X							X	
Q							X									X		X							
R																				X		X		X	
S	X	X	X	X	X																				
T	X		X	X																					

It would be unusual for you to not have fears about such a big lifestyle change. What you do with those fears is what will determine whether you get to live your dream. Each of the people in the following Road Stories had fears or concerns — or at least doubts — as to whether they could make this work. However, all of them overcame these issues and are now living the life of their dreams. Do you want to be like them, or would you rather live your life just thinking about it? Reading this book is your first step towards this freedom, as it will hopefully serve to reassure you and give you the tools you need to make the plunge.

A Profile of a Full-Time RVer

There are a few things that are important to note from the beginning. There is no "prototype" for a full-time traveler. They come young and old, working and non-working, with kids and/or pets and without kids and/or pets, with savings and without, home-owners and not. Some are solo, others are coupled, and still others are traveling as families.

The first step in our travelers' interviews was a general 10 question survey. More than 80 travelers completed this questionnaire. I will share some of their answers throughout the book. Here is the scoop on how long they've been on the road:

● < 6 mos ● 6 mos - 1 yr ● 1 - 2 yrs ● 2 - 5 yrs ● > 5 yrs

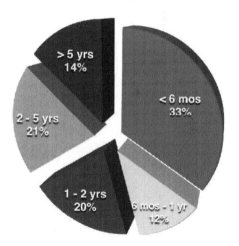

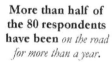

More than half of the 80 respondents have been *on the road for more than a year.*

There does seem to be a common thread in the length of time our travelers are expecting to stay on the road. Remember, I'm defining "full-time" as extended time (at least a year) but not necessarily *permanent*. Many of the travelers say they want to continue this lifestyle for one to five years. This means if you do not want to travel full-time for the "rest of your life," know that others have that desire and expectation, too.

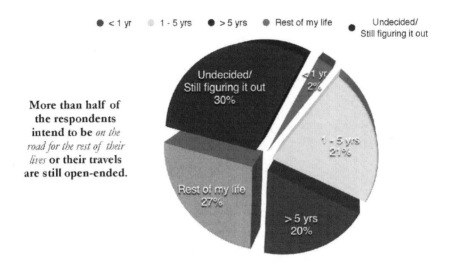

More than half of the respondents intend to be *on the road for the rest of their lives* **or their travels are still open-ended.**

In the lengthier interviews with 25 people, I asked how long it took them to actually hit the road after making the decision. I find the answers to this question really interesting as the *vast majority* of interviewees took *less than six months* to set out on their adventure, as you can see from the road stories that follow.

TheAmericanFieldTrip:

"As we were talking about our goals last year, we decided that the timing would never be perfect to leave our lives and move onto the road, and that we didn't want to put this dream off."

This resonates with my own experience, as it took us four months from our decision-day to actually be on the road full-time. What this means to you is that if you decide *today, right now*, then you could be a full-time traveler yourself in a handful of months. Just think what this change would do to your experience of life!

ROAD STORIES:
THE GENERATIONS

When we started exploring the idea of full-timing, we had the preconceived notion that most other full-timers would be retirees in their 60s and 70s. Were we too young to do this now? As we explored further, through other travelers' blogs and on Instagram, we were shocked to discover that many full-time RVers are actually in their 20s, 30s, and 40s. Here are the specifics from the survey I conducted:

● 20 - 30 yrs old   ○ 30 - 40 yrs old   ● 40 - 50 yrs old   ● 50 - 60 yrs old   ● 60+ yrs old

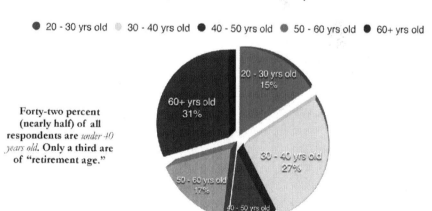

Forty-two percent (nearly half) of all respondents are *under 40 years old*. Only a third are of "retirement age."

This reality really fascinated us. We could not figure out how all these young people could afford to travel full-time, or what motivated them to seek a very different American dream from the one we grew up with. We both thought we were in a unique situation in that we had a pension to rely on for income and rental income from our previous residences. In addition, we had cut all of our other bills to zero, since we had made good money before we "retired" at young ages. How could all these young people do it, and why did they want to live this nomad existence instead of what we have all been taught to want — the 9-to-5 high-paying job, consumerism, and the house with the white picket fence?

I know of many other people — of all ages — who want to travel full-time for at least awhile, but most have excuses, or perhaps valid reasons, for why this is not possible. I decided I needed to seek out these *successful* travelers to find out their secrets and tips, so this could be done by more travel-hungry people.

I sent out and posted surveys everywhere I could think of: Instagram, blogs I had been following, people I had met on the road, Facebook, specific Facebook groups, and friends of all these people as well. I sought out people from all generations: Generation Z through Baby Boomers and beyond. I looked for singles, couples, and families. I invited people who had jobs on the road, and those who didn't need to work. I wanted as much variety as possible. More than 80 people answered this survey. Question 10 was "can we contact you to interview you further." The people who said yes to this question then got a lengthy interview to complete. The following Road Stories are the synopses of these interview questions, organized by generational category.

Some of the people who filled out the lengthier interview turned out to be travelers who had done longish stints (one month+) but hadn't yet taken the plunge to be full-time. I included one of these stories as an example of why you should "just do it now!"

I'm now raising the curtain on our performance. Please meet the cast of characters!

Generation Z/Post Millennials

Generation Zs were born between the mid-1990s to around 2009. They make up approximately 25 percent of the population, according to the U.S. Census Bureau. Generation Zs expect to work harder than their Millennial counterparts and are likely to be more realistic about life and work due to their Gen X parents — who are direct and skeptical as a whole — and to growing up during a recession.

Gen Z was born into full-time and pervasive connectivity in the form of smart phones, internet, social media, texting and instant messaging, and on-demand video. This lifestyle is all they know.

ROAD STORY 1:
Lindsey and Gerrit of **LivingLifeInBetween**

Instagram: @livinglifeinbetween

Website: www.LivingLifeInBetween.com

YouTube: Living Life In Between

AGES: Both are 24

HOW LONG ON THE ROAD: Six months to a year

HOW LONG EXPECT TO STAY ON THE ROAD: Five years or more

CHILDREN: No

PETS: Yes (two dogs)

RIG: 35-foot Class A motorhome

WORK ON THE ROAD: Yes

HOW LONG TO GET ON ROAD AFTER DECISION: Four months

After loving a road-trip vacation to the West Coast, Lindsey and Gerrit learned that full-time RVing is a "thing" and decided to look into it for themselves. Within six months, they had sold all of their belongings and bought a Class A motorhome. Their dream is to "live life to the fullest" and experience this beautiful country through rock climbing, hiking and mountain biking.

Lindsey says her favorite feature of this lifestyle is being with her husband and dogs 24/7. They are best friends, and despite living in a small space full-time, they still love being together. She says they address any conflicts immediately, so they don't develop into bigger issues.

Gerrit works a 9-to-5 job as a software developer, and Lindsey works to monetize their blog and social media. When Gerrit is done with his work day, they go out to explore their ever-changing environment. It can be a challenge to focus on work while being camped at a beautiful spot, like Zion National Park, but Gerrit does it by reminding himself that his job is how they can afford to live this lifestyle.

The Millennials

Many people think Millennials were born around 2000, but actually this generation is defined by those who became adults at the turn of the last century. People from this generation are often the children of baby boomers, which affects their collective attitude about the original "American Dream." These people grew up when their parents were getting into massive consumer debt and losing their homes. They have watched as their parents' dreams have been pushed to "some day" instead of living them today.

Like Gen Zers, they are extremely tech-savvy. They weren't born into the technology, but rather watched it unfold. They tend to job hop, overall having high levels of unemployment, probably leading to tendencies towards unconventional work and a distaste for the traditional office job.

ROAD STORY 2:
Ashley of **RVegan**

Instagram: @crueltyfree_rv

Website: www.r-vegan.com

AGE: 26

HOW LONG ON THE ROAD: More than a year

HOW LONG EXPECT TO STAY ON THE ROAD: One to five years

CHILDREN: No

PETS: No

RIG: Fifth wheel

WORK ON THE ROAD: Yes

HOW LONG TO GET ON ROAD AFTER DECISION: Five months

Ashley wants to live more simply and has a goal of saving money and creating financial independence. She is quite different from most other full-time workers in her road occupation. She works as a traveling healthcare provider. She spends three months at each spot and takes on four contracts a year. This limits her ability to move and explore often, which she hopes to change by starting her own business selling therapy materials.

Ashley lives this lifestyle on her own. She drives and sets up a fifth wheel by herself. She likes her fifth wheel despite its challenges, because it feels roomy and spacious — it even feels as large as her previous apartment. She loves the cost savings associated with living in an RV rather than paying rent.

Her greatest challenge is meeting a partner while on the road. She attends local activities when she is stationed in a particular town, but she finds that knowing she'll be leaving the area in just a few months gets in the way of developing long-term relationships.

Her favorite thing is waking up in a new spot and admiring the views.

ROAD STORY 3:
Cees, Madison and Theo of **OurVieAdventures**

Instagram: @OurVieAdventures

Website: www.ourvie.com

AGES: Both are 26

HOW LONG ON THE ROAD: More than one year

HOW LONG EXPECT TO STAY ON THE ROAD: One to five years

CHILDREN: Yes (one newborn)

PETS: Yes (a cat)

RIG: Small Class C: 1989 Toyota Odyssey mini-motorhome

WORK ON THE ROAD: Yes

HOW LONG TO GET ON ROAD AFTER DECISION: 18 months

Loving the outdoors, adventure and travel, Cees and Madison decided to set out on a journey to see all of the national parks. Along the way, they became pregnant and gave birth, not too long ago, to Theo. They are excited to be the first to show Theo the amazing sites in the U.S. and relish having him along for the ride. Their hope is to inspire others to live their dreams now. This doesn't mean encouraging a life of travel, but rather the pursuit of whatever passions others may have.

Cees didn't realize how challenging social media-related work can be. He says knowing this wouldn't have changed his decision to pursue this line of work, but he may have had more realistic expectations.

They are excited that they actually get to see their loved ones' big events more than before, given their mobility. They've made it a priority to be where they need to be to enjoy these times with their special people.

They like the simplicity of this lifestyle because they think the "stuff we 'own' can start to own us." Living small and mobile helps combat that, because there is simply no room for extraneous belongings.

Living in a small space works for them. In fact, they think it has been invaluable for their relationship. They have to work through their problems, since there is nowhere to run and hide.

Their desire is to live entirely off-grid, so all of their decisions about how to outfit their rig revolved around that goal. They have a wifi extender, a cell booster, solar panels, a bigger battery bank, and a power inverter.

Their cat had to adapt to this lifestyle but can now use the litter box going down the road at 60 mph. Theo will never have to adapt since he was born into this life. They are excited about learning what it means to be a true road "family."

ROAD STORY 4:
Heath and Alyssa

Instagram: @heathpadgett, @alyssapadge

Website: www.HeathandAlyssa.com

Facebook: www.facebook.com/heathandalyssa

YouTube: Heath and Alyssa Padgett

AGES: Both are 26

HOW LONG ON THE ROAD: Three years

HOW LONG EXPECT TO STAY ON THE ROAD: Five years

CHILDREN: No

PETS: No

RIG: LARGE CLASS C: 2016 Winnebago Brave 31C

WORK ON THE ROAD: Yes

Heath and Alyssa started traveling in their early twenties shortly after being married. This couple is planning to travel to all 50 states and much of Canada, at which point they intend to RV in Europe, Australia and New Zealand.

They disliked the heat of Texas in the summer and their office jobs, hence their decision to quit work and leave Texas in an RV. During their first year on the road they produced a documentary called Hourly America, in which Heath worked a job in all 50 states. As it turned out, they loved this lifestyle. They decided to enhance their video production business and stay on the road.

Their day-to-day life consists of editing videos in the RV, recording new podcast episodes, managing their Facebook group for RVers, and working on a software start up called CampgroundBooking.com. They exploit their tech savviness to earn a living in unconventional ways.

Work/life balance is an issue for this "team" because of Heath's passion to work 24/7 on projects and Alyssa's pull to enjoy the beautiful places they are camped (after she's finished her work, of course). Exploring national parks, kayaking, and laying around in a hammock all must be enjoyed amidst the desire to create compelling videos and online projects.

ROAD STORY 5:
"Cat" and Family of **OurIncredibleDash**

Instagram: @ourincredibledash

Website: www.incredibledash.com

AGES: 34, 32, 6, 4, 3 months

HOW LONG ON THE ROAD: Two to five years

HOW LONG EXPECT TO STAY ON THE ROAD: Rest of our lives

CHILDREN: Yes (three)

PETS: Yes (a dog)

RIG: 35-foot Class A motorhome

WORK ON THE ROAD: Yes

HOW LONG TO GET ON ROAD AFTER DECISION: One month

Catherine (aka "Cat") and crew hit the road because they were tired of the "rat race." Her husband had been in the military for years and missed much of their first two children's lives due to deployments abroad. Their goal now is to live a "fuller life, together." They strive to achieve a simpler life where family is the first priority.

The desire for simplicity is a constant theme in their interview, from getting rid of "stuff" to being less busy. She feels that being on the road full time has made them closer as a family.

They have some income from a military pension and from being furloughed from a railroad job, but they also earn a living by "workamping" (being camp hosts or doing other service work at campgrounds in exchange for a free full-hook up site and pay for hours worked). She also does some part-time blogging and related work to bring in income.

Cat got pregnant with their third child while on the road. She has complicated pregnancies, so they stayed close to her father during this time. They use Abeka Accredited Academy and have DVD lessons to school their kids, along with life lessons learned from their travels.

ROAD STORY 6:
Josh and Laura of **TravelExploreUncover**

Instagram: @travelexploreuncover

Website: www.travelexploreuncover.com

YouTube: www.youtube.com/travelexploreuncover

AGES: 33 and 29

HOW LONG ON THE ROAD: About one year

HOW LONG EXPECT TO STAY ON THE ROAD: One to five years

CHILDREN: No

PETS: Yes (two dogs)

RIG: Grand Design Momentum 349M Fifth wheel

WORK ON THE ROAD: As needed

HOW LONG TO GET ON ROAD AFTER DECISION: Three months

Laura and Josh sought the road to get away from the typical 40 hour work week and demands of a traditional life. They wanted to slow down and get back to nature. They intend to see as much of the U.S.

as possible, including Alaska, and then want to volunteer to give back to others. Laura is a physical therapist and can do contract work on the road. She intentionally hasn't been working during their first year of travel as they want the freedom to explore without the necessity of working.

They say that life on the road is "exciting, enlightening and free." They love that "every day can be new" and that every week they "have a new backyard." They travel at a fast pace, moving every few days. Most of their time is spent boondocking in private spots.

Interestingly, they didn't live together prior to moving into their fifth wheel to travel. They thought this would be a good way to learn about each other. Apparently it has been a good thing, because they are now engaged.

To those of you wanting this lifestyle, they offer this advice: "When you seriously start considering this as an option, others around you will tell you it's not possible. But it is! It takes planning, saving, and courage, but it is possible."

ROAD STORY 7:
Jessi and Valerie of **HappyCamperWives**

Instagram: @happycamperwives

Website: www.happycamperwives.com

Facebook: www.facebook.com/thecamperwives

YouTube: www.youtube.com/HappyCamperWives

AGES: Both are 31

HOW LONG ON THE ROAD: About one year

HOW LONG EXPECT TO STAY ON THE ROAD: One to five years

CHILDREN: No

PETS: Yes (two dogs)

RIG: Travel trailer (T@b TEARDROP)

WORK ON THE ROAD: Yes

HOW LONG TO GET ON ROAD AFTER DECISION: One month

Jessi and Valerie are a married lesbian couple. They decided to travel full-time when a tenant in an investment house asked if she could stay longer. They had planned on moving into that house, but figured keeping it rented would give them some income and enable them to travel and see the U.S. (and other countries).

Their goal is to "find happiness outside the 9-to-5 rat race." Jessi is a web designer with internet-based work. They are currently traveling in an RV in Spain, and intend to RV in New Zealand next. They will then return to the U.S. and continue their adventure here.

They recognize that it is scary, and sometimes dangerous, to travel as a minority couple, but they have been surprised by how friendly and kind people have been. They are so glad they took the leap of faith and actually wish they had done it sooner.

They've been able to see a lot of their friends and family since they are able to meet up with people in nearly every state across the country.

Amazingly, they travel in a "teardrop" trailer. Yes, two 5'10" women and two dogs in an extremely small space. They say that they've found ways of giving each other space and talking through any conflicts that arise.

ROAD STORY 8:
Amber and Ryan of **HotSauceHippo**

Instagram: @hotsaucehippo

Website: www.HotSauceHippo.com

AGES: 30 and 28

HOW LONG ON THE ROAD: About six months

HOW LONG EXPECT TO STAY ON THE ROAD: One to five years

CHILDREN: No

PETS: Yes (a cat)

RIG: 22-foot 1988 Lazy Daze Class C

WORK ON THE ROAD: Yes

HOW LONG TO GET ON ROAD AFTER DECISION: Five months

Amber and Ryan felt that something was missing from their lives. They both have loved traveling and figured they needed to find a way to create a life of full-time travel. They want the freedom of not being tied to a desk all day.

Something they said really resonated with me; we also tend to get used to our surroundings and take for granted the beauty around us. They say travel enables them to cherish what's in front of them, because they will be moving on to something else wonderful the next day.

They like always having a "teammate" to troubleshoot problems with and to share the experience with. They have found a richness in their relationship by being on the road.

Amber is a contract attorney and continues to work. She advises others to take what they do now, or what they enjoy, and brainstorm a way to use that to make money while traveling. She doesn't believe you have to have internet-based work, but rather that everyone has a skill that could enable them to live this lifestyle.

They live in a small 22-foot Class C and move daily. They love the maneuverability of the rig and that they can park on city streets. Like many of the other travelers, their intent is to primarily boondock, so they modified their rig accordingly, removing the microwave and air conditioner for more headroom.

ROAD STORY 9:
David, Madison, Graham, and Margaret of
TheAmericanFieldTrip

Instagram: @theamericanfieldtrip

Website: www.americanfieldtrip.com

AGES: 29, 27, 4, 19 months

HOW LONG ON THE ROAD: About six months

HOW LONG EXPECT TO STAY ON THE ROAD: One to five years

CHILDREN: Yes (two)

PETS: No

RIG: 25-foot 2007 Ford E-450 converted shuttle bus

WORK ON THE ROAD: Yes

HOW LONG TO GET ON ROAD AFTER DECISION: Six months

This family had always wanted to live on the road and see all the U.S. sites. When discussing their goals last year, they realized that timing would never be perfect to leave their stationary lives, and they didn't want to put their traveling dream off any longer. They now hope to educate others about the beauty of the national parks in the United States and advocate traveling locally (within driving range).

The four of them live in a customized converted shuttle bus that they designed to meet their personal needs. They have work space and play space, a big full-sized kitchen, and lots of storage.

They used to live in New York City and do miss some of what a big city offers. They rent their house and use the income derived from it to help fund their travels.

They say that between the road lifestyle and logistics of travel, they are busier now than they were before. They are traveling at a fast pace to see all 59 of the national parks, so they spend a lot of time on the road. The kids have adapted and spend time learning things during travel days, and the older one loves the Junior Ranger Program that is part of the national parks' system.

ROAD STORY 10:
Becky and Steve of **GoWiththeFlowandCo**

Instagram: @go.withtheflowand.co

Website: www.GoWiththeFlowandCo.com

AGES: 33 and 31

HOW LONG ON THE ROAD: About one year

HOW LONG EXPECT TO STAY ON THE ROAD: One to five years

CHILDREN: No

PETS: Yes (two dogs)

RIG: Fifth wheel

WORK ON THE ROAD: Yes

HOW LONG TO GET ON ROAD AFTER DECISION: Six months

Becky and Steve started their adventure because their lives were stagnant. They wanted change — and enjoy traveling — so exploring this lifestyle made sense to them. They love the mobility and flexibility that this life offers. They also are happy that their dogs are along for the journey.

They relish exploring the different environments with their pups and living in different weather conditions and settings.

They use income from renting out their personal residence, as well as money from their investment properties, to help fund their travels. So far they say it has worked out well for them, and they've had minimal "landlord" responsibilities.

They chose a fifth wheel, and love it, but would be more cognizant of a few things if they did it again, one being water storage. They have a 40-gallon tank and have run out of fresh water a few times, so that's a consideration if they were to ever change rigs.

Their advice is: "*Enjoy everything!* (Even when you're sweating profusely while dumping your black tank and gagging) because, come on! You could be back in the daily grind, in a building from 8-5."

ROAD STORY 11:
Matt and Amanda of **TheVanProject**

Instagram: @van.project

Website: www.thevanproject.co

AGES: 32 and 30

HOW LONG ON THE ROAD: Less than six months

HOW LONG EXPECT TO STAY ON THE ROAD: Undecided/still figuring it out

CHILDREN: No

PETS: No

RIG: Renovated bus

WORK ON THE ROAD: Yes

HOW LONG TO GET ON ROAD AFTER DECISION: Eight months

Matt and Amanda wanted to live a less expensive lifestyle that would afford them the opportunity to travel and do things that they enjoy. They work, but fewer hours than before, because they only spend $500/month on their living expenses. (This is by far the lowest monthly expenditures of anyone in our group of interviewees.) They are able to live this cheaply by camping only in free spots, eating out rarely, dumping as infrequently as possible, staying stationary and traveling less to cut down on fuel costs.

Their work is internet-based and often their internet connection is poor. They compensate for this by buckling down and getting as much done work-wise when they have good internet, or perhaps staying somewhere a bit longer than planned to get more done.

They chose a renovated bus as their rig. They outfitted it with an on-demand water heater, fully functioning toilet, a lot more storage, a queen size bed, three solar panels that are powerful enough to power a refrigerator, and LED lighting. They wish they had four-wheel drive capability, but otherwise are happy with their choice.

Generation X

Gen Xers are between their mid-30s to mid-50s. They are known for their work ethic, and as a group strive to pay for their children's college education. They want workplace flexibility and are willing to walk away from their jobs if they aren't offered this perk. Most (70% from a 2011 survey done by Center for Talent Innovation) prefer to work independently. Many Gen Xers either are, or strive to be, entrepreneurs. The vast majority are home owners and state this as a value.

ROAD STORY 12:
Gabi, Stephan and Kali the K9 of **8Paws1Tail**

Instagram: @8paws1tail

Website: www.8paws1tail.com

Facebook: www.facebook.com/8Paws1Tail

AGES: 43 and 41

HOW LONG ON THE ROAD: Six months to one year

HOW LONG EXPECT TO STAY ON THE ROAD: Undecided/still figuring it out

CHILDREN: No

PETS: Yes (one dog)

RIG: 37-foot 2007 Winnebago Voyage Class A

WORK ON THE ROAD: Some

HOW LONG TO GET ON ROAD AFTER DECISION: Four months

Gabi and Stephan wanted to get out of their long office-day jobs where they were just "ships passing in the night." They love the outdoors and their motto is "adventure is life." Full-time travel was the solution to having a fuller life.

They hope to maintain this lifestyle as long as possible, perhaps even buying their own campground. They currently work as camp hosts at a campground near Lake Tahoe. The couple want to see as much of the states as possible, with a trip up to Alaska as a goal.

They love that this lifestyle gives them a sense of freedom and lots of time to be together. Being with their dog is also very important to them, and they can do that full-time now.

They used to have a large older home, but are fine with the 300 square feet they have now.

They started their travels by living off their savings. They did this intentionally, because they felt they were really able to take in their experience and that it was worth doing so. Now, they are starting to work a bit.

They point out that there are some demands with being a full-time traveler that you don't have being stationary: being affected by the weather, time requirements for set up and travel between locations, and planning your destinations. For them, though, it's worth it!

ROAD STORY 13:
Brad and Maggie of **WanderlandTravelers**

Instagram: @wanderlandtravelers

Website: www.wanderlandtravelers.com

Facebook: www.facebook.com/wanderlandtravelers

YouTube: www.youtube.com/wanderlandtravelers

Maggie's Photography: www.margaretpitcherphotography.com

AGES: 37 and 36

HOW LONG ON THE ROAD: More than one year

HOW LONG EXPECT TO STAY ON THE ROAD: More than five years

CHILDREN: No

PETS: Yes (two dogs)

RIG: 33-foot 2003 Fleetwood Bounder 32W Class A

WORK ON THE ROAD: Yes

HOW LONG TO GET ON ROAD AFTER DECISION: Eight months

Brad has had a nomadic lifestyle in mind since attending college. He chose a major in computer science, because he knew this would give him the best opportunities to work remotely. In the beginning of their planning for this lifestyle, they were considering traveling on a boat. They intended to buy a boat in Florida (they lived in Oregon), which meant they'd need to *get* to Florida.

While looking at land travel options, they began considering full-time RV travel. This won out in the end. They still may do the sailboat one day, but for now they are quite happy. They love the variety of landscapes.

Their goals are to "stay in scenic places, camp for free as often as possible, visit national parks, see old friends, make new ones, and go on adventures in every place we visit." They created a road trip bucket list and are quickly checking off their items.

They've discovered that they can control their cost of living better while traveling in an RV than before when living in a house. They strive to camp for free, move locations less frequently for lower fuel costs, and reduce the cost of "utilities" by bundling up during the cold months.

The couple realize they are more adaptable than they gave themselves credit for. They've developed roles and systems for moving days — and just general life — which make things easier for them as a couple.

ROAD STORY 14:
Nathan, Renée, Tristan, Winter & Wylder of **Wandrly**

Instagram: @wandrly

Website: www.wandrlymagazine.com.com

Facebook: www.facebook.com/Wandrly

YouTube: www.youtube.com/user/clicknathan

AGES: 38, 35, 15, 6, and 4

HOW LONG ON THE ROAD: Eight years

HOW LONG EXPECT TO STAY ON THE ROAD: Rest of my life

CHILDREN: Yes (3)

PETS: Not now

RIG: Camper van

WORK ON THE ROAD: Yes

HOW LONG TO GET ON ROAD AFTER DECISION: Six months

This family of five has been living on the road for more than eight years now. They have primarily been in a 1978 VW Bus, although they spent small amounts of time in a small Class C, an Airstream trailer, and a bit of time in a van. Two of three children have known no other life. The oldest child is pushing a bit for a more stationary high school experience, but the rest of the crew is more than happy to have this nomadic life.

They like the van because of its ability to go anywhere. It also keeps their life simple, since they can't accumulate a lot of "stuff." The downside is that when it rains it's "kind of a bummer."

Nathan says he loves how much time he gets to spend with his family. He initiated this adventure with his (now) 15-year-old son, back when his son was 7 years old. One day he showed up at his college sweetheart's house and asked if she wanted to join them. The answer was "yes" and they made two more babies on the road.

His advice "for others who want to live a traveling life is to have some type of an income...because you just may get addicted and that whole 'sold my house to travel for a year' thing, well, a year can go by really quickly."

In regards to "road schooling," he says, "we have done everything from paying a teacher to come up with curriculum for us (first year on the road, I see that as silly now) to unschooling (basically just "not doing school" and letting the world's influences teach your child). For us, the right balance is a couple of hours a day focusing on subjects the kids actually enjoy. Everyone learns more that way."

ROAD STORY 15:
Laura J

Website: www.splashesalongtheway.com

HOW LONG ON THE ROAD: Less than six months

HOW LONG EXPECT TO STAY ON THE ROAD: One to five years

CHILDREN: No

PETS: Yes (a dog)

RIG: 22-foot 2016 Minnie Winnie 22R Class C

WORK ON THE ROAD: No

HOW LONG TO GET ON ROAD AFTER DECISION: Six months

Laura had always dreamed of traveling in an RV, and when she got laid off from her job in expensive San Francisco, she decided to make that dream a reality. Her goal is "to see as much of the country as I can by meandering the back roads, not zooming down the interstate, to stay on the road as long as I can, to see how cheaply I can live…"

As a solo traveler, she acknowledges that one of her challenges is needing to do and know everything about the rig by herself. She must drive it, set it up, hook up to utilities, fix it, etc. all on her own.

She's not working, by choice. She wants to explore as much as she can right now, without anyone having expectations of her. She is currently living off of her savings and seeing how long she can make that stretch. She mostly camps for free and cooks her own meals to keep her expenses low.

She has a dog that is her best friend. She is very sensitive to his needs in terms of water, food, temperature and attention. She sometimes misses out on seeing sites because it is too hot to leave him. She mostly tries to visit national monuments and state parks since they tend to be more dog friendly.

ROAD STORY 16:
Jax and Michelle of **Jax733**

Instagram: @jax733

AGES: 53 and 49

HOW LONG ON THE ROAD: About one year

HOW LONG EXPECT TO STAY ON THE ROAD: Two to five years

CHILDREN: No

PETS: Yes (one dog, one cat)

RIG: 32-foot Eclipse Attitude 27SAG Travel Trailer Toy Hauler

WORK ON THE ROAD: No

HOW LONG TO GET ON ROAD AFTER DECISION: Four months

Jax and Michelle had grown tired of lives of consumerism. They initially scaled down by moving to a small house, but realized they also missed nature. During one of their many camping trips, they sensed a growing need to be camping more. They saw an RV in a campground they were staying in and decided to explore the idea of living in an RV full-time for themselves.

The want to follow the weather and their intuition in a way that will allow them to have the most fluid experience possible. They seek a more simple and thoughtful life.

They love the open-ended nature of the adventure and being able to wake up somewhere new as often as they want.

They live off of rental income and savings. They own two properties that are cash positive and that helps fund their travels. The most joyous thing for them, though, is enjoying experiences more and "stuff" less. They take advantage of their locations to create a feeling of abundance rather than accumulate more things to achieve that sensation.

They recommend you get pet insurance for your pets, and use doggy day care for your dogs, so you can visit national parks without leaving them in the car or RV.

ROAD STORY 17:
James and Rhiannon of **MilesAwayEveryday**

Instagram: @MilesAwayEveryday

Website: www.milesawayeveryday.com

Facebook: www.facebook.com/milesawayeveryday

AGES: Both are 35

HOW LONG ON THE ROAD: Less than six months

HOW LONG EXPECT TO STAY ON THE ROAD: Rest of my life

CHILDREN: No

PETS: Yes (a dog)

RIG: 31-foot Class A

WORK ON THE ROAD: Yes

HOW LONG TO GET ON ROAD AFTER DECISION: Seven months

"Hell week" is what caused this couple to consider hitting the road. Several of Rhiannon's grandparents fell ill; James had to lay off a number of people — and cut bonuses and salaries as well — on his boss' behalf. After making a joke about hooking up a trailer and driving off to get away from their lives, they reconsidered the joke and made it their goal instead.

They love the freedom this life offers: that they can move when they want and leave when the weather gets bad.

They are entrepreneurs and enjoy running their business remotely. They laugh because people often wonder how they can afford to travel full-time; are they trust fund babies? But no, they just work really hard to create a lifestyle that is perfect for them.

Since their business is web-based, they rely on the internet a lot. They due ample research before moving to a new site to make sure they will have connectivity. One time they were disappointed and weren't able to get work done, so they had to leave prematurely. Typically, though, they have been lucky with their ability to get the job done.

They viewed innumerable RVs to decide which one was right for them. In the end it was a 31-foot Class A. Anything bigger, and they'd both walk out immediately, exclaiming "it is just too big." They considered a 27-foot to enable them to have more camping options. It would have required reconfiguring things, and they just didn't have the time. All-in-all it was a great decision for them, as they love the big front window, the fact they can tow their jeep, the quick set up time, and so many other features.

ROAD STORY 18:
Brittany and Eric of **RVWanderlust**

Instagram: @rvwanderlust

Website: www.rvwanderlust.com

Facebook: facebook.com/rvwanderlust

AGES: 47 and 30

HOW LONG ON THE ROAD: Two to five years

HOW LONG EXPECT TO STAY ON THE ROAD: Undecided

CHILDREN: Yes

PETS: Yes (a cat, RIP bearded dragon)

RIG: Large Class A

WORK ON THE ROAD: Yes

HOW LONG TO GET ON ROAD AFTER DECISION: A couple of years

NOTE: One person is a Millennial and one is a Gen-X

Brittany and Eric love to travel and RVing seemed the least expensive and practical way to do it full-time. They are hoping to hit all 48 continental states; they've spent at least one night in 22 states to this point. In the beginning they moved sites often, but have slowed down their travels to eradicate feeling burnt out.

They miss church, and a sense of stable community, but feel that the negatives to RVing are inconsequential compared to the returns.

They own an online marketing company, and as long as they have internet, they can get their work done. They spend time researching cellular and internet connectivity before heading to the next site.

They have five children: two grown, two in high school, and Caspian, who was born on the road. Caspian is the only full-time traveler with them, but the high-schoolers do spend some time traveling, too. Since Caspian is a baby, they work half days and then spend the rest of the time with him and/or adventuring.

They've had to develop schedules to work around having a baby in the "house." When it's his nap time, they must stay in the main room. When it is night time, they must stay in the bedroom. It took some getting used to, but they make it work.

ROAD STORY 19:
Sunny and Karin of the **Vagabroads**

* photo credits to Carolina Casas-Cordero

Instagram @thevagabroads

Website: www.vagabroads.com

Facebook: www.facebook.com/vagabroads

AGES: Both are 40

HOW LONG ON THE ROAD: More than one year

HOW LONG EXPECT TO STAY ON THE ROAD: Undecided/still figuring it out

CHILDREN: No

PETS: Yes (a dog)

RIG: 1997 Toyota Landcruiser with a rooftop tent

WORK ON THE ROAD: Yes

HOW LONG TO GET ON ROAD AFTER DECISION: Six months

NOTE: The Vagabroads are traveling in Mexico and South America. Both answered the interview separately, and I've taken the liberty of combining their answers.

Their initial intention was to travel to find somewhere new to settle down, but now they aren't sure a stationary life will ever be satisfying again. Unique to them, they chose a Landcruiser with a roof-top tent as their rig. This choice gives them maximum flexibility in regards to where they camp, since it is small, easy to maneuver and a 4-wheel drive. If they had to do it all over again, they'd pick the same vehicle sans roof-top tent. They miss having indoor space, especially for cooking, and on rainy days.

Sunny maintained her law firm and still consistently works within it. Karin looks for internet-based work. They sold their house to give them capital with which to travel. Between those funds, and their work, they can be on the road for a long time.

Living in such a tiny space means that organization is paramount. Their advice, "you can never add enough compartments, drawers, shelves, to your rig." Not only did they add extra storage, they also outfitted their Landcruiser with a refrigerator and two Duralast Platinum 31M batteries to power everything. They also have a two-and-a-half lift, winch, Slee back gate, ARB front bumper, and more. One important modification they made was to have a remote starter on the car so they could run the air-conditioning if they needed to leave their dog alone in the car for a bit.

Baby Boomers

This generation was born between the early- to mid-1940s and the mid 1960s. They earned peak levels of income, and could therefore reap the benefits of products such as food, apparel, cars, and electronics. In general, they are known for higher levels of consumerism than previous generations. Now in their retirement ages, many have good pensions, savings and social security on which to live.

ROAD STORY 20:
Jeff and Coffee Fujita

HOW LONG ON THE ROAD: Two to five years

HOW LONG EXPECT TO STAY ON THE ROAD: Five years or more

CHILDREN: No

PETS: No

RIG: 28-foot Airstream travel trailer

WORK ON THE ROAD: Yes

HOW LONG TO GET ON ROAD AFTER DECISION: Two months

Jeff and Coffee viewed his quadruple bypass surgery and his parents' passing and leaving an inheritance as signs that they needed to make some changes. After being lost in the "fog of consumerism" in "soulless" Southern California, they sold everything and started living a life on the road. Two months after deciding, they set out on an adventure to replace the American Dream for a "simpler, untethered life."

Jeff was college educated, but wanted a freer life than the 9-to-5 grind. Now they both work "common man" odd jobs on the road. I actually met him at a gas station outside of Bryce. He filled up my propane tank, and we hit it off.

In addition to odd jobs, they've also done camp hosting stints a couple of times. They enjoy the trade off of working 20 hours per week in exchange for a full-hook up site and a place to stay for a couple of months. They like the opportunities camp hosting affords them to get to know people in one town — and become part of it — before moving on.

Outside of their camp hosting jobs they mostly boondock. They have a simple set up with a strong generator, but no solar, and that works great for them. Since they are often alone where they are camping, they know their generator isn't bothering anyone.

Their favorite quality of this lifestyle is knowing that "each new day's events are unwritten."

ROAD STORY 21:
Michael and Brenda

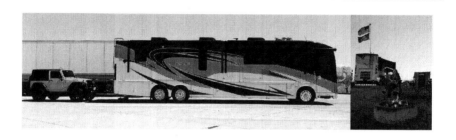

AGES: 57 and 55

HOW LONG ON THE ROAD: More than one year

HOW LONG EXPECT TO STAY ON THE ROAD: Five years or more

CHILDREN: No

PETS: Yes (a dog)

RIG: 42-foot 2015 Winnebago Tour 42HD Class A

WORK ON THE ROAD: No

HOW LONG TO GET ON ROAD AFTER DECISION: One year

Michael spent 22 years defending this country, and he now wants to see the beauty of all 48 continental states. He and his wife are looking to make memories and create new friendships.

He wishes he had started full-time travel sooner, and says it is a continuous learning experience. He admits they miss their friends and family, but he loves the freedom to create his own schedule.

They owned a home, which they decided to sell. They figured that while on the road they might find somewhere new to settle into a sticks-and-bricks home.

They travel in a 42-foot Class A that has all the comforts of home. They decided if they were going to travel like this, they'd "go big or go home."

He recommends budgeting for the unexpected.

They offer this advice: "Life is never a guarantee. Live it while you can."

ROAD STORY 22:
Leslie and Eric of SunnyJunket

Instagram: @sunnyjunket

AGE: 57 and 54

HOW LONG ON THE ROAD: Less than six months

HOW LONG EXPECT TO STAY ON THE ROAD: One to five years

CHILDREN: No

PETS: No

RIG: 18-foot vintage 1982 travel trailer

WORK ON THE ROAD: Yes

HOW LONG TO GET ON ROAD AFTER DECISION: Five to six months

Leslie and Eric once owned two homes and were financially prospering. When the crash happened in 2008, things changed. Their financial hardship eventually led to their decision to buy an RV and travel. They are looking for a simpler life, and to get out from under mortgages and/or rent. They love their current lower cost of living.

They'd like to not have to work, but as things would have it, they must. Fortunately, Eric just got a great full-time travel job, and is quite happy about it, even though it means working 9-to-5 still.

They just found out they will be grandparents in seven months. They are so excited, but disappointed that they no longer live near their oldest son who is bringing them this joy.

They have enjoyed using some free camping options: Harvest Hosts. Through this membership, they have stayed at three wineries, an animal park and the Petrified Forest gift shop.

ROAD STORY 23:
Dawn L

HOW LONG ON THE ROAD: Six months to one year

HOW LONG EXPECT TO STAY ON THE ROAD: Undecided/ still figuring it out

CHILDREN: No

PETS: No

RIG: 2001 Montana Fifth wheel

WORK ON THE ROAD: No

HOW LONG TO GET ON ROAD AFTER DECISION: Six months

Dawn was a hospice nurse and had heard many people say that what they regret most is what they didn't do. She didn't want to have any regrets, so she and her husband set out on their road travels. They enjoy the freedom of this lifestyle and meeting new people.

They had a travel trailer but it was a bit too small so they traded it for a fifth wheel. They love the spaciousness of the fifth wheel, although sometimes she wishes they had a Class A or C. They outfitted their rig with two batteries and two generators for off-grid camping.

Since her husband was in the Navy, they stay at many military campgrounds. She says they are beautiful and inexpensive. They both receive social security and he has a pension, which is how they finance their travels.

ROAD STORY 24:
Michael and Loida

Website: www.thurmond.net

HOW LONG ON THE ROAD: More than two years

HOW LONG EXPECT TO STAY ON THE ROAD: Rest of my life

CHILDREN: No

PETS: No

RIG: 35-foot Tiffin Class A

WORK ON THE ROAD: Yes

HOW LONG TO GET ON ROAD AFTER DECISION: Nine months

After Michael's first wife passed away, he decided to sell the house, buy an RV, and travel. Fortunately, he is able to work remotely. His goal was to see more of this country. He now travels with his second wife who has always dreamed of traveling.

They chose a large Class A and have a two-seater vehicle that they tow. He now wishes he had a car that seated more than two people, but he definitely recommends towing something.

He and his wife do mission work together while on the road. Doing so helps them maintain a connection to their community. They also drop in on other churches while traveling. Their desire to travel outweighed the need to stay connected to a single community. They do miss the community back home, but they find they can stay in touch with their faith and practices just fine while moving around to new places.

Loida, his wife, has grandchildren that she feels a pull to be near, and Michael has elderly parents. They wish they could move around a bit more, but these relationships are too important. They still get out and enjoy state and national parks, and they are learning to balance their time between family and travel.

When Michael works, Loida uses her sewing machine. They have an easy relationship and travel well together. They turn to God for any problems that may arise.

ROAD STORY 25:
Mandy J

This traveler opted not to include her photo.

HOW LONG ON THE ROAD: Two to five years

HOW LONG EXPECT TO STAY ON THE ROAD: Rest of my life

CHILDREN: No

PETS: No

RIG: 40-foot Fifth Wheel Toy Hauler

WORK ON THE ROAD: Part-time

HOW LONG TO GET ON ROAD AFTER DECISION: "Not long"

Mandy has always loved to travel. She and her significant other have Harley motorcycles and use them to explore new places. They love the freedom of this lifestyle and use it to see new places and make new friends.

She recommends creating a checklist before getting on the road.

She is retired, but does work a bit on an internet-based business. She recommends setting up a separate space in your rig to use for work, and to try it out before starting your travels.

They have a 40-foot fifth wheel toy hauler that they like because it can haul their bikes around. They've modified the inside to include a reclining sofa in place of the fold-up sofa and storage instead of the overhead loft bed.

Her advice is: "Have fun and don't sweat the small stuff."

Just Do It!

Once you read the Road Stories you see one very common denominator: Most of these travelers got on the road within about six months of deciding. They didn't wait for "the right time." They decided the right time was *now* and they made it work.

If you wait, your time will slip away.

My grandmother died with dozens of "special occasion" wines in her basement, because she was always waiting for the right time to drink them. Now is the right time! This final story illustrates this lesson and should encourage you to *just do it*!

ROAD STORY 26:
Steve K

AGES: 56 and 50

HOW LONG ON THE ROAD: Five years (on and off), not full-time

HOW LONG EXPECT TO STAY ON THE ROAD: Rest of my life

CHILDREN: No

PETS: No

RIG: 45-foot 2015 Entegra Coach Anthem Class A

WORK ON THE ROAD: Not yet on the road

HOW LONG TO GET ON ROAD AFTER DECISION: Not yet on the road

Steve has been preparing for a life on the road for 56 years! He is a classic example of waiting for the "right time." He has taken many lengthy trips alone, and now with his husband, but the idea of not having roots somewhere makes him nervous. For this reason, he remains a "part-time" traveler (by my definition).

He and his husband travel in a very large Class A. He has traded up rigs several times and loves this one. It is new and has all the bells and whistles he could possibly want. He chose this RV because of its floor plan and power. He warns, though, that buying an expensive rig doesn't necessarily mean fewer maintenance issues. In fact, you may have more because there are more fancy things to break. His advice is to be prepared for some down time when the rig is getting fixed.

He feels very lucky to have met and married someone who loves to travel as much as he does. He also feels fortunate that they are compatible in a small space. They even find themselves spending time in the RV when they are at their sticks-and-bricks.

He is waiting to become a full-timer until his retirement savings is where he wants it to be. He knows he could do workamping on the road, but would prefer to not have to work. He is an administrator for a family-owned medical practice and finds that with today's internet-based technology he could continue to work, even when he is on the road.

WHAT ARE YOUR GOALS & DREAMS?

While our travelers are all very unique in their life experiences and situations, there are definitely some similar themes that run through their stories. Some commonalities are:

- the desire for freedom
- wanting to explore the world or our nation
- seeking nature
- escaping the mundane
- getting away from the "9 to 5 grind"
- returning to basics
- leading a simpler life
- delving into themselves
- reducing their consumerism and expenses
- having more time with family or spouses

This lifestyle can afford full-time travelers any or all of these goals. Why are you reading this book? What compels *you* to travel full-time? Here is what one of our travelers had to say:

> **Jax733:**
>
> *"Now that we are on the road, we want to see and explore the United States. Our intention is to live simpler and more thoughtfully. We want to spend time in nature and explore the less traveled parts of the country. We want to be flexible and plot a course based on weather, intuition, and random chance. We want to be open to what the road brings us, both in terms of people and of places."*

Your first step is to identify *your* goals and dreams, because doing so will guide your decisions for how to structure your experience. Be as specific as you can during this part of the planning process.

Jeff and Coffee:

"Full-timers are different in what they want out of their life on the road. Some want the company of others and others want the seclusion. Some want to stick to asphalt, others follow the dirt roads. I would say the best advice is to know one's limitations...but also to push them a bit. That's adventure."

Let's look at some of the similarities and examine how our travelers have accomplished these goals.

Finding Freedom

It is interesting to me that we live in a country founded on freedom, and that is what all of the interviewees seek to find in their individual lives. Freedom takes many forms for our travelers, but it is absolutely the common thread that weaves through all of the desires, and what appears to me to be the New American Dream.

If *your* goal is "freedom," what does freedom look like to you? Is it the absence of work? Or the option to work when you want, doing what you want? Is it that you still want to work, but you want to work less and spend more time hiking with the family or visiting our national parks? Or is freedom simply having a picnic table to work on and an RV window from which to look out?

Freedom takes many forms, but you have to know your version of freedom in order to create it. All of the above scenarios have been created by our storytellers in their lives; I know you can do the same in your life.

Here are some additional thoughts from our travelers.

HotSauceHippo:

"Our main goal was for freedom. We wanted to not feel tied to a desk each day. As we have settled into road life, we have picked up the additional goal of helping others find their freedom, in whatever sense they see best fits their life."

Michael and Brenda:

"What I like the best is that I make my own schedule. I go when and where I want with no issues."

TheVanProject:

"A big part of getting on the road was living a less expensive lifestyle that gives

us more freedom and time to pursue the things we love to do. Because we save so much money not paying rent, we can afford to work fewer hours for others, allowing us to spend more time on our own creative endeavors."

I know my idea of freedom was similar to this next one.

MilesAwayEveryday:

"We love…that we never feel stagnant or stuck with this new life. We also really love that we have the ability to chase the good weather and move on when it's bad."

Life was a bit routine for me before hitting the road. It certainly was not a bad life; in fact I'd venture to say it was exceptional by many people's standards. I didn't work full-time then, either, so I had free time during my day to do as I please. But "free time" isn't the same thing to me as "freedom." "Free time" means you aren't chained to someone else's schedule. "Freedom" means the sky is the limit, that whatever you can imagine can be achieved. At least that's what it means to me. Instead of simply not living by someone else's rules, freedom is not having rules. Since our location is constantly changing, our experience of life is also always changing.

Even with a freer life, there are still responsibilities that must be addressed. When asked what a "day in their life" is like, most travelers make the claim that every day can be truly unique, but many acknowledge they still have responsibilities.

OurIncredibleDash:

"A day in our life might include a day trip to explore the area we are in, or it might include just regular life stuff — laundry, school, hanging out at home. It really depends on the day, as each day is never the same."

Exploring the World or Nation

I think a full-time traveler would have to have a desire to explore the nation (or the world) or else why would they leave stationary life? In fact, more than half of those interviewed explicitly stated a goal of traveling the U.S. and seeing as much of it as possible.

Laura J:

"My goals…are to see as much of the country as I can by meandering the back roads, not zooming down the interstate, to stay on the road as long as I can, to see how cheaply I can live, and to not get a blowout!"

Michael and Brenda:

"[My goal] is to see this beautiful country that I spent 22 years defending….to see all 48 continental states, make lots of memories and friends."

RVWanderlust:

"We'd love to eventually hit all 48 continental states, but we're in no hurry. We've spent at least one night in 22 states so far. If we don't spend a night, then we don't count the state!"

While traveling is an element of freedom, the dream of travel is also about living life to the fullest.

HappyCamperWives:

"Our dreams are to travel the world by car, camp, explore, and to live life to the fullest."

LivingLifeInBetween:

"Our dream is to live life to the fullest and to enjoy every minute of it doing what we love to do, and that is seeing and experiencing this beautiful country."

But for some, this life of travel is also a practical decision.

Heath and Alyssa:

"Summers were blistering hot, we didn't love our post-college office jobs, and [we] desperately wanted to get out and travel."

Michael and Loida:

"My first wife died, and I decided that rather than maintain a house, I would buy an RV and travel. ...[I] hoped to see more of this country. Then I met my current wife, who always dreamed of traveling."

Steve K:

"There is so much of the country to see and RV people are the 'kind' of people I find myself wanting to be around. My goal is to... choose my travels and destinations."

Most of the interviewees explicitly stated they love to travel, and that travel was a primary motivator.

HotSauceHippo:

"We originally were planning a trip abroad, but one night we decided that neither of us had seen much of the U.S. ...And what better way to see our country than in an old school RV?"

MilesAwayEveryday:

"We absolutely love travel and this was an ultimate way to do that."

TheAmericanFieldTrip:

"We love traveling, and especially seeing all the 'in-between' places that we wouldn't experience if we traveled another way...Living on the road and traveling full-time have always been goals of ours. We wanted to travel more in the U.S. and specifically, to see all the national parks, and we knew driving was the best way to do that. As we were talking about our goals last year, we decided that the timing would never be perfect to leave our lives and move onto the road, and that we didn't want to put this dream off. Our goals have evolved over time; after the election, we wanted to do something that would help us understand better the current moment in the U.S., and we wanted to try to document different cultures and people within our country. We have also learned much more about public land issues since we started and are working to educate other people about the current issues and legislation surrounding the public land in the U.S."

OurVieAdventures:

"We both love being outside and are stoked on adventure in all of its forms, so I think the trip was born from our passion and love for the earth. We also love to travel, so we thought that we should try to see as much of our own country as possible. We thought, 'well maybe we could visit a bunch of the national parks?' Then when we found out that we would graduate during the 100 year anniversary, we thought — why not try and get to all of them?! So we went for it!"

Finally, there are those that want "no regrets."

Dawn L:

"I'm retired and wanted to see the country. I'm a hospice nurse and noted that what people regret the most is what they didn't do; I wanted to not have that regret."

Experiencing Nature

RV life is certainly different from backpacking, tent or car camping, but it still forces you to stay more in touch with nature. Whether it is hiking, having fires in your fire pit, eating at your picnic table, doing your work outdoors, taking walks, swimming in the lake by your campsite, or merely following the weather, RV life does encourage a connection to nature that sticks-and-bricks life does not.

8Paws1Tail:

"We love the freedom and being in nature."

Being tuned into nature is part of what I was seeking. At my stationary home, I tended to stay inside my house or inside a restaurant. I lived in a beautiful part of the country, but rarely got out to enjoy it, even though I would claim it was important to me. It was just too easy to not do it. RV traveling, without a doubt, has nudged me outdoors and into nature much more regularly. In fact, as I write this I am sitting outside in my camp chair in front of Lake Superior. Not a bad way to write a book!

Jax733:

"We were doing a lot of camping and no matter how long we were gone we never seemed to want to go back home, even though home was a fun and enjoyable place to be. We liked waking up in nature and having the flexibility to do whatever we wanted to do that day."

TravelExploreUncover:

"We wanted to slow down, get back into nature, and enjoy our lives."

HotSauceHippo:

"The best thing [about this lifestyle] is being close to nature and seeing a new place every few weeks."

LivingLifeInBetween:

"I also love not just seeing our beautiful country, but experiencing it by rock climbing, hiking, and mountain biking."

Escaping the Mundane and Grind

The Old American Dream was one of working a (preferably) high-paying 9-to-5 job, getting married, buying a house, and having 2.5 kids. It was about following orders and following others. That dream has left many feeling unfulfilled, inspiring the birth of the New American Dream. In this new dream, work is done in a different way, with fewer hours, less stress, around your family, or perhaps not at all.

HappyCamperWives:

"We were tired of being sick and sick of being tired. Our goals were to find happiness outside the 9-to-5 rat race and see if there was more to life than working."

OurIncredibleDash:

"We were tired of the rat race. My husband was military for 12 years and missed the first part of our two oldest children's lives with back-to-back deployments where his life was at risk daily."

TravelExploreUncover:

"We hit the road to get away from a traditional 40-hour work week and the expectations of life."

GoWiththeFlowandCo:

"We were also getting tired of 'living for the weekend' and the 'daily grind' eating away at our mental and physical health."

Laura J:

"I hit the road for a number of reasons: I was laid off from my job and couldn't face the prospect of looking for a new one; I was renting a place in the Bay Area and the cost of living is very expensive there...I'd always dreamed about traveling around in an RV.... I like being in control of where I am, where I'm going next, when I go.... not being tied down to others expectations or schedules (like work, school, etc)."

Leading a Simpler Life

One of the fascinating things that I discovered from conducting the interviews is that people from each of the generations expressed the same desire: to live a simpler life.

> **Jeff & Coffee (Baby Boomer):**
>
> *"Our goal was to exchange the paradigm that is formerly known as The American Dream (go to college, work a life-long career, buy a house) ...for a simpler, untethered life. We chose to accumulate experiences over material things...and full-timing in a travel trailer helps one discard the unnecessary."*

SunnyJunket (Baby Boomer):

"We hit the road for a simpler life and to get out from under mortgages and/or rent and to take on the challenge while enjoying our passion for travel."

Jax733 (Gen-X):

"We both love to travel, and the older we've gotten the more we have valued experiences over things. The more things we accumulated, the less fulfilled we were...If your life and days are filled with beauty and adventure, you need less stuff to make you happy. Putting ourselves on a limited budget has made me appreciate things more and think through purchases more carefully. It feels good to not be as much of a consumer. I take more pleasure in the smaller things in life like a beautiful campfire, a frosty drink on a hot day, and feeling more in tune with nature and the natural rhythms of the seasons."

WanderlandTravelers (Gen-X):

"Another lesson we've learned is that we are far more adaptable than we give ourselves credit for! With RV living, you'll be in a smaller space, have a much smaller shower, and if you're boondocking a lot, it becomes very important to be much more conservative about water and power usage. These are pretty inconsequential when you consider the richness you gain in this new lifestyle. Those things that we thought would be difficult adjustments (navy showers, less frequent showers, limited energy to power our devices, limited fridge space) just became our 'new normal' and we just moved forward and accepted it for the reality that it is. We wake up every day excited about our life, the places we're in and the places we're going."

OurIncredibleDash (Millennial):

"What I like best is that life is less busy and more simple."

RVegan (Millennial):

"I wanted to live more simply, with the goal of saving money and creating financial independence."

Increasing and Improving "Family Time"

When asked what they like best about this lifestyle, many of our travelers mentioned the perk of being with their family/spouse/pet all day, every day.

LivingLifeInBetween:

"The best part about this life is being with my husband 24 hours a day seven days a week. He is my best friend, and we have grown so much in the short time we have been on the road. Being with our dogs all day long is awesome, too."

8Paws1Tail:

"We also love that we are together a lot more. When in the city, I (Gabi) worked extremely long hours and it felt like Steph and I were sometimes two ships passing in the night. Now we're exploring together, working together and love discovering the world together. With our dog, we're a happy little family of three."

One couple had never lived together before and used this RV lifestyle as a way to see if they were compatible. Apparently they are, because they are now engaged.

TravelExploreUncover:

"During this journey, we hope to find out more about ourselves, create a strong foundation for our relationship, and see our country."

Another couple had experienced intense times apart, while the husband was deployed. They were sad that he missed out on much of their first two kids childhoods and wanted to change that for the future.

Our Incredible Dash:

"Ultimately we just wanted to be together and to not have to worry if he was going to come home alive. Our main focus and goal is to live a fuller life, together. To get back to the basic principles of a close knit family and a simple life."

Another traveler, who has been on the road for more than eight years, loves the amount of time he gets to spend with his family.

Wandrly:

"I sit outside at campgrounds and work the early part of the day away designing websites or writing articles. I see my kids scoot by on their bikes or skateboards. I taught them to do both, heard their first words, saw their first steps, taught them to swim in Cenotes in Mexico and just more or less am not missing everything because I'm off at some job."

Always Seeing Something New

I've always lived in beautiful places: Washington, D.C., San Diego, San Francisco, Pismo Beach, and Portland (Oregon), to name a few. I've also always become somewhat jaded in my *experience* of these areas, because I saw them every day. At one point, I lived within 10 minutes of Muir Woods — with its spectacular massive trees — and I had stopped seeing them as their amazing selves. Pismo Beach is perhaps one of the most beautiful coastlines in the world, but it became commonplace. Being on the road with an ever-changing view has enhanced my recognition of, and appreciation for, the awesome-ness that is our world. Other travelers also seem to cherish that this lifestyle allows them to always see the world through fresh eyes.

HotSauceHippo:

"The best thing about this life is the changing scenery. We lived in a beautiful area of the country, but found ourselves not enjoying its beauty because it became 'normal.' Now, as we're driving to different spots each week, we get to experience that place's beauty for the first time. The newness, and the knowledge that we won't stay forever, conjures up a true appreciation for a location. We cherish what is right in front of us because we know we're on to the next beautiful place tomorrow."

GoWiththeFlowandCo:

"The best thing about this lifestyle is the mobility and flexibility. If you don't like a location, move! ...We've never really not liked a neighbor, but, if you don't...beep beep! It's also great to experience the different weather in such extremely different locations — from the dry heat of the desert, to the damp, tree covered coast line...I love it! Also, we are very active and always walking the dogs in new environments — it's so enjoyable to always have something new to look at or experience!"

WanderlandTravelers:

"We love the constant variety and changing landscapes. We love getting to experience places that we never would have thought to visit in our previous life. Some of our most favorite spots are those that we just happened upon when looking for a place to camp along our route. There is immeasurable beauty in the desert and mountain landscapes of eastern California, Utah, and Arizona."

We actually have had the same experience. Two of our favorite campgrounds in Canada were ones where we didn't plan on staying. We were looking for a stop along the way and were pleasantly surprised by these two special locations. (In case you are going to Canada, the two "surprises" I just mentioned are Buffalo Pound Provincial Park in Saskatchewan and Aaron Provincial Park in Ontario. If you want specific site suggestions, go to my blog. Blog address is at the end of this book.)

Waking up in a new place is exciting. Having the opportunity to change your scenery whenever you want is a thrill that I cherish. I bore easily, and with this lifestyle I am never bored.

Jax733:

"[What we like] best: The open-ended adventure of it and being able to wake up in a different place and explore different options."

TravelExploreUncover:

"Life on the road is more exciting, enlightening, and free....Everyday can be new. Every week we have a new backyard. ...To be honest, our days often look different because we travel at a fast pace. We generally only stay a few days at a time. Our day may include a quick morning workout, a motorcycle ride, kayaking, walking the dogs, and settling in to work on our social media."

RVegan:

"The coolest feeling is the day after moving, waking up with a brand new view."

Vagabroads:

"I decided to hit the road because we only live once. There is so much to see, and it is all so different than you can imagine sitting at home on the couch. I originally wanted to travel and find a place to settle down, but now after traveling this way, I just want to explore more. I don't know if I'll ever be content just being in one place."

Jeff and Coffee:

"We have been very fortunate the last 2.5 years. The first year we stumbled into a camp hosting stint: 20 hours work in exchange for a beautiful site with full-hookups in a southern Utah state park for three months. The remainder of that year was spent traveling the western states, boondocking 75% of the time. The next year, we decided to remain in one our newfound favorite areas: Escalante and The Grand Staircase National Monument in southern Utah. The typical day of the first-year nomad was either total relaxation or exploration; every day was something new. The second year we spent seven months in a small town of 800 to really feel that small town life. The biggest realization of life on the road is that each new day's events are unwritten."

Inspiring Others

A few of our travelers mentioned the desire to inspire others to pursue their dreams. Not necessarily to travel in an RV, but rather to strive towards whatever is important to them.

OurVieAdventures:

"On a larger, and probably more important, scale — We want to inspire people, as corny as it sounds, to live their dreams! We couldn't care less about convincing people that life on the road is the number one thing… we just wanted to show people that if you are serious about making something happen, you can. We had no idea how we were going to make it all work… we just went for it. Since we were serious about making it happen, things fell into place, and we learned a lot along the way. We want people to realize that no matter what you come up with — writing a book, going to med school, or living in an old RV with the love of your life — it is possible. We want to push people to let go of excuses and get out and live your dreams! We want more people to have 'I can't believe this is my life right now' moments!"

I suppose that is the motivator for me writing this book. I feel so fortunate to have this lifestyle — to have made the leap of faith to explore this opportunity — and I want to encourage and inspire others to pursue their dreams, as well.

WHAT'S YOUR STYLE...

Let's assume that you're hooked (or almost hooked) on the idea of living the dream in an RV. The next step is realizing that your *reasons* for wanting to do this will dictate *how* you go about making it happen. For example, if your main priority is to explore nature in relative solitude, then you will want to explore how best to do this and what that means from a practical point of view.

Boondocking Versus Formal Campground

Boondocking, for those of you who don't know, is camping outside of formal campgrounds on public land owned by agencies such as the U.S. Forest Service, Bureau of Land Management, Army Corps of Engineers, and some state agencies. These lands offer legally free (or dirt cheap) camping with little or no amenities (such as hookups, trash receptacles, toilets, water, etc.). Agencies usually call this "dispersed camping." There are often rock-rimmed fire-pits indicating spots where others have camped. While it is free, it is not without rules. Go to the organizations' websites to learn their specific regulations, which often include guidelines on where to camp, pack-in pack-out rules, fire regulations, time limits, etc.

On-grid (in campgrounds or RV parks with services) options include everything from national, state, county, or municipal parks to KOAs and other independently owned and run parks and campgrounds. These range from very natural settings to concrete slab parking lots with no greenery and everything in between.

There are also the in-between options: parks and campgrounds that offer some amenities, but not all, or that have no amenities (except perhaps a drop toilet) but still charge a fee.

The type of environment that you will seek out depends on your goals and dreams. If you are looking for a "back to nature" experience, you may want to outfit your rig for more "dry camping" (without hookups). This is also helpful if you are on a budget, as you can live off-grid at little or no expense. For a detailed discussion about RVing off the grid, see the later discussion ("Outfitting Your Rig") under Nuts and Bolts.

If, on the other hand, you seek a social environment with other like-minded people, and like the security or amenities of full-hookups, wifi, laundry, showers and the like, then you can select parks that offer these services, and you must budget for the additional expense. These private RV parks can cost as little as $25 but usually run upwards of $50/night or even more. (In Florida, in the winter especially, you can expect to pay more than $100/night even at the "cheap" parks, and they book-up nine months in advance). There are clubs that you can join which offer discounts at these types of RV "resorts:" Good Sam Club, Passport America, KOA, and sometimes AAA provides members with discounts as well. Also ask about AARP discounts, if it applies to you.

You will either pay for the modifications, enabling you to be off-grid more, or you will pay more at the campground or RV park to have the services provided to you. You just need to decide which experience is more "you."

RVWanderlust:

"We haven't put a huge emphasis on being able to wild camp (also known as dry camping or boondocking) because our work schedule requires a lot of stability. Since it isn't a priority right now, we don't have solar and we haven't upgraded our batteries. Maybe we will with our next RV!"

Obviously, there can be a balance between the two as well. We usually dry camp for two to six weeks, and then stop off in a full-service park for a night in between locations to fill up our water, dump our sewer, charge our devices, take showers, and do laundry. It's a system that works for us, but again, everyone is different!

By the way, I'd be remiss not to mention another type of boondocking that does get us all through long-travel days, and in some cases, travelers make it a lifestyle choice: boondocking at Walmarts, casinos, and travel stops. There are plenty of places to crash overnight for free, the ones mentioned a minute ago being the most common. These are not places that you would normally "set up camp," but if you are in a pinch to break up a drive and only need a place to sleep, all of these are options.

One Instagrammer (**@AdventuresOnWheels**) who was surveyed, but not interviewed, said this in a post, "On our way north to Maine, we stopped to spend the night at one of the best stops ever! Mohegan

Sun Casino. They have a dedicated RV parking lot overlooking the river. And to top it off the casino was gorgeous! We got there around 3 p.m. and spent the evening enjoying the casino before leaving early the next day. Highly recommend this spot for boondocking."

I met a couple who boondocked at Walmarts across the country, never stopping at a formal campground or dispersed camping location. Some other businesses will allow overnight camping, if you ask them. You could also join "Boondockers Welcome," a membership website that encourages people to post their own property for RVers to boondock on. Another membership based program is Harvest Hosts which lists wineries and vineyards that allow people to stay one or two nights. If you use one of these latter two options, bear in mind it is polite to give a gift to your host (or in the case of Harvest Hosts, buy wine) as a thank you.

Social Versus Private

As you've read in the stories, some people do this lifestyle for solitude and privacy or escaping the rat race, and others do it to socialize with like-minded individuals. Your inclinations will influence your choices as to where you stay and how you structure your experience.

I used to sell real estate, and I always told my clients that in buying a house they were buying a lifestyle. If they bought a house on acreage, they would have privacy, but may have to drive a long way just to buy milk. If they bought a condo in the city, they'd have a "walking lifestyle," where they could walk to restaurants and bars and shops, but they'd have little privacy. If they bought a house in the "burbs," they might be surrounded more by families with younger kids. If they bought a house with a view, which are typically high on hills, they'd have their view to enjoy but would likely have to drive down their hill to do any community activities like dining and shopping.

Choosing where to camp is much the same: You are choosing a lifestyle. The benefit to RV traveling over a stick-and-brick house, though, is you can mix things up whenever and however often you want. We love boondocking in the middle of nowhere. We can hang out in our hammocks or camp chairs for days, playing with our dog or playing card games. But eventually we have to shop for food or dine at a restaurant, and we have the luxury to move to a more urban spot when this need arises. For us, it's the best of all worlds! Also, you can have a beach "house" one week, a desert house another, a mountain home the following month, a lake house after that, and so forth. The environmental and social choices are endless.

We have friends back home that meet us on the road, too. Sometimes we will stay at one location for a month so that waves of friends and family can join us at the same spot. We did this in Sedona, AZ last winter and it was so much fun.

Planned Versus Spontaneous

I'm a self-proclaimed planner, for better or worse. I tend to like to know where we are going next, or I get a little anxious. My wife, on the other hand, likes the spontaneity of being able to move when she feels like it and go where weather dictates and interest lies. We've learned to strike a balance between the two.

Jax733:

"Be flexible in your travels and don't map out every step if you don't have to. Be open to staying longer at certain places if you want to. Pick areas where there is a lot to do, and stay in one place and explore."

Summer is a hard time to be spontaneous, because campgrounds are booked up, far in advance of the season. This means that during the summer we follow a plan that we book in the winter or spring. I use the (free) Roadtrippers app for this purpose. I've tried many, many apps and websites for trip planning, and they've all fallen short except for Roadtrippers. With Roadtrippers, you can put in your locations and it will tell you how far each spot is from the next. You can click and drag to change the order. You can write in notes and dates. You can turn locations off and on to play with whether you will go to a particular area or not. You can also post it to your blog, so friends and family can find a spot to meet you. It's a very flexible trip planning tool, and I can't recommend it enough.

In exchange for planning a route to alleviate my stress during high season when it is hard to get a spot, we've agreed that off-season will be spontaneous. We check weather reports daily and check our moods, and then we decide when it is time to leave and go somewhere new. I have to admit it is an awesome way to live, once I relax and let go of the planner in me.

Jax733:

"We want to be flexible and plot a course based on weather, intuition, and random chance. We want to be open to what the road brings us, both in terms of people and of places."

Weather is a huge factor for us (and for most other RVers). Some people chase the sun, which we don't, but we also don't want to be towing the trailer in wind, rain and snow. That is why we are so reliant on weather apps to influence our decisions.

Our favorite weather apps are Dark Sky (a paid app, but worth it), Wunderground (aka Weather Underground), The Weather Channel, and Rain Alarm. Dark Sky and Rain Alarm both have radar displays and alerts that you can program. This allows you to know when temperatures will be dropping below a set level or when rain or wind is in the area, for example. Dark Sky is also unique in that it has weather satellite for the forthcoming days, whereas most satellite weather apps only have the past up to "now." We like Weather Underground, because you can "change stations" to choose a spot closer to you or more indicative of the weather you will be experiencing. The Weather Channel offers a 15 day forecast which is five days longer than most other apps.

I just discovered a new website called www.weathertab.com. This website provides free long-term weather projections. By long-term, I mean months and months in the future. I'm not sure yet how accurate it is, since I just started using the site, but I'm excited at the possibility!

It is strange to be so reliant on weather apps and so influenced by weather, but that is a part of this lifestyle. It does make me feel more connected to the earth though, in a funny way.

Move a Lot Versus Move a Little

Whether to move infrequently or often is one choice that may change for you once you are on the road. It is hard to know how long you want to be somewhere until you experience that place.

Vagabroads:

"I've learned that you can go at your own pace, but if you like a place, be prepared to spend more time than you thought there."

We know people who move every few days and some who stay in the same spot for four to six months at a time. We have found our rhythm to be boondocking somewhere private and quiet for 10-20 days, then stopping overnight at an RV park with utilities and hookups, followed by going to our next dry camping destination for another 10-20 days. Obviously, there have been times when we've been disappointed in a place and have left sooner. There have also been times where we've been pleasantly surprised and extended our stay. But our typical rhythm is the ten to twenty days in one spot.

TheAmericanFieldTrip:

"We're traveling at a pretty fast pace in order to visit all 59 national parks, so we spend quite a bit of time driving. The kids do really well in the car, but we have moments where we all get cabin fever. We listen to a lot of music, play a lot of road games, and try to have a sense of humor about things."

Keep in mind that moving days can be stressful. Every time you move you must secure your belongings, including dishes and pots and pans, turn things off (refrigerator, water heater). If you are in a place with hook-ups you must unhook; if you are towing something, you have to attach, and later detach. If you've been dry camping, you need to find a sewer dump and potable water station. If it's a long travel day, you likely need to stop for fuel, which can be its own stressor. It's truly a process.

Now that we are in a groove, we can pull up our roots and be on the road in 45-60 minutes and then set back up at our next destination in about 20-45 minutes. We tend to drive no more than five hours, and prefer three.

When we started our travels, it took us much longer to get ready to move and then to set back up. I would estimate the numbers at twice as long on both ends. That makes for a really long day! The whole family dislikes moving days, but it is a necessity in this lifestyle. It's probably the only thing I don't love about being on the road, and it influences why we tend to stay places longer than some people.

We've gotten really skilled (in my humble opinion) at hooking up our trailer to our truck. When we first purchased our trailer I thought there was no way we'd remember all the steps and get it right. I was stressed out every night before a travel day. Now, it's not a big deal at all. We have our steps that we do the same way every time. We use walkie-talkies for communicating during hook-up, pull-out, and pull-in, so we aren't yelling at each other and trying to decipher hand signals. By the way, that alone (the walkie talkies) have been a life saver. Get some. Another tip: when guiding the driver, use "to the driver's side" and "to the passenger's side," instead of "left" and "right." It is clearer for everyone.

MilesAwayEveryDay:

"We used to take a lot longer to get ready when packing up and in, so we could move to another location, but we've really come together well with that. Now it takes us very little time to get everything ready inside and outside of the RV and to hook up our tow car. We get excited and high five each other when we are all done, and again when we are rolling down the road."

Tour Versus Live

Some of us want to visit all the national parks, national monuments, state parks, national forests, etc. Others just want a relaxed lifestyle in which they can connect with their partner or family during a hike or a game or a nap in a hammock. This, too, is a lifestyle choice. It's not an all-or-nothing situation, though.

RVWanderlust:

"Like pretty much everyone else, we were overeager to cover a lot of miles when we first started. That burned us out quickly. We went from traveling every Saturday, to moving every other Saturday. That gave us more time to relax, live 'real life,' and see each area. It really is not sustainable to play tourist all the time."

We have struck a balance between being a tourist and living a "normal" life. The first five days at a new destination (if it's a national park, for example), we spend getting the lay of the land and doing the touristy things. After that, for the next 5-15 days, we usually relax, perhaps do a hike in the morning and a fire at night. Maybe we play some card games. If we are near or on the water, we take our dog (and us) for a swim.

Laura J:

"A typical day involves reading/listening to the news, walking/hiking/exploring with the dog, tidying up/sweeping, making meals, planning where I'm going next, watching downloaded Netflix."

Steve K:

"My favorite days are waking up to sunshine, a palm tree, and water. A nice relaxed morning having coffee, reading an online newspaper, Facebooking, and emails and then a slow bike ride around the campground. Finding new restaurants and shopping in the afternoon and relaxed evening by a campfire are high on my list."

GET RID OF YOUR "STUFF" AND THEN CUT IT IN HALF

Even those who want to "live large" talk about the need to get rid of "stuff" once they commit to getting on the road. There just isn't enough room to store a sticks-and-brick's household-worth of belongings.

OurIncredibleDash:

"We don't need as much as we have. We still have too much stuff! I wish we'd gotten rid of more before we started, but we were under a time crunch, so we have quite a bit still in storage."

Michael and Brenda:

"[It took] about a year [to get on the road]. The last six months was the most stressful and crazy. Trying to sell everything; *deciding what to keep and not."*

Jax733:

"Really pare down your life and bring as little as possible: you need less than you think."

I posed the question in follow up interviews, "what did you bring that you don't need," because we *all* brought things on our adventure that we later found were unnecessary. Here's the list of what our travelers brought that they later got rid of:

- Kitchen items: plates, bowls, pots and pans, steamer, crock pot, infrared turkey fryer, toaster oven, baking dishes, muffin pan, carbonated-water maker, juicer
- Clothes and shoes
- Christmas decorations
- Twelve person tent
- A tiny clothes washer
- Jigsaw puzzles
- Books
- Outdoor mat
- Second TV
- Bedsheets, towels, blankets
- House plants
- High heels
- Robes

WanderlandTravelers:

"I don't think I've cracked a single book that we brought! We've listened to our audiobooks while driving, but in our down time we tend more towards digital hobbies or finding great hikes. We also have more bedsheets, towels, and blankets than we need. And I'm still carrying around a muffin pan — surely some day it will come in handy!"

HotSauceHippo:

"Ryan and I envisioned we'd have these luxurious mornings lounging around in our robes, sipping coffee as the sun rose over the trees. This was a lofty dream, especially since Ryan and I aren't morning people. Waking up is usually more of a, 'make the coffee and down the first cup as fast as possible' situation, so that we can actually function as human beings. We also are really horrible at lounging. We like to move, get going, or do some work of some kind."

TravelExploreUncover:

"If you haven't used it after a month of traveling, you really won't need it! So ship it somewhere safe or sell it!"

RVWanderlust:

"We go through everything every six months and are always amazed at how much we get rid of. Our rule of thumb is that if we haven't used something in a year, we automatically get rid of it. We have a ton of storage in our diesel RV, so it's easy to keep items we don't actually need."

MilesAwayEveryDay:

"We literally gave away the majority of our kitchen... we realized how little we actually needed."

About three months into our trip, we met up with family and gave them several items to keep for us: a crockpot (what were we thinking?), an extra dog bed (again, one is enough), and some other miscellaneous items. Really think through what you are bringing. Where will you store it? Think about whether there is some way to double the use of things you are bringing or that are built in to your rig. For example, I saw an ingenious idea on Instagram: someone wrapped a metal table leg with rope for their cats to use as a scratching pad. Think like that, and you'll be in good shape.

Keep in mind, there are things you "just have to have" with you, even though they may not make sense.

Wandrly:

"I don't absolutely need a bunch of books on tree identification and birding...but I like them. Same with my guitar, our iPad, but these things make life more enjoyable. We really do try and eliminate everything we don't need. We're a family of five in a van, after all."

What to Bring That You May Not Expect

I also asked our travelers what they wish they'd brought and what they purchased while on the road. Here are some of their comments, which are good suggestions to consider (in no particular order):

- Solar panels and solar chargers

- Tiny shop vacuum

- Low-flow shower head and faucets

- Cast iron skillet

- Copper chef pan

- Instant hot water pot

- Electric blanket or a 12V heated mattress pad

- Items to make outdoor experiences better: anti-gravity chairs, big rug, nice grill, propane fire pit

- Outdoor activity items: hiking boots, walking poles, water belts, water shoes, inflatable kayaks

- A generator

- Cell phone battery pack

- Full ratchet/wrench set

- MaxxAir fans (built-in high efficiency fans)

- Battery-powered (or 12V) fan

- Step ladder/stool

- Hotspot

- Guitar

- Computer

- Sewing machine

- Coffee pot

- A bug zapper wand

- A veggie spiralizer

- A backup camera

- Reusable bags

- Good camera with plenty of SD cards

- Extension cords

- A dash-cam

- A GoPro camera

- Dual USB cigarette lighter charger for the car

Many people said solar is a great addition, and the other suggestions that got multiple "votes" were a vacuum, step ladder, outdoor activity items, electric blanket of some variety, some version of a fan, and a generator. I also highly recommend a Mr. Buddy Propane Heater, a long power strip (to plug in all your devices and charge at once and in one place when you are able), and some NASA approved "No Rinse" Body Wash and Shampoo. Definitely consider those purchases!

CAN I LIVE THIS LIFE IF I'M...

A Family ("Road Schooling")

Children are a common excuse people make for not being able to live this lifestyle: wanting to have babies, needing to wait for the kids to leave home, educating their children on the road, etc. I interviewed three families who gave birth to kids during their travels. Several families offer education solutions. All of the families feel that traveling as a family has brought them closer.

OurIncredibleDash:

"We are so much closer as a family."

Our "road families" offer good advice and share issues.

RVWanderlust:

"Caspian has always lived in an RV! Because Eric and I had been living the RV life for three years, adding a baby was pretty seamless. We knew what to expect and planned accordingly. We've been very minimalistic when it comes to baby items and clothing. The biggest issue is juggling his sleep schedule. When he naps in

the bedroom during the day, we can't go in there. When it's time for him to move to his crib in the living room at night, we have to retire to the bedroom. It took some figuring out, but we have a good rhythm now."

Parents with older (and school-aged) kids argue that allowing "the road" to educate their children is a unique and amazing thing.

TheAmericanFieldTrip:

"Our kids are 4 and 19 months, so they're not officially school-age yet. But we do love the opportunities our lifestyle gives us to learn about all kinds of things. Our 4-year-old loves the junior ranger program from the National Park Service and learns a lot from the booklets they give him at each park to fill out. We also practice his reading and writing while we're driving. Mostly we follow the kids' lead — if they are interested in something, we use whatever resources we have to learn more about it."

Wandrly:

"We have done everything from paying a teacher to come up with curriculum for us (first year on the road, I see that as silly now) to unschooling (basically just "not doing school" and letting the world's influences teach your child). For us, the right balance is a couple of hours a day focusing on subjects the kids actually enjoy. Everyone learns more that way... Our teenager has gone to public school a couple of times, when we were cooking our other youngsters, and he has absolutely destroyed any notions I have had that a public schooling setting can ever fully meet the needs of most children. They're either going to be 'too smart' intellectually I guess, and so be held back by those children who don't get stuff as quickly, or they'll need a different approach to learning than this factory life, sit-down-at-a-desk-all-day-and-absorb-largely-pointless-facts. Some kids just don't work that way. Those are the best kids, in my opinion..."

Some "road parents" show us that a traditional education can still be achieved while traveling and learning from the world.

OurIncredibleDash:

"[We have] three kids. We use Abeka Accredited Academy and have DVD lessons. We mail in the work and receive feedback. We have visited the academy in Florida and met the teachers, and love the school! [Our] best tip is to just learn from where you are! The world is your classroom — take advantage of every opportunity as a learning experience!"

RVWanderlust:

"Eric and I have five kids together. Two are now grown, two are in high school in California, and Caspian is with us all the time. Caspian will be home schooled when he's old enough. I home schooled all the way through high school before attending The University of Texas at Austin, so I'm very comfortable with how it works and what to expect. There's also a huge community of families on the road now, and I look forward to building friendships with other parents and learning from them."

The bottom line is, using the excuse of "after my kids leave home" as a reason to not follow your dream may prevent you from ever pursuing this unique opportunity. If you believe in "traditional" education, home schooling on the road can be achieved. If you'd rather develop your child's knowledge by learning from the world, that is an option as well. A combination of both is a possibility, too. While I don't have children, I can agree that by being on the road and visiting national parks, new communities, big cities and small, and meeting a wide variety of people has increased my personal education in a very real way.

Providing a "road education" doesn't mean there aren't challenges, but these issues can lead to positive results, too.

Wandrly:

"Our biggest 'issue' right now is that our teenager wants to live a more stationary life, so we're figuring out what that's going to look like. He's got about two years left of high school, and we think we can make it work for everyone. But with our younger ones, both of whom were born on the road, there is nothing different or special or weird or 'needs adjusting to' for them. This is the only life they've known and it's as natural as anything, more natural I think because having five people in a van forces you to live outside, to accept hot days and find a swimming hole or go for a bike ride to cool off, rainy days where you play in a tent with your brothers and have to learn to get along or get wet, and cold days where we make lunch at some place with a heater last for three hours."…Things like breaking down and the kids occasionally needing stitches or whatever we've faced, we've learned it's all just a process. Problems seem insurmountable until you just sit down and make a list of what needs done with a reasonable outcome...things somehow do always work out in the end."

A Couple

I've heard people say, "I don't know if I could live 24/7 in such a small space with [insert partner's name here]. We'd probably kill each other." Certainly there can be challenges unique to living in a small space, but interestingly, most couples have nothing but great things to say about living in tiny quarters. Of course, it's probably not a good idea to take it on if you are struggling in your relationship, as traveling full-time in an RV will likely exacerbate any existing problems. However, if your relationship is strong, it is likely to get stronger while on the road. The one key, which all our couples and families mention, is immediate communication when challenges arise.

Jeff and Coffee:

"Photographs can lie on Instagram or Facebook; life together as a couple 24/7 definitely has its challenges — there are bound to be arguments. Our [RV] dealer was very wise when he advised us to get our older 28-foot trailer over a newer 19-foot trailer...if we wanted to stay married. But square footage doesn't necessarily solve differences...it's the realization that we both need each other, and that always [comes] to both of us within a half a day."

Some couples have actually used the road as a way of peeling back the onion of their relationship to learn their compatibility.

TravelExploreUncover:

"This RV is the first place we've lived together. We both left our separate homes, and moved into the rig. This was wonderful, yet also challenging. Communication is key. Luckily, we had a strong foundation of communication, but it's a whole new level when you're together 24/7. When a conflict arises, we address it immediately. Both being very receptive, we offer strategies to improve the situation and implement it quickly. This has been successful for us."

Many years ago, before my wife was my wife, she told me a story about friends of hers. She described their decision to "test" their relationship by spending a year traveling in an RV. They believed that if their love could survive living in a tiny space with the stresses of being on the road, then they could survive anything. It is true that the road reveals underlying behaviors affecting your "couple-ship," but it also provides ample opportunity to learn how to grow and communicate as a couple.

HotSauceHippo:

"Since life is changing constantly while on the road, stress can be high and challenges often, but being a couple on the road, we tackle these problems together. It's like having a teammate always at your side. We have twice the brainstorming ability and always have another person to bounce ideas off of. It's awesome to always have someone to laugh with, share a new sight with, or discuss weird thoughts with."

Despite the incredible opportunities to grow as a couple, the challenge of having alone time is still present. As a couple, you may need to learn how to give each other space in a small space.

Jax733:

"[One issue is a] lack of alone time/space. We [deal with this by] doing things separately occasionally. We have our defined tasks that we've gotten good at. We divide and conquer errands and chores. Give each other space."

WanderlandTravelers:

"Traveling as a couple, we've fallen into our different roles and we each have certain duties or chores. Brad handles the outside of the rig while I tend to things inside. We both work on trip planning: how many miles we want to travel and whether there's free camping at the destination, figuring out dump stations along our route, and researching hikes or activities to do once we're there. Any issue that might arise between us can usually be solved by being a better listener and not letting emotions flare. If at least one of you can keep calm, it helps to bring the other one back down. I'd say that's the same as life before. It's just so important to be respectful and be sincere."

GoWiththeFlowandCo:

"It is just Steve and me, our 12-year-old golden retriever (Lenny), and our yellow lab (Maybel). So, we definitely see a lot of each other, but, luckily we like each other! But, like I said earlier — everything in moderation! It's important for us to have time away from the pups — and they do a good job staying in the RV when we go into national parks, or out for a happy hour drink. Also, we run errands separately sometimes and work on different projects or activities for our 'alone time.'"

8Paws1Tail:

"Knowing how to respect and trust each other is first and foremost. Communication is key and knowing to give yourselves time for enjoying each other's enjoyments as well as your own."

Compatibility is certainly important. If you don't communicate well in your "sticks and bricks" home, then that will be intensified on the road. If you have a strong foundation of mutual respect, traveling full-time can truly enhance your relationship.

8Paws1Tail:

"We really haven't had any issues as a couple on the road. We're both pretty calm and know when the other needs extra space or time out."

Vagabroads

"I get along with my partner really well. I am surprised that we haven't fought more, but we've both learned what is and isn't actually important on this trip, so that has helped a lot. Typically when we do fight, we just need a little bit of space from each other for a little while. Sometimes I will stay down in the car or go to the beach, and she will stay in the tent or vise versa. Knowing that space is a good thing on occasion is key. Also sometimes adding another person or two to our situation is helpful because we can focus on other things."

Single

Singles on the road certainly have ample alone time; their challenges are different.

Laura J:

"I'm a solo traveler, so the biggest impact is that I have to know how to drive, set up, attend to the systems, and troubleshoot the vehicle. There have [also] been a few times when I haven't done something, because I didn't want to leave the dog alone in the vehicle. ...if I was traveling with someone, one of us could stay with him and the other one could explore....As a solo person, there is no way I could do [these travels] without my dog. He helps provide structure during the day, and because I want him to get out and about, [this] also helps determine where I go. National parks aren't very dog friendly, so we go to more national monuments and state parks."

Being young and single on the road can make developing new, or romantic, relationships a bit harder.

RVegan:

"I am 25 and single, and it is difficult to meet people for dating. I have just been trying to meet people from activities around town — guitar, dancing, etc. It's hard knowing that I won't be in the town for more than 13 weeks. So far I've been on the road for one year and haven't found a partner."

Certainly ample single people (men and women) travel full-time on the road though, particularly in the "Van Life" lifestyle. If you are someone who cherishes your alone time, this may be the perfect life for you.

CAN I LIVE THIS LIFE IF I OWN A HOME?

The decision to sell your home or rent it out is a tough one. We opted to rent ours out and are happy to have the extra few dollars a month that decision has afforded us. However, if what you owe on a monthly mortgage is more than what you can get in rent, then leasing it out is not likely the best option. In that case, selling the home may make more sense.

Most of the interviewees who opted to sell were happy with their decision, and most of those who chose to rent out their home were also content they did the right thing. There is no "cookie cutter" answer to offer, but here are some considerations.

Should I Sell?

I found it very interesting that just as many homeowners decided to sell their homes as those who opted to rent their home out. Those that sold did so to alleviate the stress of maintaining the home, finding renters, and having a mortgage while on the road.

TravelExploreUncover:

"Josh owned a house, which he decided to sell. ...He didn't want the headache of being on the road and needing to fix problems thousands of miles away. He also didn't want the concern of draining his bank account if issues arose."

RVWanderlust:

"We sold our house. For us, we didn't want to worry about any possible home repairs, yard maintenance, or even just keeping it rented. We knew we'd be on the road for several years at a minimum, and we figured if and when we got another house, we'd go with something smaller, and we didn't want to keep a storage unit with all the furniture, etc. We just got rid of pretty much everything! It was quite liberating."

Some full-timers sold as a matter of practicality.

Michael and Loida

"[I] decided to sell; [we] couldn't support the RV and a house...I would rather travel while I can."

Other people thought they might find somewhere to settle down during their travels.

Michael and Brenda:

"We sold. We plan to buy again when we have done all we want with the open road lifestyle. We should know then, as well, the best places to settle back into a sticks-and-bricks home."

8Paws1Tail:

"We debated both. We ended up choosing to sell our home. We knew that we no longer wanted to live in California and wouldn't be coming back to our previous home. We also wanted the money to help fund our travels and purchase our RV."

Not everyone was perfectly happy with their decision, though.

Vagabroads:

"We decided to sell but looking back, we should've kept our house and rented it out. It was nice to have the money up front, but in the long run the investment in the house would've made more sense. I can say this mostly because our property value went up a lot while we were on the road...I might not feel the same way if that were not the case."

Hindsight is always 20/20, right?

Should I Rent It Out?

Travelers who decided to rent out their home did so for the income, despite the challenges of finding renters, dealing with home repairs, and covering (or exceeding) their mortgage payment every month.

GoWiththeFlowandCo:

"Along with our home that we rented out, we have a total of six rental properties. We manage them all from the road, and (fingers crossed) we have been successful at being on top of it! We had two leases ending (luckily at the same time), and we were able to complete most of the process from the road, but, Steve did end up flying back to check on them as well as a project house that we were 'flipping.' We have a work partner who does the construction while we're away, and we will go back to Ohio for the summer to work on the construction, as well. Then — back on the road!"

TheAmericanFieldTrip:

"We own our apartment in New York and are renting it while we're on the road. The rental income helps with our expenses."

Some use homes they've inherited or bought for other reasons as a way of generating income.

HappyCamperWives:

"We rent out a home we've never lived in. We had plans to move to Florida so bought a house with a renter in it because we were going to Alaska for the summer. When that renter asked to stay longer, we saw it as an opportunity to travel while also having investments."

Jeff and Coffee:

"We inherited my parents' home, and first we thought we should sell it to start our journey, but later deciding to rent it, immediately paid dividends. A very reliable and experienced property manager led to a dream tenant, and that person unknowingly has been paying for our adventure. Definitely a win-win situation."

Jax733:

"We live off of our rental income and savings. There certainly are downsides to renting out your home (or maintaining other rentals for income), but for us, the pros out-weigh the cons. We've been pretty lucky with tenants. We've had to hire people to make some repairs, but our tenants have been very cooperative and have helped make it smooth."

These decisions show that both scenarios can work. Pick what is best for you and move forward to your life of freedom!

CAN I LIVE THIS LIFE IF I CONTINUE TO WORK?

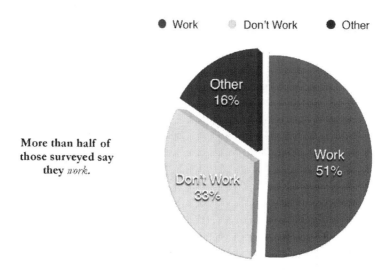

● Work   ◌ Don't Work   ● Other

Other
16%

Work
51%

Don't Work
33%

More than half of those surveyed say they *work*.

I thought most full-time RVers would be retired, but more of our travelers work than not.

MilesAwayEveryDay:

"We definitely work! Hahaha. We have often been asked, since we are younger than the typical RVer, if we are independently wealthy, hit the lottery, are trust fund babies, or just have wealthy parents footing the bill. All you can do is laugh it off, tell them they guessed incorrectly and explain that we have done this all on our own, and we continue to work really hard to make this life possible."

Making a Living on the Road

So, how do you pay the bills while living the dream on the road? As you would expect, many of our travelers work in internet or tech fields.

MilesAwayEveryDay:

"Our main company provides all elements of branding for your business, as well as web applications and more. We love that we are so fortunate to work remotely."

WanderlandTravelers:

"Brad works as a web developer at a small company where all employees have been working remotely for a couple years now. He worked remotely out of our house for almost a year when we started taking the idea of going nomadic seriously. Once we had made up our mind, Brad let his manager know our plans and she was really supportive and excited for us."

COMMON JOBS

Of the 80 full-timers who work, the most common jobs are:

- Tech jobs (10)
- Social Media/Blogging (nearly everyone, many for income or sponsorship)
- Photography (6)
- Online marketing (5)
- Writing (5)
- Business consulting (4)
- Workamping (4)
- Craft items (3)
- Legal (3)

But what is interesting to me is the variety of other jobs that people are doing from the road. Here's a list of some:

- Film
- Contract healthcare
- Railroad work
- Raft guide
- Farm work
- Motel maid
- Convenience store clerk
- Power plant labor
- Engineer

- Occupational therapist

- Health consultant

- Rental properties (managing their own)

Even if you don't plan on working, you may wind up extending your trip which may cause you to have (or want) to work. We set out on a year-long adventure, but I must say that a year goes by incredibly fast. After seven months, I panicked because we had barely gotten out of the southwest and central northwest areas. We had intended to go across Canada — how were we going to work that in with only five months left? I asked my wife how she was feeling about it, and we quickly agreed that one year just wasn't enough. We modified our plan to two years, with next summer being a trip to Alaska. Traveling full-time does get addictive. In fact, we may extend our adventure even longer!

Wandrly:

"The best advice I have for others who want to live a traveling life is to have some type of an income...because you just may get addicted and that whole 'sold my house to travel for a year' thing, well, a year can go by really quickly."

8Paws1Tail:

"We just started working, prior to that it was just money management and working off our savings. You can start this RV life by just working off a savings. You'll see so much, and you won't regret taking that vacation of a lifetime. Life is about taking chances, and if you're resilient you can survive. Ideas change along the way, and sometimes destiny has a different plan for you."

TravelExploreUncover:

"We plan on working next year. Laura is an occupational therapist and can complete short, contract positions all over the country."

Other people seem to have been planning for a traveling life for a very long time.

WanderlandTravelers:

"Brad had a nomadic lifestyle in mind over 15 years ago, when he was choosing his college major. He went with Computer Science, thinking that someday this might lend itself to working from anywhere."

RVWanderlust:

"We own a boutique online marketing company and work with small businesses. We started our company in January 2011, and built it up before we started RVing. Our long-term clients had learned to trust us, so they didn't have any issue with our travels. As long as we have an internet signal, we can do our work. We plan all of our stops ahead of time, to ensure we'll have connectivity."

WHERE CAN I FIND WORK?

There are websites and services that help travelers find work. Workamping is a popular option that many travelers seek.

Jeff and Coffee:

"We have camp hosted three winters in southern Utah at a state park....It provides us with electricity, water, and sewage, and a relatively mild winter in exchange for 20 hours per week of cleaning camp sites. We get to work together, and it's relatively easy work, while enjoying being outside among red canyon walls. We have stumbled onto the other temporary jobs by talking with locals and staying long enough in an area to better know the community. There are plenty of online sources to find work, either the traditional minimum wage jobs or camp hosting in national parks. Even the most tedious jobs are manageable with the right attitude in trying something new and knowing one can move on at any time."

Here are some of the Camp Host and other Workamp job websites. These sites help you find work in exchange for a campsite, often with hook ups, and sometimes with extra money paid.

- www.workamping.com
- www.work-camping.com
- www.coolworks.com
- www.volunteer.gov
- www.workampingjobs.com
- www.workamper.com
- www.work-for-rvers-and-campers.com
- www.workamp.com

Workamping is by no means the only option.

RVWanderlust:

"Full-time RVers Heath and Alyssa Padgett have developed some fabulous resources for working RVers. The RV Entrepreneur Podcast showcases people who are living and working on the road. Xscapers is also my top recommended membership program for working RVers. It's an arm of Escapees."

Some travelers sell their photographs on websites, such as:

- www.istock.com
- www.istockphoto.com
- www.123rf.com

Freelance writing is another big one — online blogging as well as travel magazines and business writing. A few of the websites featuring travel writing needs are:

- www.earthisland.org/journal
- www.gogalavanting.com
- www.literarytraveler.com
- www.matadornetwork.com
- www.sierraclub.org
- www.thetravelwriterslife.com

Of course you can always pursue more well-known travel or RV journals, such as Conde Naste, Sunset Magazine, National Geographic, RV Life Magazine, Trailer Life, Motorhome Magazine, and Camping World.

If you prefer blogging jobs, check out the e-book at www.beafreelanceblogger.com.

If you have experience in website development, graphic design, logo design, or any of many other "creative" skills, you can set up an account on one of these websites to get work:

- www.fiverr.com

- www.99designs.com

- www.Odesk.com

- www.Elance.com

One more source of work is Amazon Camperforce (www.amazondelivers.jobs). On this website, Amazon lists hundreds of postings nationwide for seasonal and part-time work. Everything from Fulfillment Associates to Campus Associates, and even Spanish-speaking work-from-home customer service positions are listed here.

In addition, some full-time RVers look for sponsors to provide them with free products in return for mention or photographic feature on their blog or in their Instagram posts.

Many travelers have created different avenues for making money on the road, including odd jobs in the service industry, manual labor, and working at the camps where they are staying. Blogging, life coaching and other personal services are additional sources of income for the travelers who took part in the survey.

Jeff and Coffee:

"We wanted to try the common-man jobs. So far we have worked as line cooks, motel maids, camp hosts, a tiny bit of carpentry, and a convenience store clerk."

TheVanProject:

"Diversify yourself. Give yourself lots of options for earning income, especially passive income, if possible. Be prepared to take on unconventional work, too."

OurIncredibleDash:

"Find what works for you. There is a way to make this work for everyone. Be frugal and be determined."

Several travelers have sought multiple sources of income.

OurIncredibleDash:

"Currently we workamp — only accepting jobs that offer site plus hourly pay for all hours worked. I do offset some expenses by helping people rid their homes and bodies from toxic chemicals, as well as coaching those who wish to start a travel blog. I blog, and that brings in income for us, and I also do social media work."

Heath and Alyssa:

"We spend most days editing videos in the RV, recording new podcast episodes, managing our Facebook group for RVers, and working on my software start up — CampgroundBooking.com."

One of our travelers, a contract attorney, believes that anyone can work on the road, if you think outside the box.

HotSauceHippo:

"Don't reinvent the wheel. You don't have to go out and look for a 'road life job.' Take what you're doing right now, or what you know you're already good at, and turn that into a job. Finding a job on the road is not difficult, you just have to change your mindset that it is possible and the opportunities will present themselves."

Another road attorney offers this advice.

Vagabroads:

"I maintained my law firm back home where I am able to complete a small bit of remote work — document preparation, etc. The biggest challenges have been our 'road schedule' — not having one, really, but being dictated by safe times to travel, weather, wifi. I try to get as much done as I can while in comfortable places. That may mean working 16 hours in one day so that I don't need to worry for the next 3. My advice would be to schedule your work time and stick to it as closely as you can. It's okay to stay at a campsite for an extra day for the peace of mind of getting something accomplished or to get an Airbnb or hostel bed for a few days to ensure good wifi. The more money you make, the more sustainable this way of life becomes — it's about priorities."

Our travelers offer some good examples of taking a job that you already have and turning it into traveling income.

RVegan:

"Traveling healthcare is very well paying, and the job requirements can range from an associate degree to a doctorate. The pay is excellent for travel therapy, I bring home around $85,000 per year after taxes. I am trying to transition to starting my own online business selling therapy materials, so I don't have to take four contracts a year and I can take advantage of my RV to travel more!"

SunnyJunket:

"Eric recently, miraculously, got a full-time travel job. We are just learning about our challenges such as not going exactly where we want to go!....As much as we want to be completely carefree, we still need to make money, but this lifestyle will enable us to save more money."

TheAmericanFieldTrip:

"David sells prints of his photography online and does a little graphic design freelance work. He spends a lot of time editing photos. We also spend time working on our website and social media in order to get sponsorships for our trip. We mostly work at night, after the kids go to bed. The hardest part is making enough time for work, since one of our primary goals was to spend more time together as a family."

As you can see, the options abound! It's just a matter of deciding for yourself what to pursue and then going for it! If you are creative, there are jobs to be found. Don't use needing to work as an excuse for not pursuing this lifestyle. Working on the road is definitely a different (and I'd argue better) experience than working at a place of business or even at your home office.

WORK/LIFE BALANCE

Finding work/life balance can be just as challenging for full-time travelers as it is for those that live stationary lives.

Heath and Alyssa:

"The hardest part about working and traveling is just striking the balance. I could work 24/7 and sometimes that leaves Alyssa begging for us to take the kayaks out and enjoy wherever we're camping. But the best part of working from the RV is when I can take an afternoon break and nap in the hammock or hike around a national park."

OurVieAdventures:

"The most difficult part of what I do is balancing work and life. It is very easy for me to get totally enveloped in a project and lose sight of the world around me. This was true prior to us hitting the road, so working on a contract basis, as opposed to a full-time basis, is one way I have overcome this. Also, working remotely has helped to physically remove myself from the case I'm working on. If I want to enjoy life outside of work I can simply close my computer, whereas when I was in an office, I couldn't just walk away."

LivingLifeInBetween:

"The biggest challenge with working remotely is being self-motivated. If you're going to work remotely when you're parked in Zion National Park, you need a lot of discipline to keep you on track. It's very tempting to just drop everything and go explore. This hasn't been too much of an issue for Gerrit. He simply needs to remind himself that his work is what gives us the opportunity to live this amazing lifestyle. It's also nice when, at the end of the work day, you get to go explore. It's not the simple 'work grind' that everyone is used to."

This lifestyle can be a perfect balance of work and life.

LivingLifeInBetween:

"While Gerrit works full time 9-to-5, I work on YouTube videos and our blog. When the work day is done we head out and explore whereever we are. We will either go for a hike, rock climbing, off roading, or mountain biking."

TECHNOLOGY SOLUTIONS TO WORKING ON THE ROAD

Heath and Alyssa:

"A lot of people assume that internet on the road is the biggest hurdle to working from our RV, but this really isn't a big deal. We have an unlimited Verizon plan and a cell booster that give us service almost everywhere. If you want to work from your RV, don't even try it without this!"

Cellular, wifi, and hotspot strength varies tremendously when on the road, but not always as you would expect. There have been more times than I can list in which we've been camped in the middle of nowhere and had an incredibly strong cellular (and hotspot) signal. As I've mentioned, we periodically stop in formal RV parks to dump, get water, charge devices, do laundry, take long showers, and use the park's wifi. Many, many times these parks claim to have hi-speed wifi, but in reality that wifi is only strong at one spot (usually the office) in the campground.

We've been sorely disappointed before, so we've learned to really probe the reservationist if it is truly necessary to get wifi at this location. Since cellular strength is important to many people and can be so unpredictably good or terrible, we now add that as a part of our campground/boondocking reviews on our blog (www.toystrailsandtails.com) in hopes that information will help other travelers.

If you need consistent connectivity, though, there are several steps you can take. First, get a cellular plan that has unlimited data and enable the hotspot function on your phone or get a separate hotspot device (or both). Second, have multiple service providers available to you. We have four devices on a Verizon shared unlimited data plan, one phone that works as a hotspot on an unlimited AT&T plan, and a

T-Mobile hotspot that has unlimited streaming capabilities.

This strategy has helped us have some amount of cellular at all but two locations in the last year, and, remember, we like to be in the middle of nowhere as much as possible. Lacking cellular only twice is pretty impressive, considering our preference.

Verizon does have the best coverage in the U.S., it seems, but it is beneficial to have other options, too. The third solution is to use a cellular booster and a wifi booster. These are separate devices, and you may want both. Finally, read reviews in advance of moving to a new spot to see if any reviewers mention the cell and wifi strength at that location. Often, reviewers will provide guidance on this matter. One other strategy is to use public wifi. Most towns, even small ones, have wifi available at coffee houses, laundromats, libraries, cafes, and some other random spots, so check with locals and business owners to find a good place for you to work. The website campendium.com includes cellular signal strength of the U.S. major carriers in their reviews.

LivingLifeInBetween:

"Sometimes maintaining a stable internet connection can be a challenge, but so far it hasn't been that much of an issue. We have a Verizon unlimited plan that we consume through a Netgear Jetpack. We have a 4G booster, but so far we've only needed it a couple times in six months."

RVegan:

"For internet I have a T-Mobile hotspot and an AT&T hotspot."

HotSauceHippo:

"For internet, I use a hotspot on my phone, or we spend time at a local coffee shop. Documents, or the research assignment, get sent to me by email, and I send the completed project back by email as well. Sometimes a phone call is required to ask for supplemental information or to explain my results, but mostly everything can be completed online."

WanderlandTravelers:

"The biggest challenge is having good internet. Brad needs to have a pretty strong internet connection (most public wifi won't do) for his daily video conferences with coworkers. We use our cell phone hotspots for most of our internet needs, supplementing with wifi when feasible. We have a mobile booster for when the mobile signal is too weak, and a wifi booster for when the wifi signal is weak. Both have come in handy innumerable times. We use the unlimited plans on Verizon and AT&T and have never run out of data, though we occasionally have spotty connections, even with the booster. The best advice we can give is to use boosters, they help a lot!"

MilesAwayEveryDay:

"We research as much as possible when planning our routes and potential places to stay. When we arrive somewhere, we scout the area for a spot that works for us. We've only had an issue once where there was absolutely no signal. We had to leave after one day, because we had client meetings we needed to conduct, and files that needed to be sent. Other than that, we've been really lucky. We have gone off grid before for days at a time, but only when we know we have nothing scheduled and time sensitive. There's plenty of work that can still be done offline. We had lightning fast service out in the middle of a forest once, that was the most surprising for us yet. So you never know what you're going to get, and plenty of times we've been pleasantly surprised."

TheVanProject

"We overcome the problem of poor internet connection, [by getting] as much work done as possible when the connectivity is good. Sometimes this means staying in one place for a little longer than we want. It's not a bad trade-off."

CAN I LIVE THIS LIFE IF I DON'T WORK?

People who don't work on the road either live off their savings, or have income from a pension, social security, or rental properties. If you live frugally, you can travel for quite some time on a modest savings account, according to our travelers. If you want to "live large," though, it will often take some other source of income, at least for the average full-timer.

To live frugally, you will need to consider boondocking often (or utilize military campgrounds, if that's an option to you), preparing your own meals, and staying in one place for a longer period of time to reduce fuel costs. In a future section, we will look at what our travelers say is a typical budget (there is a large range, of course). Our travelers offer good advice and insights.

TravelExploreUncover:

"Save more than you think you'll need. Campground, gas prices, propane, and unexpected expenses can add up very quickly."

Laura J:

"I could work remotely, but there would be impacts from that that I don't want right now: I'd need to be connected more consistently, I'd need to have more of a schedule/availability to others; and that's what I'm enjoying being away from! I also try to be pretty frugal: boondocking as much as I can, preparing my own food...live in a way that is most comfortable and feasible for [you], and don't feel like you have to live how someone else thinks you should."

Some travelers rely on social security, disability income, pension benefits, and the like.

Michael and Brenda:

"I have retirement income, 401, social security, and disability income."

OurIncredibleDash:

"My husband receives monthly disability for his injuries. He is also furloughed from the railroad for the last two years....When he is recalled, we will travel from station area to station area as he works."

Dawn L:

"We both get social security. My husband has a Navy pension and this helps. We actually stay on a lot of bases, the campgrounds are beautiful, and they are usually very nice."

NUTS & BOLTS

What Rig Should I Buy?

Most books about becoming a full-time traveling RVer have a section that details the differences between each of the "Classes" of RVs. This information is important to have, because you will be researching what is best for you. Rather than overlap these books with technical information, I will let our travelers share with you their reasons for picking their rig and any shortcomings or surprises they faced as a result of their decision.

There is no common RV type within the different generations. The age of the traveler doesn't seem to determine the type of rig. Even "family status" (i.e., couple, single, family with kids) doesn't seem to dictate the type of rig. There are families in small vans and large Class As and everything in between. The "must have" list seems to be based on factors that don't correspond to generational category or family status.

Here is a breakdown of the rigs driven by the 80 people surveyed:

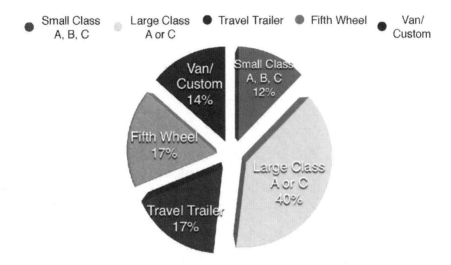

As you can see, there is no one-size-fits-all rig. What works for one family or couple, may not work for you. You must look back at the early section on dreams and goals first to start your examination of what RV may work best for you. After this step, make a list of lifestyle priorities. Then glance at the table at the end of this section to narrow down your options. Here are a few criteria to get you started thinking about what your priorities and lifestyle preferences are, but this is not an exhaustive list:

- Fastest travel

- Ease of parking

- Ease of set up at camping spot

- Most storage

- Largest interior

- Accommodations for guests

- Work space (like an office)

- Smallest to fit in any camping spot

- Largest (maximized) living space

- Convertible space (bedroom by night, living room by day)

- Most easily outfitted for off-grid camping
- Needs an attached tow vehicle
- Already have a strong towing vehicle
- Only want one vehicle to manage
- Nice amenities (such as dishwasher, clothes washer/dryer, air conditioning, kitchen counter space, etc.)
- Convertible bed vs. permanent bed
- Least expensive to buy up front
- Least expensive to maintain
- Money is no object
- Ability to go off-road
- No need to go off-road
- Big bathroom (with large shower and/or with bathtub)
- Small but functional bathroom
- No bathroom needed
- Have access to the interior of the unit while driving
- Separate motor from "house"
- Self-contained motor and "house"
- Easy to maneuver

Whichever "Class" of RV you decide to investigate, you should definitely consider using RV Consumer Group's site at www.rv.org for their analysis and reviews of specific brands and models of RVs. You do have to pay for their information, but it is extremely thorough and gives you great details regarding safety, quality, economy, and other factors. The cost of the service off-sets any mistakes you might make in choosing your rig without this valuable information.

CLASS A

*   photo courtesy of MilesAwayEveryDay

Quick description: Similar looking to a modern commercial bus with a huge window in the front and a blunt nose.

The vast majority of our full-time travelers decided on purchasing a Class A, and most have been very happy with their decision.

Michael and Brenda:

"We have a 2015 Winnebago Tour 42HD. We bought the Winnebago because of the quality of the product,...layouts and detail. We decided if we were going to do this, either go big or go home."

Steve K:

"Our current RV is a 2015 Entegra Coach Anthem 45-foot. Other than an awful lot of maintenance issues, we absolutely love it. We chose this particular coach for its floor plan and power. ...This was an ideal coach for entertaining and dry camping for an extended period of time. The ride and handling are exceptional. The engine is one of the quietest on the market. It is a joy to drive."

New and upscale Class As are often quite pricey. This is because they contain an engine (as opposed to a trailer or fifth wheel), often have high-end amenities (clothes washer/dryer for example), and are large (typically 30+ feet). However, many of our travelers made the initial decision to buy their Class A, because they found a good deal, and one that was in their price range.

LivingLifeInBetween:

"We chose a 35-foot Class A motorhome and a Jeep Wrangler [to tow]. ...We didn't go looking for a Class A, necessarily. We set parameters for ourselves and when we found a rig that met those, within our price range we pulled the trigger. The advantages we see are that set up and tear down are very simple. We also get to have our favorite vehicle with us for errands, and adventuring."

8Paws1Tail:

"We bought a 37-foot 2007 Winnebago Voyage. We purchased a used model, because it was within our budget. We knew that we personally no longer wanted to tow our home. We've had trailers and fifth wheels, and I think we also just wanted something different. We are Jeep people and enjoy off-roading so felt that an RV and tow would be a better setup for the lifestyle we wanted. [The advantages are]: comfort, easy leveling system, luxury residential amenities... [The disadvantages are]: fuel economy, two motors so more maintenance, [and a] bigger rig means [we are] unable to get into more rural locations.... We love Winnebago, but would probably go with a newer model [if we were to buy again]."

WanderlandTravelers:

"There were many factors influencing our decision. We needed something that could propel itself because we didn't own a vehicle that could tow, so that ruled out trailers and fifth wheels. We liked the giant front windows and the spacious rooftop space and bays...One big disadvantage is the long length, which prevents us from staying at many state park campgrounds, as well as some boondocking sites which have narrow roads or small sites...If we could do it over, we would get a smaller rig with four wheel drive. We're currently drooling over Sportsmobiles. Thirty-three feet is a lot bigger than we need, and it's a gas hog. A smaller 4x4 rig would enable us to camp almost anywhere as well as being a little stealth if necessary."

MilesAwayEveryDay:

"We did tons of online and onsite research...[we decided our] dream home on wheels was a 31-foot Class A. When we first started looking, we thought the only option that fit our needs was a fifth wheel, but we could not have been more wrong. We looked at and walked through every type and size option RV out there. When we actually decided to walk through the Class A options, we realized how well it would work and fit our needs. We knew we didn't want to go too big because national parks tend to have size limits, and we knew we didn't need a ton of space. In fact, anything we looked at that was larger than 31, we would both exclaim that it was just too much room and [would] walk right out. We would have gone for 27 feet, but it would have involved a lot of renovations that we just didn't have time for with everything going on. We were able to get everything we needed without renovations when we saw ours at the dealership. We love the huge windshield, it is amazing when you're driving, and it's even better when you camp somewhere with a gorgeous view. Our rig is gas, which we like as well. We can have the perfect tow car for us, which is a Jeep, instead of having to drive around in a huge truck that tows an even bigger fifth wheel. With our Jeep, we can go anywhere."

You don't necessarily have to choose a *gas* Class A to be happy though. Remember that everyone's needs are different.

RVWanderlust:

"We chose a used Class A diesel, and we would do it again if we could go back in time! Diesels are built for full-time travel. The heavy duty chassis can support the weight of possessions and sturdier building materials, like real tile and real wood. Gas models and trailers are typically full of flimsy material that can't withstand the wear and tear of full-time travel. ...The downside to diesel is that it's more expensive to repair. But we plan ahead and it's not a huge deal."

Michael and Loida:

"[Our rig] is a class A motor home by Tiffin, [a] 35-foot long front engine diesel. [It's] almost nine years old, so we don't have all the latest technical gadgets. It is a good size for two people. The price was right."

Most of the interviewees were happy with their decision to get a Class A and would buy the same again. However, one family differs.

OurIncredibleDash:

"We chose a 35-foot motorhome (Class A) because the timing and price were right. It's not our first choice in an ideal world, because we don't want the kids riding in it, so we drive separately. However it has worked well for now, and we own it free and clear which is important to us. Eventually, we will upgrade to a truck and a fifth wheel, probably a toy hauler."

CLASS B and CLASS B+

Quick description: These rigs are small and do not require a tow vehicle, and do not usually tow a vehicle. These RVs are usually no longer than 25 feet and can be as short as 15 feet. They do not have an over-the-cab bed like Class C's do. They do not usually have a blunt nose like Class As do.

Most full-timers don't choose to buy a Class B due to their compact size. Many Class Bs are limited in their interior space and amenities. The new ones are also often very expensive, partly because they tend to be built on a Mercedes chassis. The older ones are often more affordable.

TheVanProject:

"We chose a 1964 Clark Cortez ...It's limited in terms of the terrain that we can take it on, but it has way more character than any sprinter. It has a fully functioning toilet and on demand hot water heater. There is ample storage, and we fit a queen size bed in it. We also have a two burner propane range and [a] basin sink. Based on our experience so far, I think I would choose a four-wheel-drive vehicle next time."

There are also Class B+s (see photo on right above). These are, not surprisingly, larger than Class Bs and smaller than Class Cs (or Class As). They often have more headroom and a slide, unlike Class Bs, which typically don't have slides. (See later discussion about slides.). Interestingly, none of our travelers said they have a Class B+. I think this might be because either they are drawn to the spacious size of rig options much larger than a Class B, or they like the lifestyle associated with the more nimble Class B or traditional van.

Another anomaly is that Class B+ vehicles are typically too small for towing a vehicle but too large to maneuver easily in and out of a city parking lot. I suspect there is probably a huge appeal to them for medium-term travelers, such as one to two months. However, it is hard to say, since I didn't interview anyone with one.

CLASS C

* photo courtesy of OurVieAdventures

Quick description: These RVs look like U-Haul trucks. They have a bed (or storage) over the cab.

Class C's are also frequently considered by our interviewees for their full-time life. One of our solo travelers, has a 2016 Minnie Winnie 22R, and she doesn't tow anything, but rather uses a bicycle for supplemental transportation.

Laura J:

"I originally wanted a Class B van like a Roadtrek, but I just couldn't afford it. At the end of the day, I think the Class C is better for a full timer in that it has more room and you don't have to make the bed to eat dinner and then clear off the table to go to bed! If I did it over again, I might not pick the same rig because

driving this is a bit cumbersome. There are some vehicles that are a bit bigger than a B but smaller than a C [these are the B+] which I might investigate, but I know I don't want to tow a travel trailer or a fifth wheel."

Class Cs range dramatically in size. There are smaller (approximately 20-foot) ones, but there are also large 32+ foot ones.

HotSauceHippo:

"We chose a 22-foot 1988 Lazy Daze RV (photo above), which sits on a Ford E350 chassis. We chose this rig, because we wanted a single-unit, all-inclusive rig (as opposed to a truck and travel trailer combo) and we wanted something under $10,000 with less than 100,000 miles on it. We contemplated buying a Class B or van, but after touring a couple rigs, we realized that we liked to be able to stand up in our home and have a living area that was separate from the bed area...The advantages of our RV are the size and maneuverability that a truck and travel trailer combo, Class A, or larger Class C wouldn't have. We can drive through most cities and park on the street (although sometimes we have to feed two meters). We feel that we are at the max size capable of doing this, and anything larger wouldn't fit. The disadvantage of our rig is that once we are parked, leveled, and hooked up for the night, we feel a bit stuck. If we had a truck and trailer combo we could unhook the truck and take it to dinner or grocery shopping, instead of having to take our entire RV along with us...[We] are happy with our decision overall [and we would buy the] same RV again because the advantages of our rig fit our lifestyle significantly more than the disadvantages. We aren't hooked up very often, and we move locations most nights. We do very little city driving, and we fit in the areas we want to explore. If we were to park for longer periods of time or want to explore large cities, having a separate vehicle from the living quarters might be a better way to go."

Several travelers mentioned considering (or using) Class Cs at one point, but opted for a Class A instead.

MilesAwayEveryDay:

"Class Cs weren't an option as soon as James tried to sit in the cab of one. There's just no room, and the view isn't there. When you have our view while driving, it helps us in more ways than one to ensure we are safe on the road."

Heath and Alyssa:

"After living in a renovated 1994 Class C motorhome…for a year and a half, we switched to a Winnebago Brave 31C motorhome. We wanted more work space and a dependable rig to continue traveling. We fell in love with this retro version of the iconic Winnebago Brave and have already put close to 20k miles on it."

TRAVEL TRAILER

Regular Travel Trailer

* photo courtesy of Jeff Fujita

(NOTE: This is a "special" type of travel trailer called an Airstream.)

Quick description: The difference between a travel trailer and a fifth wheel is where it attaches to the truck. Travel trailers hook on to a hitch attached to the bumper, hence the term "bumper pull" that is used to refer to them. The front part of a fifth wheel extends over the bed of the truck and attaches into a hitch within the truck bed.

Jeff and Coffee:

"We like to hike and fish, and after seeing the RV, trailer, and fifth wheel setups, we chose a 28-foot Airstream that was nine years old when purchased, and a two year old Toyota Tundra 4WD for the tow vehicle. We can explore much more with our 4WD truck, but still have all the comforts of a tiny house with our Airstream. We are not big people and lived the apartment life our entire adult lives, so the move into a trailer was more lateral than say, a couple used to a large house. We have no regrets and would do it all over again with no changes. The size of our trailer has proved to be not too small and not too big."

SunnyJunket:

"We have an 18-foot vintage 1982 trailer. We wanted a small trailer so we can boondock and be more flexible than in a large rig. With a trailer we can leave it parked and we can go places in our car."

This logic is the reason we chose our trailer as well. We wanted to be able to dry camp or boondock for long periods of time. Our trailer has a large fresh water holding tank (100 gallons) that is much larger than most other models of RVs. The other factor that is very important to us, especially in hindsight, is that when we've found a great place to camp or boondock, our rig stays in place to "mark our spot," whereas if we had a Class B or other RV that didn't tow a vehicle, you have to take your entire rig with you, which means someone else can come and claim your spot if you leave it temporarily to run errands or explore.

Trailers come in all sizes from small tear drops and "casitas" to larger 30+ foot ones.

HappyCamperWives:

"[We chose a] t@b teardrop because our small truck could pull it and the bathroom/kitchen were located inside. We love the t@b, no regrets, it's perfect for us."

It is interesting to note that they are both taller women (5'10" I believe) and have two dogs along with them, all fitting comfortably in a small teardrop. That just exemplifies how everyone's criteria and needs are different, and there is no one-size-fits-all RV.

Travel Trailer/Toy Hauler

* photo courtesy of Jax733

Quick description: These units are bumper pulls that have been outfitted to accommodate a "toy" (such as an ATV) with a "garage," "garage door" and extra high head room.

One of the least expensive RV options is a travel trailer. You can choose either a regular one as described in the last page, or one that is a "toy hauler."

Jax733:

"[We have an] Eclipse Attitude 27SAG [toy hauler]. It's supposedly harder to drive than pretty much anything else from what we've been told. Even though it's not huge, its size still limits us to what parks we can go to and small, windy roads are stressful. [The pros, though, are] we have the ability to detach, and if our vehicle breaks down we still have a house. For a not-huge rig, it has a lot of storage space and the ability to carry our toys. It was affordable and doesn't have a motor to break down. It's rugged enough that we can go to boondocking spots and be 'off grid.' Because of our budget I'd pick the same rig. I think the only other thing I'd consider would be a fifth wheel version of this, but I'm not sure we could justify the extra expense."

This is one of the differences between a travel trailer (toy hauler or regular) versus a fifth wheel — the expense. Fifth wheels are typically at least $20k more to buy than a similar length and quality travel trailer.

FIFTH WHEEL

Regular Fifth Wheel

* photo courtesy of GoWiththeFlowandCo

Quick description: These RVs are towed rigs that attach with a "tongue" to a truck bed.

Another frequently chosen RV for full-time travel is a fifth wheel. Their size, cost, and amenities make it a great option for someone on the road for a long period of time. Interestingly, though, many RVers would consider other options if they could choose again.

GoWiththeFlowandCo:

"We think about other rigs daily, but, love ours. The under belly storage is lovely, it tows wonderfully. We love that we have a 4x4 truck along with it — it makes getting through tough terrain much easier and allows us to get to some amazing boondocking spots. If we do it again (which, we will), we would definitely pay more attention to the tank sizes because it is only 40 gallons and sometimes we run out of fresh water. We also think we may get a toy hauler to get some fun little scooters or off-road motorcycles to explore with (to keep miles off the truck and cut down on diesel costs — and it'd be so fun)!"

RVegan:

"I have a fifth wheel and Ford F-250. I like that the fifth wheel is like a mini apartment with tons of storage, and an 11-foot ceiling makes the place feel big. My kitchen is bigger than my old apartment's, and this is the first queen size bed I've ever had! A used fifth wheel is quite cheap, mine was $13,000, so I'm saving a lot in rent. I like being able to take my truck as my daily driver. The truck is a little too big for me in some cities I am in, so if I could do it again I would do a used class C and a small daily driver."

Dawn L:

"We have a 2001 Montana fifth wheel. We love it. I sometimes wish we went with a Class A or C but think I really like the room we get in the fifth wheel. We started in a travel trailer. We found it was just a tad too much togetherness. The fifth wheel is just right."

Fifth Wheel/Toy Hauler

* photos courtesy of TravelExploreUncover

Quick description: These Fifth Wheels are outfitted to accommodate "toys" (like an ATV) with a "garage," "garage space," and extra interior height.

The difference between a regular fifth wheel and the toy hauler version is the garage space and garage door. A plus to the toy haulers, both the trailer version and the fifth wheel, is that the garage door can also be turned into a patio with an optional package (see photo on left). With this package, you maintain the ability to use the garage door as a ramp to get your toys into the RV, but also have the option of adjusting the ramp to be parallel with the ground to use for outdoor relaxation. The patio option has a screened fence around it and a screen that drops down between the patio and the rig, so bugs won't get in. One other significant difference is the toy hauler versions of RVs typically have radically higher head room. The difference can be 6-foot ceilings as compared to 8- or 9-foot ceilings. This is partly because toy haulers usually have a set of bunk beds in the garage area that raise up to the ceiling so that the "toy" can fit underneath them when the beds aren't needed.

TravelExploreUncover:

"We chose a Grand Design Momentum 349M. We chose a toy hauler for a few reasons. It has a large garage area that we can use in a variety of ways, such as a guest bedroom, storage, or a place to let wet dogs dry off. The toy hauler also has a patio/ramp that extends out the back which we love. A disadvantage is while we are towing, we aren't able to get out of seat and be in the rig, as you would in a Class A, B, or C rig. If we did this again, we both agree that we would pick the same exact rig. We were lucky in the sense that we didn't pick a rig that was too small or too big for our needs."

OVER THE CAB TRUCK CAMPER

Quick description: These camper units attach to the back and top of a truck. The truck is typically a "dually" (with four tires in the back and two in the front). The camper unit can be removed from the truck. From the front of the vehicle, the look resembles that of a Class C because of the "over the cab" bed.

Surprising to me, none of our full-time travelers chose an Over-the-Cab camper. We actually considered one, and came very close to buying one, until we thought through the storage issue. We realized there would be no where to easily carry our "toys" — kayaks, SUPs, and bikes — and that overall storage was very limited. Perhaps that is why none of the people I interviewed went that route.

The plus, as I see it, is that the truck camper is very durable on dirt roads, especially if you buy a 4x4 truck, which is what is generally recommended (dually trucks are ideal). This quality makes them perfect for off-road boondocking.

Disadvantages, though, are they also tend to have smaller fresh water, gray water, and sewage holding tanks, which limit the length of time you can be without hookups or dumping. Another con is that you must get adept at taking the camper off, if you want to travel in your truck sans camper. The appeal is definitely its maneuverability and durability, however, so it could be a good option for you if those are some of your criteria.

OLD SCHOOL VAN (VAN-LIFE)

* photo courtesy of Wandrly

Quick description: "Van Life" has become a popular term for people who reside in an "old school" van full- (or most-) time. Examples of these vans are the VW Van, Vanagon and Westfalia. They have "convertible" interior space that is a bed by night and a couch or dinette by day. They typically do not have any type of bathroom inside.

Wandrly, a family of five, started off their adventure in a Class C RV but decided it was "too big and bulky." He admitted that the bed was very comfortable, though.

"After a year, I ditched [the Class C] for a 1978 VW Bus. I also convinced my college sweetheart to move into it with me at the same time. We chugged along happily in that for years, making two more babies in it before we decided to 'upgrade' to a 1976 Airstream, which we lived in for three years before finally admitting that we loved space less than convenience, and so ditched that Airstream to climb back into our Volkswagen."

I know what you are thinking, "five people in one van?" This is the whole point though: everyone has different needs and priorities. Maybe living in a van would suit you, too!

Wandrly:

"RVs are cumbersome and vans make life easy …Buying old and cheap means spending a lot of your travel time working on your rig instead of exploring. Everything is a trade off (vans are kind of a bummer when it rains, for example, and the newer your ride, the more you've got to work to pay for it), but I'd say those are about the only two things that have really frustrated us over the years."

MODIFIED BUSES AND OTHER RIGS

There are many, many custom versions of RVs that can't possibly be covered in this section. Modified buses are a big category, though.

TheAmericanFieldTrip:

"We chose a 25-foot 2007 Ford E-450 shuttle bus. We're really happy with our choice and would pick it again. We liked designing a layout that met our needs and building the bus ourselves. We also liked the safety of a bus. The size of the shuttle bus was perfect for us, too."

* photo courtesy of
TheAmericanFieldTrip

Vagabroads:

"We chose a 1997 Toyota Landcruiser [with a rooftop tent] because it has solid axles and lockers. My main goal was to be able to get out of any situation if needed, and also not to break down. We had the top end of our engine rebuilt before we left the states just to make sure everything was tip top. I would pick our rig again, however, I wouldn't go with a rooftop tent. I miss having "indoor space." It would be nice to be able to cook, etc. inside versus in the tent if it's raining…Even with our awning, it's still a task being outside all the time."

QUICK GLANCE TABLE

The table below is intended to help you sift through your priorities and rigs to consider. Bear in mind that the determination of whether a priority fits a Class is somewhat subjective. What I, or our travelers, may feel is a lot of storage may be different from your opinion, for example. This table is merely a starting point, but should help weed out some of your options, at least.

	Class A	Class B	Class B+	Class C	TT	5th Wheel	TT/Toy Hauler	5th/Toy Hauler	Over-cab	Van
Fastest travel		x	x						x	x
Ease of parking		x	x						x	x
Ease of set up at camping spot	x	x	x	x					x	x
Most storage	x					x	x	x		
Largest interior	x				x	x	x	x		
Headroom	x					x	x	x		
Accommodations for guests	x			x			x	x		
Work space (like an office)	x				x	x	x	x		
Smallest to fit in any camping spot		x	x						x	x
Largest (maximized) living space	x						x			
Convertible space (i.e., bedroom by night, living room by day)		x	x	x	x					x
Most easily outfitted for off-grid camping	x				x	x	x	x		
Needs an attached tow vehicle	x			x						
Already have a strong towing vehicle					x	x	x	x	x	
Only want one vehicle to manage		x	x						x	x
Upscale amenities (such as dishwasher, clothes washer/dryer, air conditioning, kitchen counter space, etc.)	x					x		x		
Permanent bed	x		x	x	x	x	x	x	x	

	Class A	Class B	Class B+	Class C	TT	5th Wheel	TT/Toy Hauler	5th/Toy Hauler	Over-cab	Van
Least expensive to buy up front					x		x		x	x
Least expensive to maintain					x	x	x	x	x	
Money is no object	x	x	x	x	x	x	x	x	x	x
Ability to go off-road		x					x	x	x	x
Big bathroom (with large shower and/or with bathtub)	x					x				
No bathroom needed		x								x
Have access to the interior of the unit while driving	x	x	x	x						x
Separate motor from "house"					x	x	x	x	x	
Self-contained motor and "house"	x	x	x	x						x
Ground clearance for off-road driving							x	x	x	
Easy to maneuver		x	x							x

Slide or No Slide

A much debated topic among RVers is whether to buy a rig with a slide or without one. A slide is a part of an RV that "pops out" from the side of the rig to add extra interior space. These pop-outs can be along any side of the vehicle other than the front. Some slides are not very deep (maybe a foot-and-a-half) and others are so deep that when they are retracted, there is no room inside to move around because the slides take up the entire space.

We special ordered our trailer so that we could outfit it the way we wanted. When we originally placed the order, we requested a rig without a slide. The dealer told us they had one on order that was exactly like what we were customizing with the exception that it had a slide. If we waited for our custom order, we would receive the trailer in October. If we went with the one with the slide that they had on order already, we could take delivery in July. We opted to take delivery earlier, so we got the slide. We are so happy we did! We have one of the smaller slides (only about one-and-a-half to two-feet deep) but it adds a much more spacious feeling to our living space than if we had gotten it without the slide. I don't think I would buy one now that did not have a slide, even though slides make me nervous, because they are one more thing that can break on the rig.

If you do get a rig with a slide, most people will tell you to *not* get a slide that has a refrigerator or other heavy piece of furniture in it, as this tends to increase the likelihood of the slide breaking.

Outfitting Your Rig

You can literally make as many changes to a rig as you can contemplate. Some changes are cosmetic — new carpet, linoleum, tile, paint — others are functional — size of tanks, appliances, type of bed — and some are mechanical — type of engine, solar, batteries, generators. That list of priorities you made earlier will dictate what modifications need to be made.

OurIncredibleDash:

"We have completely renovated our rig to make it fit our needs. As our needs change, we make more changes."

TheAmericanFieldTrip:

"In the bedroom, we built bunk cubbies for the kids next to our full-size bed, and the big bed lifts up so we have a lot more storage underneath. Our kitchen has a full-size counter, so there is plenty of workspace, and a huge apron-front sink, which has been really functional for us and makes the space feel like a real kitchen. The whole rig runs off 600 watts of solar power, a small propane tank, and a 40-gallon freshwater tank (stored under our bed). We have a self-contained toilet for emergencies (we haven't had to use it yet), and an outdoor shower that runs off a propane tankless water heater."

Rather than modify a rig by adding elements, you can also change things by taking something away.

HotSauceHippo:

"The two things we did to the rig to fit our lifestyle were removing the microwave for more storage space in the kitchen and removing the air conditioner for

more head room in the main living space. To use these appliances, we needed to be plugged into electricity and we knew we were primarily going to be boondocking. So, removing them for the extra space and discarded weight was the way to go for us." Note: They did, however, add *"two solar panels (not attached to the rig) for off-grid electricity and bought a gym membership for off-grid showering."*

Wandrly:

"[We added] 100 watts of solar, wooden floors,…a custom bed, [and] 12 volt fans [for] on or off grid depending on where we are or what we want to be doing."

Customizing the rig to your needs and tastes is what makes it functional and feel like home.

RVWanderlust:

"There's hardly anything I don't love. Every day is an adventure when I step out my front door. When I step back in, it's home. I have everything I need here: the food I like in my fridge, my pillows, my books, my family. It's the best of both worlds."

STORAGE

With the exception of the larger rigs (and even sometimes then), storage is an issue. Adding storage, or organizing storage areas, is a common theme from our travelers.

Jax733:

"We use crates to organize everything: jars in one, canned goods in another, and we store those in our 'garage' area in the back of the toy hauler. In our overhead cupboards, we use crates for our pots & pans, dishes, extra glasses, etc. Crates are invaluable. We use our bunk beds in the garage area to store our camp chairs and off-season clothes."

Vagabroads:

"It's about organization — you can never add enough compartments, drawers, shelves, to your rig. Open storage space is messy storage space. We took out the backseats and had a steel locking storage box built in its place. We have an ARB drawer system for our kitchen and clothing, a locking storage box with several compartments — oh, and packing cubes are the best thing ever."

OFF-GRID OPTIONS

Most of our travelers either have off-grid options or wish they did.

OurVieAdventures:

"We wanted to stay completely off the grid. We wanted to move around wherever we want, and not be connected to a concrete pad in an RV park. So, we had to make adjustments for internet, water, and power. We have a wifi extender, a cell booster, solar panels, a bigger battery bank, and a power inverter all to accommodate that style of travel. We also had to bring all of our outdoor gear — so that meant big storage boxes on the top of the rig along with bike racks."

Jeff and Coffee:

"One of our first purchases was a 2000-watt Honda generator, which supplies all our needs, specifically our television monitor and LED interior lighting. We wanted 4WD for mountain roads. We purchased four freshwater containers and two gasoline containers. We hope to install solar panels some day but we really haven't needed it since we boondock most of the time and our generator doesn't bother anyone in isolated areas."

LivingLifeInBetween:

"In the future we would like to add solar an inverter and better batteries, but as of right now we rely on our generator to boondock."

Dawn L:

"[I have] two batteries and two generators."

8Paws1Tail:

"We did purchase a 100 Watt panel and inverter for energy to be off-grid."

Jax733:

"We outfitted our trailer with a composting toilet, strong solar system, and extra batteries."

TheVanProject:

"We have three solar panels that are powerful enough to power a refrigerator, LED lighting, and to charge all of our electronics."

TravelExploreUncover:

"We have a solar and lithium battery set-up for off-the-grid. We have a garage that we can use as storage for our two motorcycles, but also as a workplace with a desk and chair."

WanderlandTravelers:

"We made sure to get a rig that already had some solar set up, and bought a couple extra panels to get more watts (we have 535 watts). [We also] installed a larger inverter (4000 watts) and set it up so that we can plug our shore power cable into it to power all the outlets in the RV...We wanted to be as self sufficient as we could, so we could comfortably boondock and save money on campsites, as well as enjoy the more peaceful solitude that we find in our great country's public lands. We spent 200 days dry camping over the last year and it was mostly pretty comfortable."

Vagabroads:

"[We outfitted our Landcruiser with] a refrigerator and two Duralast Platinum 31M batteries to power everything. We have a two-and-a-half lift, winch, slee back gate, ARB front bumper, etc. You can see more on our website at vagabroads.com/our-build."

Wandrly:

"We have only had a solar setup for about a year and a half and it has changed our lives, as far as where and what we could do, and never needing to be the annoying folks running a generator."

To fully outfit your rig for off-grid experiences, I recommend considering a composting toilet, a strong solar and battery system, a large fresh water tank or supplemental jerry cans, two 30-pound propane tanks (instead of the smaller 20-pound tanks found on some rigs), an inverter, and a generator. You should also have a decent gray water tank, and/or outfit your rig to use the black water tank as a supplemental gray water tank.

In addition, it's wise to have high ground clearance since boondocking usually involves dirt, gravel, and/or rocky roads. We flipped our axles to raise our trailer up an extra few inches. Be careful doing this, though, because it will likely void a warranty on the chassis, but it was worth it to us to take that risk. Make sure you have great tires, too. Most stock tires are rather mediocre.

One more item that we invested in that is very inexpensive but highly effective and efficient is a Mr. Buddy Propane heater. We use our furnace in cold weather to keep the pipes from freezing, but it's not that efficient at keeping the trailer warm. The Mr. Buddy is amazingly efficient, using only one 20-pound propane tank every two to three weeks, even when it is on for 10 hours a day or more, every day; well worth it. The company also offers small versions of Mr. Buddy which we haven't experimented with yet.

Composting Toilets

Composting toilets have come a long way. The new ones use peat moss or coconut coir (coconut shell shredded and packed hard) to compost the solid waste and have separate jugs for the liquid waste. The key to a composting toilet being effective is keeping the liquid waste separate from the solid waste. This, in combination with the moss or coir, creates an amenable environment for the solids to compost. (We use, prefer, and love the coir option over the peat moss. You can buy it in a compacted brick-form from Amazon. You can use a knife or sharp instrument to break apart the coir into small bits and then mix it with a bit of water until it is just damp. This mixture is placed into the waste receptacle and then it goes to work against the human waste.)

I am amazed at how quickly the waste composts. We've cleaned it hours after using it (sorry for the candor), and the compost is never gross or smelly. I've been very surprised! The liquid waste goes down into a separate jerry can type of plastic container, which you then empty periodically by either dumping it into a public toilet or sprinkling it in the grass and plants around the campsite. Urine isn't problematic to plants, and actually contains some beneficial minerals and nutrients, so no harm is done.

For the two of us, the urine usually needs to be emptied once per 24-36 hours. I usually dump it every night regardless of how full it is, just to have a routine. The solid compartment can last anywhere from two weeks to many months, depending, of course, on how often you use it. We usually try to use an available toilet for that activity, when it is an option. Doing so means we only have to dump our solid container once every few months, or even less frequently than that. I've noticed people with regular RV toilets and black tanks also try to use the publicly available restrooms for their "solids," so I don't feel like I'm being inconvenienced any more than any other RVer.

Solar System

We purchased the Renogy 500 Watt 12-Volt Eclipse Solar Premium Kit. We combine this with six 6-volt batteries. Some say that amount of battery power is overkill, and perhaps it is, but it has worked well for us.

As I write this, I am dry camping in Saskatchewan, Canada and have been living off my solar for three days now, without running my generator once. I love solar! Note that most dealer supplied solar packages come as one hundred watt systems, which typically do not provide enough power to be off-grid consistently (without a generator or some other power-source).

We added a small inverter (which is used to power outlets when you don't want to use the generator) with two outlets to power our TV and one other device like a DVD player or a phone charger. We initially installed a huge inverter that in theory would power our entire trailer for everything except microwave and air-conditioning, but we had so many problems with it (brand was Samlex), that we took it out and replaced it with the smaller one, which has worked great. I would certainly love to have all of our outlets powered by an inverter, but it is very expensive and not really necessary. We do have one DC outlet as well, to charge phones and tablets and other devices like these, and I highly recommend at least one. I actually wish we had a few more DC outlets scattered throughout the RV.

Fresh Water, Gray Water, and Black Tanks

We have a 100-gallon fresh water tank (this is for drinking water, dishes, and shower), a 50-gallon gray water tank (waste from kitchen and bathroom sinks), and a 50-gallon (unused) black water tank (toilet). We've considered modifying our system to enable the black water tank to be an overflow for when the gray water tank is full, but we've been afraid to do this for resale reasons. Therefore, our boondocking time is limited by the size of our gray water, but we have learned to be very sparing with what water goes down the drain.

We use a dish tub sink insert to wash our dishes and dump the water on the plants outside (unless we are in bear country during bear season!). We take "space baths" (which is what we call them), using NASA approved No Rinse Body Shampoo and No Rinse Hair Shampoo. The only liquid that goes down the drain is water from brushing our teeth and some small amounts of coffee and remnant liquids from meals. We can live on our 100-gallon fresh water tank/50-gallon gray water tank combination for up to three weeks or a bit more without dumping the gray water or refilling the fresh water. We have used our jerry cans for extra fresh water, but that's only been on rare occasions.

Generator

Usually, we run our generator for about 20 minutes in the morning to make coffee and to use the microwave or toaster. Our batteries are usually already charged by our solar from the morning light, so we don't need to run the generator to charge the batteries in the morning unless it is very overcast or shady. We can go all day on our solar/battery system without using the generator (unless, again, we need to use a huge power-sucking appliance such as a microwave or hairdryer). We typically run the generator again in the evening while we cook dinner for about 20 minutes or so. With the systems we have in place, that's all the generator we need. Our fuel for our generator can last us months.

The disadvantage to using your generator as your primary powering source is that it is noisy. Because of this, many formal campgrounds or parks have "generator hours," limiting the noise to only certain times during the day. If you plan on boondocking the majority of the time, you must remember that if you rely solely or mostly on your generator, you may bother *yourself* with the noise, even if no one else is around.

Cellular Service, Wifi, and TV

I've been shocked at how often we have good enough cell reception to stream Hulu or Netflix or the like. We have three cell services between us: Verizon for a phone and three iPads (that can all act as hotspots), AT&T for another phone, and T-Mobile for a hotspot. We experience the best reception typically with our Verizon service, but there are times when Verizon isn't good and AT&T comes to the rescue. For this reason we have intentionally kept both services. We got the T-Mobile hotspot for the unlimited streaming the plan offers for services like Hulu, Amazon On Demand, Netflix, Pandora, etc. However, we have not had consistent reception with the T-Mobile, so we are undecided as to whether to keep it and the $20/month expense.

We used to stream off our 30 GB Verizon plan, and then Verizon released their unlimited data plan, so we switched. The trick to Verizon's unlimited data plan (as it was explained to us) is to use different devices as hotspots, if possible. The way that data plan works is this: for the first 10 GB used you have 4G streaming speeds. After 10 GB, it drops to 3G or 2G speeds (which, incidentally we have streamed off of with no buffering). If you have multiple devices on the same plan (which we do; we have the four devices all with hotspot capabilities), you can rotate through each device giving you much more 4G access. What this means is, with our four devices, we get 40 GB of 4G! This system works really well for us.

I need to note that what I have just outlined is how our services work in the United States. We do have a Verizon plan that covers Canada and Mexico, but no one explained to us that the data is not truly "unlimited" in these other countries. In Canada, we get one-half GB of high-speed data per day (it's amazing how quickly that goes), and then it drops down to a speed so slow I can't load a webpage. AT&T's roaming service does seem better in Canada, but we don't have an unlimited data plan with AT&T, which means we run out of data fast on that device as well. T-Mobile has been mostly useless in Canada for streaming and data.

In terms of TV throughout the continent, our stock digital TV antenna has rarely provided us with channels, but we check at every new location, because we have been surprised before. We do not have satellite, although I've heard good reports about some of the newer models. Ask around and read reviews before you select one, if this interests you.

FOR WORK

One thing to consider: If you are going to be working on the road, where do you want your office to be? Do you want to work outside at a picnic table? Inside at the dinette? Or would you like to have a dedicated space? Do you need that space to be separate from others? You also may prefer to always work at a coffee shop, library, or the like.

If the latter is the case, you will need to be camped or boondocked near towns that have public wifi. If you'd rather your office be in your rig, you need to think through any modifications you will need to make a hospitable place for you to get your work done.

TheAmericanFieldTrip:

"We built our bus with a separate 'garage' and office space in the back. We have a desk back there, along with a pegboard where we store most of our gear. Having a separate space for work makes it much easier for one person to get things done, while the other hangs out with the kids in the main part of the bus."

WanderlandTravelers:

"He was accustomed to a stand up desk in the house, and it was important for him to keep using a stand up desk. He spent some time retrofitting the TV area over the dash to have a drawer that pulls out into a desk where he can work standing up....Brad installed the stand up desk, and set up a curtain that he can close behind himself to section off the area and make it more like an office. He also replaced the old box TV in the front of the RV with a flat screen on an adjustable arm."

Personally, I've always liked being mobile when I work. Even in my sticks-and-bricks, I'd work various places (sofa, chair, dining table, patio) depending on my mood, rather than work in a separate office space. For me, working in different places on the road is preferred. I like being able to take my computer out to the picnic table in the morning and move to the camp chair in the afternoon. The next day I can hang out inside on my recliner. That's how it works for me. However, if you like a separate work space, you need to plan for that before you hit the road.

FOR PLAY

Understandably, most of the "for play" modifications involve the outdoors in some way.

Steve K:

"We added more electrical outlets and more circuits to the outside entertaining area for catering. We had power slide trays installed in the storage bays. We bought NuWave induction cooking units to add to the outdoor cooking options."

8Paws1Tail:

"We bought two kayaks for some better exploring and fun in the water. We are usually always parked by a body of water."

RVWanderlust:

"We've spent time gathering items to make our outdoor experiences more pleasant. For our patio, we have four anti-gravity chairs, so friends can be comfortable when they visit. We have a big rug, a nice grill, and a propane fire pit."

Jax733:

"We specifically custom ordered our 'garage door' on our toy hauler so that we could have the outdoor patio option."

I suspect that if you are considering this lifestyle, you like the great outdoors as well. You may want to think about what you can bring or add or how you can modify your rig to enjoy being outside the most.

Outfitting Your Life

One of the road blocks I hear many wannabe travelers talk about is how to structure their lives to make full-time travel work. What do I do about my mail? How do I care for my pets? Can I keep schooling my kids? Will I kill my spouse living in such a small space? This section is designed to address these questions.

RELATIONSHIP MANAGEMENT

Probably the biggest concern I've heard expressed by those wanting this lifestyle is whether they'd be able to live in such close quarters with their spouse/partner/kids/pets.

OurVieAdventures:

"We get asked all the time 'how do you live together in such close quarters?' It hasn't bothered us one bit! But, that may just be our personalities. I honestly think it has been invaluable for our relationship. We have to work through our problems, because there is nowhere to run and hide. We are always right there together. We are still adjusting to adding the newborn to the mix. So I have a hard time talking about how that has 'changed the game.' We are excited to show him the world and really learn what it means to be a road family."

Our travelers say they have learned communication skills that allow them to resolve conflicts more quickly and give each other "virtual space" even when remaining in close quarters.

HappyCamperWives:

"Living in a tight space with your significant other has its challenges for sure. We've learned communication and still learn to just stop talking if need be. Sometimes it's best to just take a time out, even if you're in the same room. Awkward but effective."

OurVieAdventures:

"You have to work out your problems because there is nowhere to go."

TheVanProject:

"Living in such close quarters means you're in each other's faces all the time. For us, if we ever have any disagreements or conflicts, we deal with them right away."

Finding ways to have alone time and respect each others' space is paramount to some of our interviewees.

Jax733:

"We have found ways to have time alone. We have quiet time with each other, yet not interacting. We sometimes will take turns playing outside with the dog. Occasionally, we'll do separate bike rides or walks."

RVWanderlust:

"Eric and I are best friends and we genuinely never get sick of each other's company. We do things on our own from time to time. Eric loves off-roading with his Jeep, and I enjoy quiet reading time at local coffee shops. But we mostly do everything together, and prefer it that way."

Some of the Road Stories mention relationship *benefits* to living on the road and in a small space.

Heath and Alyssa:

"Living in a small space during our first year of marriage forced us to learn how to resolve conflicts."

LivingLifeInBetween:

"It has affected us very positively. It is a lot harder to avoid the other person when your house is only 272 square feet, so we talk out our disagreements much quicker and more efficiently now than we did before."

HotSauceHippo:

"Ryan and I have lived in no more than 500 square feet for our entire relationship, so space, or lack thereof, is not a problem. If one of us is annoyed or grumpy, the other usually opens space by simply not butting in verbally. The silence gives both of us time to think about what the truth is behind our frustration at which point we're able to rationally discuss the real problem or emotional reaction taking place. When your partner truly listens to you, respects what you're saying, and honors your feelings about an issue, then living in small, ever-changing, cramped, sometimes stressful spaces is not a problem."

Having a division of responsibilities also seems to help keep the relationship running smoothly.

HotSauceHippo:

"Ryan and I share responsibilities related to our rig and life in general. We switch off driving, cooking, cleaning dishes, cleaning the bathroom, etc. Ryan primarily is in charge of dumping our sewage (because chivalry isn't dead) and I make our bed each morning (because Ryan can't quite fit in the overhead space without just laying down). We each have our role and respect the other person's roles. Chores aren't necessarily 50-50 because we believe that keeping 'count' or 'track' of what each person does just leads to a tally that can cause resentment or frustration. If one person feels they are doing more than the other, we simply discuss this and shift responsibilities around until it feels right for us. Our relationship is about love, mutual respect, and not taking anything too seriously."

WanderlandTravelers:

"We each have our roles and duties, and this works quite well when getting the rig ready to move, keeping our home clean, and taking care of our pets. Brad is the driver of the rig, basically because he's so much more comfortable behind the wheel than I am, so I'm the navigator and DJ, and I capture video along the drive for our episodes."

In some cases, our travelers say nothing has changed by being on the road.

MilesAwayEveryDay:

"We do all of the same things we did before RV life. We have date nights out and date nights in. We love to cook together, and we come together for the regular day-to-day stuff like washing vehicles and cleaning the house. We make it fun….We still do nights in where we veg out and just talk, communication is a huge piece of the puzzle. We love campfires. We would say we do movie nights in, but the beauty of this new life is that we so rarely watch anything anymore. We've only had one movie night, but it was great! We curled up in bed at a rest stop after a long day of driving and watched Tombstone... after we stayed in Tombstone, because it makes sense to watch it afterwards and it before."

TheAmericanFieldTrip:

"Living in the bus actually hasn't felt much different from living in our apartment, in terms of our family relationships. Maybe because we've always lived in small spaces, maybe because, having kids, we're used to not having much alone time, we really haven't experienced an adjustment. Kindness, consideration, and a sense of humor are key. We also know our limits as parents; if one of us needs some time, the other makes it happen."

HotSauceHippo:

"My travel companions are Ryan (my husband) and our two dogs (Nelson and Gizmo). I manage these relationships just as I would if we were not living on the road — I spend quality time with each of them, make sure I focus on their needs, and we respect each other's space."

Remembering to keep up with the good things in life always helps.

Wandrly:

"[We manage our relationship] with lots of sex and hugging and poems and beer and patience and remembering that we are the primary example to our children. If there's one thing we need to do it is to slow our roll when things get heated, step back and wait until we can make that example work in their favor."

Jeff and Coffee:

"We listen to a lot of music, enjoy whole foods, and just know deep down, we really need each other. We go through the whole gamut of the couple relationship: shared laughter, very hard arguments, and the constant realization of just how lucky we are."

Another couple, **@rvlovetravel**, who was surveyed but not interviewed, posted a photo of wildflowers and said this on Instagram, "I love that after almost seven years together…and three of them living in a 350 square foot RV together — romance is still alive in the #RVLove bus! Sometimes Marc needs to get out on his bike to decompress and recharge his introverted batteries, but he almost always stops along the way to take photos of something beautiful to text me. Most often flowers. It's a beautiful, simple, yet thoughtful way to keep the love alive and keeps us appreciating one another. It really is the little things that make all the difference."

PET MANAGEMENT

The first step in a pet's life on the road is the transition from sticks-and-bricks to a life of moving. Some animals have not had trouble adapting. My dog was only nine months old when we started the adventure, so she hasn't really known much else. My cat has been tent camping since he was nine weeks old, so he is a very adaptable little guy. But not everyone is so lucky. Sometimes, you have to work with the pets a bit, especially if they are a little older or less flexible.

MilesAwayEveryDay:

"We have a rescue dog who just turned 16 on June 9th. Her name is Chloe. She's a Jack Russell/Beagle mix, and she's been an amazing addition for all these years. Rhiannon adopted her early on, before we got together. She spent a lot of time working with her, since she was abused before, to make her feel comfortable and be able to do normal dog stuff like car rides and walks around the park. When we chose this new lifestyle, there was definitely a transition period for Chloe. Not just because it was a new home, but occasionally the house moves and that's a lot to process....It's one of those things that you simply need to be patient with. When Chloe steps outside to new places she can get confused, and there's sensory overload. We work with her to make her feel comfortable and remind her that we are all still here. We try to play with her as much as we can, if she has the energy in her old age. Most spots she loves."

RVWanderlust:

"Until last year, we had two pets with us: a bearded dragon, and a feral cat, whom we rescued as a kitten in rural Kentucky. The bearded dragon passed away last year from old age. Rhythm, our cat, is easy to travel with. She hides under the sofa as soon as the RV engine comes on, and we don't see her again until the engine goes off! We are very careful about her getting out of the RV. Since we're always going to new places, she may have a hard time finding her way back to the RV if she ever gets lost."

There is definitely an adaptation period for most furry kids. This was posted on Instagram by **@lietco**, one of the people surveyed, but not interviewed. "And then there were three! Today we picked up our sweet little rat, Mewan ...He's incredibly happy and comfortable in the van when it's not moving — so much to explore, so many windows! — but each time we start rolling, he poops. Baby steps."

The good news is there's hope for all pets to adjust.

OurVieAdventures:

"At first, our cat didn't really know what to expect. The first few days he had a hard time walking when the RV was driving. He would just curl up in my lap as I drove. But after a few days, he got his 'sea legs' and was able to move freely about the cabin! He runs and jumps and chases the wipers all along the road. He even has learned to use the kitty box at about 60 miles per hour!"

Road safety should be addressed. Two of our nomads (**OurIncredibleDash** and **Laura J**) recommend using a crate for your dog while driving. **HotSauceHippo** suggests pet seat belts. Personally, we use a crate for our dog and a seatbelt for our cat (he is in a "Puppia" harness with a leash attached to the passenger-side seat). Having an accident while driving can easily propel a dog or cat from the moving car, typically resulting in a fatality. You wouldn't drive your kids without seat belts, so consider protecting your pets in the same manner.

Another one of the major concerns that our travelers express regarding their pets is temperature regulation.

WanderlandTravelers:

"I suppose our main tip is if you leave them alone in the RV, be thoughtful about what the weather is doing. Make arrangements (open windows, run A/C, etc.) to make sure they will be comfortable until you return. If you can't make sure they will be comfortable, then either take them with you or don't leave the RV."

HappyCamperWives:

"Temperature control is our number one [concern]. Make sure to have a good working air conditioner and heater."

8Paws1Tail:

"During hot days we make sure the RV has plenty of ventilation, and we keep the fan on if she has to stay in the RV."

Even the **Vagabroads,** traveling in their Landcruiser and rooftop tent, were able to make modifications to their rig to make it comfortable for their dog.

Vagabroads:

"We did a lot of planning and research as it relates to our dog but overall, it was easy. We just tried to keep in mind that the car would become a huge part of my dog's world — we made it as comfortable inside for her as possible — we gave her the things she would have had at home — nice bed, blanket, toys, good food whenever possible. And we planned a lot for weather contingencies. We put a remote starter on our car so that we could let the air conditioner run when we went places she could not go. We got her a heated mattress pad for cold nights. She is part of our team and needed to be treated as such. Take plenty of flea meds and heart worm meds. Make sure you are aware of a good vet in each town and don't forget that the expat Facebook pages are a great resource."

Medical care on-the-road is another chief issue to address. One piece of that puzzle is the care itself. All of interviewees with pets say it's important to learn the location of vets when you move to a new spot. Many of us have had to use vets when on the road.

Another piece is how to pay for it.

Jax733:

"Get pet insurance! We use HealthyPaws which is super easy. When we get the bill at the vet, we open the app, take a photo and press send. Then a check arrives about a week later (to our friends, who receive our mail) with whatever reimbursement we are owed. It has been a lifesaver. We have needed vets a number of times on the road."

Yet one more piece is the record keeping. Here are some suggestions:

HotSauceHippo:

"We have two small dogs with us – Nelson and Gizmo. I would recommend finding a vet that has multiple locations throughout the United States, so you can easily find a vet if your animals get sick or injured. We use Banfield Pet Hospital (they are located inside of most PetsMart stores). This has saved us the hassle of transferring our dogs' records from one vet to another each time we take them in. It has also saved us from having to research local vets and compare prices. All Banfields are the same price whether you're in Vermont or Texas."

Jax733:

"Get your medical records from your vet back home in a digital format, so you can give these to vets on the road, and scan in the "road vets'" reports (we use the Scanner Pro app) to have an ongoing record of your pet's care."

WanderlandTravelers:

"Another good idea is to get copies of the pet medical records from your vet. This can be helpful and more efficient when you need to see a new vet on the road."

8Paws1Tail:

"We had her previous vet records emailed to us so we have them on hand at all times."

Food can be a big deal, too.

8Paws1Tail:

"Making sure that when traveling you are able to get their specific food regularly is important. We have two 10-pound storage bins for her dry food and make sure where we go has a store that sells her food. We ran into an instance being in a small town that didn't have her food, and we had to pay a high price for some other type of kibble."

Jax733:

"Our dog has lots of allergies and our cat has had crystals in his urine, so both of them are on special diets. We've learned to plan ahead and order their special food from Chewy (which has an app and a website) and have it delivered to a UPS or Mailing Store in a larger town we are headed to. Chewy shipping is free at a certain dollar amount (which we always exceed), and it's fast, too (FedEx). But they don't deliver on Saturday, Sunday, or Monday so plan ahead!"

Laura J:

"The biggest adjustment has been his diet which previously was raw food. I've had to find new food sources, and now we do more freeze dried or dehydrated."

Finally, there is the need to be sensitive to your ever-changing neighbors. One campground where we stayed had one dog that got off leash and attacked two other dogs. A separate group of pet owners let their dogs bark continually. A third group's dogs ran away from their campsite into ours on several occasions and created a huge disturbance for both our dog and our cat. We felt really sorry for other campers that didn't even have pets.

LivingLifeInBetween:

"We have two high energy dogs with us: an Aussie and a small cattle dog mix. My main tip for bringing your dogs on the road with you is to have respect for others. There are a lot of people out there that do not like dogs, especially ones that run right up to strangers and bark in delight at a new face. We love dogs, and our dogs love to play with other dogs, but there are some that don't. Just being mindful of how other people may feel about your dog running off leash goes a long way."

MONEY MANAGEMENT

These are expenses you need to factor in when planning for this lifestyle. Not all of these will pertain to you, and the dollar amounts will vary, but if you factor these in, you will be in better shape than most newbies:

- Mortgages for homes you are keeping during this adventure
- Property taxes for these properties
- RV or car loans
- Camping fees
- Hotel (often full-timers will stay in a hotel from time-to-time for a night to shower, do laundry, or when their RV needs repairs, etc.)
- RV or truck repairs or maintenance (this has been higher for us than we expected; "it's always something.")
- Auto fuel and/or RV fuel
- Generator fuel
- Propane
- Groceries
- Restaurants
- Liquor
- Pet care/food (We've had more vet bills than anticipated as well. We do have pet insurance which is a lifesaver and highly recommended!)
- Doggy day care (Bear in mind that most national parks don't allow dogs on trails. You may need this service to enjoy the parks yourself. Some national parks do offer crating in a cool room (for a fee) to prevent you from

leaving your dog in the car.)

- Clothing

- Household goods

- Health and personal care

- Showers (usually about $3-4 for 6-8 minutes)

- Laundry (we usually spend about $10-20/month for two of us)

- Sewer dump fees ($5-10/dump; if you stay at some campgrounds or full-service parks you won't have this expense, and there are other free places to dump if you do some research: use the Sanidumps app.)

- Entertainment (Park fees, kayak rentals, museums, tours, etc. Pro-tip: buy the "America the Beautiful" annual park pass to eliminate fees at national parks. Many states have similar passes.)

- Prescriptions/medications

- Postage or mail service

- Firewood (bundles are usually $4-8)

- Insurance (health, life, pet, auto, RV, umbrella)

- Roadside services (AAA, Good Sam, etc.)

- Technology (cell phones, satellite, wifi hotspot devices and service, Roku/Hulu/Amazon Prime, etc.)

- Emergency fund

- Gifts for friends and family (especially during holiday and birthday months)

- Donations/charities

- Estimated income taxes if you are self-employed

- Miscellaneous

We use an app called "EveryDollar" which is free and provides us with an adaptable way of planning and checking our expenses every month. Another good app (recommended by our travelers) is Mint.

LivingLifeInBetween :

"Track your expenses. All of them. You'll want to know how much you are spending on gas and campgrounds and park fees. We like to compare what we spend now to what we spent while living in a house on a regular basis. Usually we spend less while living on the road, but that is only because we are stingy. It is very easy to treat this lifestyle like a vacation and spend a lot of money."

WanderlandTravelers:

"We've learned that we really have the ability to control our cost of living, much more so than when we lived in a house. Our biggest costs are gas and camping fees, and those are really within our control. We try to stay in places that have National Forest or BLM land that allows free camping. If you drive fewer miles between destinations, or stay in one place for a longer period of time, you'll spend less on gas than if you're hopping around every few days. You can even control your "utilities" cost by layering up instead of blasting heat when you're in cooler areas, and by finding free dump and water fill stations. Our RVing experience so far has been in the western half of the United States and the opportunities for free camping, and free dump stations, are quite plentiful."

WanderlandTravelers:

"The two biggest costs in our life are gas and campground fees. You can save a significant amount of money by spending more time in each spot, keep the distance between each spot short, and try make each spot free (BLM, National Forest Service land, etc.). We have a couple of campground memberships (Good Sam and Passport America), so that if we do stay at one, we can usually get a discounted rate. Another benefit of the reduced driving of course is reduced maintenance costs.

Before we hit the road, we also made sure to have a savings account set aside just for repairs — that can really help ease the stress when you have to get in to a mechanic."

MilesAwayEveryDay:

"Budget and spreadsheets! Rhiannon [is] wonderful at keeping us organized and maintaining structure all across the board. She's really great at it. It's so important, especially when traveling full-time, to keep up on every expense. Sometimes you travel more often in a month or you do more activities in certain areas. If you're somewhere visiting family or friends, you can safely assume a higher expense report. Managing your money is crucial...Come up with a very realistic budget, and then add more to each category just to play it safe. Rhiannon makes time to update everything multiple times a week. That may sound like too much, but when you are in this lifestyle, you can easily lose track quickly. Your schedule is always full of work or play, and if you get distracted at a national park for days on end, and you don't make the time to update everything, it just adds more work and second guessing in the end. A receipt may get lost, you forget you paid a bill, or you forget about that bear spray you had to buy."

HotSauceHippo:

"My biggest tip for money management is to actually look into what you're spending each month. Ryan and I use an Excel worksheet where we type in every purchase for that month, the amount of the purchase, and the category of that purchase (e.g. household, dining out, groceries, vehicle, etc.). Then we look at each category and see where we're spending the most, where we can cut back, and where we're hitting our goals. There are programs that will go into your banking statements and create these breakdowns for you, but we think that the process of actually typing in each purchase makes you really digest what you are spending your money on. Other tips we use for money management are using credit cards that provide the best rewards for your lifestyle, don't eat out at restaurants too frequently, use apps like Gas Buddy to find the cheapest gas or Sanidumps to find the cheapest

dump stations, and use websites that show you free places to park (e.g. freecampsites.net)."

Keep in mind that this lifestyle does not have to be expensive.

8Paws1Tail:

"We enjoy being outdoors and most outdoor exploring doesn't require spending a cent. Hiking, kayaking, packing a lunch spending time outside is free. That doesn't mean you shouldn't treat yourself. Allow a couple of treats once or twice a month so you don't feel the urge to splurge."

Budget for emergencies and adjust your expenses when they occur.

RVWanderlust:

"One of the things we love about this lifestyle is how flexible our budget items are. If we ever had emergency expenses or lost a client, our spending on food, fuel, and lodging (campground fees) could all be scaled back. We chose not to get an extended warranty for our used diesel RV. Instead, we keep $5,000 in an emergency fund. We also have redundant roadside emergency memberships, with AAA and Good Sam. If we were to ever break down in the middle of nowhere, the towing costs could be exorbitant without these services."

Jeff and Coffee:

"Life on the road is much more simple: fuel, propane, food, search for water, and the cell phone/data bucket bill."

It's important to budget for the unexpected.

Michael and Brenda:

"Unexpected situations will occur. Just handle them when they arise and figure out your recovery plan afterwards. If it means boondocking for awhile — that doesn't cost you anything. Or staying longer where you're at until next payday. It's all workable and can easily be done."

Certainly there are campground fees or RV park fees if you go that route, but most of our travelers try to camp for free.

TheAmericanFieldTrip:

"We very rarely pay to camp; instead we find free campgrounds or dispersed camping on the AllStays app or online. We also save money by cooking all our own meals and avoiding processed food."

A final strategy, mentioned specifically by **Jax733,** as well as **TheVanProject,** is to avoid buying more "stuff."

You May Ask: "What is an expected budget for this lifestyle?"

RVWanderlust:

"This is a common question, but it's like asking what the budget is for someone who wants to buy a house or live in an apartment. There are people who (mind-blowingly) live on $500/month. And there are people who live on $5,000+/month. For the most part, I think people keep their same budgets from before they go on the road, but the money is shuffled into different budget line items. There's no more mortgage or utility bills, but there is fuel, camping fees, and maybe an RV loan payment. Many people switch to RVing to save money or pay down debt, which they can easily do depending on their desired standard of living."

It amazes me how cheaply some people are able to live.

VanProject:

"We're getting by on roughly $500/month total (for both of us). But we also stay at mainly BLM/free campsites, only dump maximum one time/per month and only eat out for about one meal and a few coffees, max per week. We're living a bit of the dirtbag lifestyle I guess, but we love it."

Michael and Brenda:

"[I] estimated $800, but I now think it more like $1000 to $1200. Repairs to RV and truck; combined with mission trips."

It's common for people to underestimate what they will be spending, which is why the list (in the above section) of possible expenses is helpful in making a realistic budget. Also, keeping track of your expenses month-to-month will help you learn where to "trim the fat" when necessary.

Our two solo travelers are able to maintain this lifestyle on about $1500 per month.

Laura J:

"This really depends on how much you move, the types of places you camp, how much you eat out, if you have a pet to feed and care for, etc. My budget goal is $1500 (not counting certain fixed costs like insurance, phone, some previous outstanding bills). As a solo person, I've been close, but haven't hit it yet!"

RVegan:

"From my experience, monthly rent in an RV park in the south east is about $500 on average, including all utilities. I hear that if you head to the southwest, you can live for free or cheap — like $100 a year type of cheap. All things included (gas, rent, repairs, food, fun, taxes, etc.) I spend an average of $1,586 a month."

The fact that she knows her exact average, down to the dollar, means she is a great money-manager!

> It appears the average is around $2000/month for our nomads.

Heath and Alyssa:

"Our living expenses are in between $1500-2500/month."

OurVieAdventures:

"We try to do things as cheaply as possible. We knew we were going to be driving around a lot, and that a big chunk of our budget would be devoted to fuel. All-in-all, we averaged about $2000 a month for the last year."

Vagabroads:

"[We spend] $2-2500 per month — but Karin and I are bougie girls. We like to eat out, and we drive a Landcruiser, so gas costs are high. We know people who do it on a lot less."

Jeff and Coffee:

"We thought we could make it on $1,200/month by really living minimally. It could be done, but for a couple to live a simple life comfortably with insurance, eating healthily, and a bit of traveling, it requires about $2,300/month."

Some of our travelers break it down for us into specifics.

WanderlandTravelers:

"This is going to be completely different for just about everyone! If you're boondocking most of the month, then your camping expenses could be next to nothing. In our most expensive month, we spent over $1200 on campgrounds alone! Yikes! That was along the California coast: LA, Malibu, Morro Bay, Monterey. Some of those campgrounds were around $50/night. It was an incredible month of travel, but way too expensive. Our campground costs over the whole year averaged to be around $700/month. We average about $350/month on gas."

HotSauceHippo:

"$2840 per month is what it costs us to live on the road: $480 in gas, $60 in oil changes, $30 in tolls/parking, $180 in RV parks, $70 in utilities (gas, water, sewage), $1000 in food, $50 in ubers/taxis, $100 in entertainment, $70 on the gym, $100 on cell phones, $400 on health insurance, $100 on the dog's food, $200 in car insurance."

Like **RVegan**, the fact that they know their exact expenses is impressive, helpful and indicative of their awareness of the finances. That's a good way to live while on the road!

Wandrly:

"It completely depends on the amount of paid camping, going out to eat, doing things like alpine slides or whale tours, etc. you want to do. You can literally live as cheaply as you'd like, given the plethora of free camping options, free firewood, dumpster diving...or you can live like a king and spend thousands and thousands every month. We personally spend around $600/month on camping and something similar on gas. Everything else depends entirely on how much we're out doing touristy stuff vs. just making our own food around a campfire or staying with friends..."

Rather than trimming the fat, if you have the ability to add funds to the equation, you can expand your spending options. Some of our travelers pick up odd jobs to enable them to live more "comfortably."

The best advice I can offer, from my personal experience, is to estimate your budget and add about 20% on to it for good measure. We may be unique, but in the year we've been living this way, we've had at least that amount in unexpected "emergency" expenses every single month. If you plan for that, it won't be as challenging, and if you get lucky and don't have those expenses, then that money can go into savings, charities, or fun.

KEEPING IN CONTACT WITH FOLKS BACK HOME

When asked, "what did you think you'd miss that you actually don't miss while on the road," many travelers said they miss friends and family, as they expected to, but that they miss them less than they thought they would. They explain that they are staying so connected with them, and in some cases even seeing them more often, while on the road than before. The time spent with friends and family when on the road is often more "real" because they aren't casual interactions, but rather planned and intensive.

We stayed in Sedona for a month and had different people visit us each week. Many other spots have been great places to connect with people. We have experienced a rich deepening in our relationship with one set of friends, in particular, as a result of them visiting us in several spots on the road. We had a strong connection with this couple prior to leaving on our adventure, but now that they have visited us during our travels, we have had some intense conversations that likely wouldn't have ever happened had we just been meeting them casually for drinks or dinner, as we did back in our hometown.

Nearly all full-time travelers have blogs that they use for various purposes, keeping family and friends back home apprised of what they are doing. The use of social media to stay in touch is also widespread, which is to be expected. The dominant sites are Instagram and Facebook. Texting is another commonly mentioned method of keeping in touch, with phone or FaceTime calls after that.

Wanderland Travelers:

"Social media is a pretty amazing tool to stay connected with friends and family and feel like you're not so far apart. We like to text with people, and that's a fun way to get real-time interactions or get updates. We've actually seen more of our families since we started traveling! We lived in different states before, but now

we have the freedom to spend a month with each side of our family. That's been really amazing. We've also met up with some of them at different locations we've been. Another bonus has been visiting old friends that are now spread across the country, and that's been really special."

Laura J:

"I am in regular (almost daily) contact with my mother; my sister and a friend have me on the Find Friends app, so they can see where I am as long as I have cell service. I have a group of about six family and friends who I inform whenever I arrive somewhere new. I also have a blog, so friends can follow my adventures."

RVWanderlust:

"It does take work to maintain friendships when we're away. For our friends who have shown a desire to stay in touch, we love to do so. It takes two to make and keep a friendship, so we can only do our part. Though we have had friendships quietly fade away since we've started traveling, we've also been able to reignite friendships by meeting up with old friends on the road, who we never would've been able to see otherwise."

Wandrly:

"I lost a few friends over this, but anyone who doesn't support our life's decisions, probably isn't a great friend anyway. And we actually get to see friends more often, because we can drive around and visit these people who are scattered all over the U.S. — old, really good friends we wouldn't have seen for years, maybe decades, if we weren't moving around like this."

GETTING YOUR MAIL BACK HOME

Everyone says that it's easy to keep up with their bills on the road because they simply manage them using Bill Pay and other internet-based banking. Mail is handled a couple of different ways. Either they use a family member or friend to take care of their mail, or they use a professional service.

Bear in mind that where you receive your mail can have consequences on income taxes and sales taxes (in the case of states without sales tax, in particular). We wanted to maintain our Oregon address because it enables us to save on sales tax when we order from Amazon. We also purchased our travel trailer and truck without paying sales tax, because of our Oregon residency, and we didn't want that to be an issue if we shortly thereafter weren't maintaining a primary residence in Oregon. You will also need to consider that the state you receive your mail in is usually where you will be registered to vote, have your car registration, and so forth.

RVegan:

"My mom handles all my mail. My mom's house is my official address, with my car's registration, my voting registration, etc."

HotSauceHippo:

"We receive mail at my mom's house back in Washington. It is still technically our 'permanent address' for purposes of our IDs, credit cards, and other important documents."

MilesAwayEveryDay:

"We have our mail sent to a family member, and if it's worth keeping, they will either send us a digital copy or ...a package of mail to a particular stop somewhere on our route, whether it's another family member or a UPS store of some kind."

Jax733:

"We have some really close friends who receive our mail and open and sort it. We pay them a nominal amount to do this. They deposit rent checks and any other checks into our bank accounts. They alert us to any urgent mail. Anything else they send to us when we are somewhere that we can easily receive mail."

You can also use a P.O. Box service from a private company like UPS.

RVWanderlust:

"We have a box at a UPS Store in downtown Austin that we use for business and personal mail. They forward our mail to us whenever we ask them to. All of our regular bills are managed online."

TravelExploreUncover:

"We have a Traveling Mailbox account. All of our mail is sent there, where the company scans the front of the envelope and emails us the scan. We are then able to choose whether this mail should be opened, shredded, or forwarded to a location that we can pick it up."

WanderlandTravelers:

"We use one of many mail forwarding services called Anytime Mailbox (anytimemailbox.com). They partner with mail collecting services throughout the country, and they happened to have a partner in our home state of Oregon, so we went with them. ...About once a month, we'll have our mail collector forward our mail to our current location. If we are near a friend or family, we'll have it shipped there, or if we're at a campsite we'll ship it there. If neither of those are an option, we'll use USPS General Delivery, a wonderful option that we didn't discover until halfway through our first year."

Wandrly:

"[We use] Escapees.com, it'll change your life with mail on the road. All of your mail goes there, you technically become a Texan (which means no state income tax), and you just shoot those guys an email, and they'll forward it wherever you are. For us, this usually means a General Delivery address, which basically just means they send it to the local post office where we are. In Mexico or further south, we just don't get mail. We spent 16 months there and aside from needing to order some parts, we never saw our mail for the entire time and yet somehow the earth kept on a-spinning."

Finally, here's an innovative strategy.

Jeff and Coffee:

"We made friends with our winter location postman, and he forwards our mail as needed with our pre-paid envelopes."

GETTING MAIL ON THE ROAD

Several of our travelers above mentioned using the USPS' General Delivery option for receiving mail. To do this, you simply use an address like this:

Your Name

c/o (Name of town) Post Office

"General Delivery"

City/Town, State, Zip

You then keep track of when your package has arrived using the USPS tracking website, go into the USPS office with your ID, and grab your mail. It's that easy.

The advantage of General Delivery is that it is free. The disadvantage is that they usually don't take delivery of mail from UPS or FedEx or other private carriers. For mail being delivered through one of these private companies, you will need to have it sent to a UPS store, or some other mail storefront. Call in advance and ask that location how they want the package addressed and what the fees are. Often they charge a daily fee plus a pick up fee, so it can get pricey if you don't time it right. Many small town mail stores, though, may do it for free, if you ask nicely.

Another solution that many people utilize is to time their mail deliveries to when they will be going to the house of a friend or family member on the road. They will then use that address and have their mail delivered while they are visiting.

One other method we've used to receive mail on the road is by taking advantage of a stay at a formal campground. We simply ask the campground manager if we can have a package sent to their office, and they usually agree, with no fees attached.

For Amazon-specific purchases, you can consider using the Amazon locker option. Amazon lockers exist in most large cities, and there is no additional fee associated with this service.

MEDICATIONS

When we were on our "shake down" trip (the extended trip you should take before you set off on the full-time adventure), we met a woman who had been a full-time traveling RVer for the last couple of years. She told us about a solution she uses to get her medication on the road. She said the easiest way was to have your prescriptions transferred to a Walmart. Since Walmarts are so prevalent throughout the U.S., it is then easy to have the prescriptions transferred between Walmarts for you to pick up at a new location, when you are in that town.

I have three prescriptions that I take daily. I began my travels using her suggestion, but later my insurance company changed, and Walmart was no longer a preferred carrier. This led me to research other options. I now have to do the same thing, but using Walgreens instead. It isn't quite as easy, because not every state has Walgreens, where it seems every state does have Walmarts, but it is working so far. I just have to do a lot more planning ahead with this provider.

LESSONS FROM THE ROAD

Before starting off on your full-time adventure, most travelers will advise a "shake-down" trip be taken. Our RV dealer told us to drive our trailer on bumpy roads and spend some a couple of weeks or more camping within 100 miles of the dealership (we bought our RV in Utah and live in Oregon). He recommended this so that we could "shake out" any defects or problems with the RV before we set out full-time. This recommendation proved invaluable, as we did have some issues that needed to be remedied.

There have been so many helpful pointers that we've received while on the road, or that we have discovered on our own. Inevitably, when we are camped at one spot and get to talking to someone from around that area, we learn an invaluable tip about where to go next. Therefore, one suggestion is to talk to people around you — both locals and travelers passing through. The second suggestion is to listen to what they have to offer and be flexible enough in your plans to take advantage of their advice.

For example, we were camped in Manitoba, Canada and I started chatting with a camper. He said that we *have* to go to Prince Edward Island. He explained that there is a big lobster dinner that goes on there (I thought he said every Sunday), and that the lobster is so good and affordable that we'd be remiss in not going. We were not planning on doing so, but I mentioned this to my wife, and she started to research.

Turns out, what he was referring to is a town on the way to PEI called Shediac that has a lobster festival around July. This town is considered the "lobster capital of the world." We couldn't be there in July, since it already was July, and PEI was thousands of miles away still. But what my wife did discover was that we could time a visit to PEI for their Annual Shellfish Festival in which they have 20 different kinds of oysters served. Well, we are huge oyster fans, so that really excited us.

We moved our plans around, changed campground reservations, booked a hotel in downtown Charlottetown, and now we are going to the festival! In addition, we are camping in New Brunswick near the town of Shediac, so we will get to enjoy their lobster, too. It's experiences like this that you can have on the road — ones that are irreplaceable and unforgettable.

After traveling for just a short while, you will find there are things you wish you'd known before you started. Some are lessons for things to avoid; some are things you must do. Here are some suggestions from our travelers.

HotSauceHippo:

"Don't put your sink water down the toilet! There are many places on the internet that suggest you do this to save room in your grey water tank (since the black water tank is larger than the grey). However, we did this and it caused the worst smell either of us have ever experienced. Seriously, the smell was wretched. After further research, we learned that there is a delicate balance of bacteria that takes place in the sewage tank and putting rotting food, coffee grounds, and toothpaste spit really messes with that balance. It took us weeks, and many gallons of vinegar, to get that balance back. Now, we use a bin in our sink to collect water from washing our hands, washing dishes, or rinsing vegetables, and simply dump it outside to save space in our grey tank. (Note — if you're going to do this, make sure to use an eco-friendly soap and pour it somewhere it is not going to leak into a water stream.)"

WanderlandTravelers:

"Take your time and think things through while dumping so you don't make mistakes! One tiny mistake can result in crap in your face (not kidding)."

Personally, this statement explains our decision to have a composting toilet. Black tanks are unpleasant (polite understatement). Composting toilets have come a long way and if you set it up correctly, they are easy to get used to and much more pleasant to empty. Funny note: I just checked our compost part of our composting toilet and discovered a few sprouts! Apparently, since it has been awhile since we've "used" it, the compost has had time to grow a thing or two. Guess it's either time to harvest, or time to dump it!

RVegan:

"[When purchasing your rig] avoid dry rot on your camper. Make sure there are no soft spots, push on the walls and make sure you can't see the outside at the seams. If there are any smells at all — walk away and do not buy that rig because there will be an identical rig right down the road in better condition."

HappyCamperWives:

"[During your travels] avoid tourist traps as best as you can, but also listen to recommendations — we've found the best kept secrets from recommendations."

GoWiththeFlowandCo:

"Visit national parks on weekdays!"

I would personally add to this to do *most* of your tourism activities in the off-season, and save your less-touristy endeavors for the summer and holidays. We started our travels in September and were pleased with how empty all of the national parks were — until spring break and summer when they became so packed it was hard to find parking.

The difference is shocking and unpleasant. You will enjoy yourself much more, in my opinion, if you bundle up and hit sights during the fall, winter, and early spring months. We plan on spending most summers camp-hosting to enable us to stay in one place for a couple of months and not have to worry about finding campsites during the busiest time of the year. During the non-summer months we will be able to tour national and state parks and won't be caught in the midst of a million other tourists.

WanderlandTravelers:

"Get a smaller rig than you think you need. You'll thank yourself later when you have a larger pool of campgrounds to choose from when searching for a place to stay."

I agree with this as well, as I long for the capability to fit into more sites more easily. We are absolutely limited by our size (32-foot trailer plus 20-foot towing vehicle). If you can squeeze into a smaller RV, then you'll expand your options dramatically.

Michael and Brenda:

"Be sure to have a roadside assistance plan."

While we have been fortunate enough to not need this too often, we, too, have had to use our AAA membership and have had numerous other times where we've been lucky to get to a repair shop without needing AAA. Just by virtue of the fact that you will typically be driving more than you used to, things will happen. We've had parts fail, damage done, regular mechanical breaks, and unusual problems.

Plan for it with extra funds, extended warranties and roadside assistance.

WanderlandTravelers:

"Bring bikes. It's great exercise, and it's one of our favorite ways to explore a new (or old) town…drop into the local tourism office for maps and local tips on some of the best things to see and do in a location."

Ditto and ditto.

OurVieAdventures:

"It is all about being off-grid. Boondocking is the way to go. Sure, it is fun to bounce from one RV campground to the next, but you are still tethered to a concrete pad! If you can make it happen, set it up to where you can experience the more secluded spots of the country. It is absolutely amazing."

Our intention from the beginning was to boondock as much as possible, too. Remember, though, everyone is different. Like many of our travelers, we enjoy solitude and nature. However, if you prefer a more urban environment, full-hookups, and like to socialize with other RVers, then boondocking may not be your cup of tea.

RVWanderlust:

"This lifestyle is not for everyone. It comes with a lot of instability and requires constant flexibility. If you don't get along with your partner for long periods of time, you're going to have issues. If you don't have an emergency fund for repairs, you're walking on thin ice. Having said that, if you've done a thorough self-evaluation and think RVing is a fit, there comes a time when you have to take a leap of faith. I wouldn't trade our leap for anything."

SECRET SPOTS FROM
OUR TRAVELERS

Everyone has their special spot. It might be a campground that has a special feel. It may be a magical and peaceful boondocking spot. Or perhaps it is a luxurious RV Park. Whatever it is, I wanted to know the secret places that everyone wants to return to. Here is what our travelers revealed.

SunnyJunket:

"Our funnest [camping spots] have been through Harvest Hosts. We've stayed at three wineries, an animal park and the Petrified Forest gift shop."

Campgrounds

Three of our travelers offered stories about campgrounds, although two of them are outside of the U.S.

Wandrly tells a tale of an experience at a small campground in Mexico that is their favorite.

Maya Belle

Palenque Mexico

No address given.

"It's a little campground in Palenque, Mexico by the name of Maya Belle. It was a gorgeous little place, and we met so many families. The town and ruins of Palenque were so full of hippies from all over the Americas, and there were just some exceptional experiences there...including howler monkeys screaming into the every evening's sunset. Our favorite part of all of that, though, was this traveling Mexican couple. They were a band and had a young daughter. They invited us out to these amazing waterfalls where their uncle lived. It was our 5-year-old, Winter's, birthday, and they had setup a piñata. No one except the dad of the little girl spoke English, but my Spanish is pretty good. We all did the best we could to hang out and conveyed most things pretty well."

The **Vagabroads** give us a short story about their favorite spot in El Salvador.

D'Takito Horizonte Surf Camp

El Zonte, El Salvador

No address given.

"I guess one of my favorites is for sure, D'Takito Horizonte Surf Camp in El Zonte, El Salvador — it is proper overlanding there — close to the beach, pool, fruit and veggie truck visits daily, giant iguana named Paco — what more could you want?"

These are the kind of memories that *you* can create.

For the U.S., **Laura J** provides us with a short review on a campground in California.

Rincon Parkway Campground

4668 Pacific Coast Hwy, Ventura, CA 93001

"Just north of Ventura, CA. Great sunsets, beach in the front yard, bike path!"

Boondocking Spots

Our travelers were sometimes secretive about their boondocking spots, for obvious reasons.

Jeff and Coffee:

"Our all-time favorite places to boondock must necessarily remain secrets; otherwise, they will cease to be favorites...sorry."

LivingLifeInBetween:

"In general our favorite place has been Utah, we do a lot of boondocking, and half of the adventure is discovering those amazing spots on your own. I don't want to give too much away."

OurVieAdventures:

"We are as cheap as it gets, which means we only boondock. During our entire national park trip, we never paid for a campsite for the RV. Which means, we spent more than a few nights in Walmart parking lots. But, that also means we spent even more nights in secluded spots on our public lands. We found so many amazing spots along our journey! One of our favorites was a spot outside of Grand Teton National Park. I can't give you the GPS coordinates, because the spot is pretty secret. But, we had a clear view of the Tetons and when the sun would rise, it lit the mountains up all kinds of magical colors."

Then there's the neighborhood boondocking.

Michael and Brenda':

"[One of our favorite experiences was] boondocking for six weeks across the street from a cousin in central California. Nice wide road and of course home cooking. Location is a secret."

A few of our travelers did give us some specifics, however.

WanderlandTravelers:

"Since one of our goals is to stay in the most scenic places, this is a tough question! We've loved so many spots! Our favorites are always free boondocking — quiet, secluded, and full of stars. Our top places are: the Carrizo Badlands in the Anza Borrego desert, Mittry Lake near Yuma, and the Alabama Hills in Eastern California. You can look up photos and reviews of all of these on Campendium.com or you can check out our videos of these spots on YouTube!"

HotSauceHippo:

"[There's a place in] nowhere Virginia on Chichahominy WMA (GPS: 37.300923, -76.899026). This is a boondocking spot on public land near a boat launch outside of Jamestown, VA. There was no one there when we camped, and it was the most serene, peaceful site we've experienced. It's surrounded by woods, and a river runs through the land. There were birds and frogs singing away, and the sunset was a spectacular orange!"

MilesAwayEveryDay:

"As far as boondocking favorites go, we just spent as much time as possible at the Upper Grand Teton View Point in Wyoming, near Jackson Hole and it was stunning. We also really fell in love with Dixie National Forest near Bryce Canyon NP, specifically Tom Best Springs. It's absolutely beautiful and peaceful. Wildlife were always around somewhere. We made so many new friends in both of these spots that we love them both even more for giving us those experiences and new relationships."

TravelExploreUncover:

"[Our favorite boondocking spot is] the Badlands of South Dakota! We had an awesome boondocking spot, on the ridge of the badlands, two miles outside of Badlands National Park. There were no neighbors. Just grass, sun, and an amazing view of the badlands."

Vagabroads:

"Camping at Playa Perla of Bahia de Concepcion, Baja California Sur, Mexico."

There are innumerable apps and websites offering campground and boondocking reviews. Some of the big ones are Campendium, Allstays, Ultimate Campground (U.S. and Canadian versions), Campground Views, freecampsites.net, or my favorite — my own blog! Yes, that's right, I have reviews on it, too. www.toystrailsandtails.com. The best advice, of course, is to find your own favorite spots! That's half the fun.

RV Parks

Florida is known for its RV "resorts." Three of our RVers give us specifics about Florida spots, one tells us about a Colorado Park, and the last is a KOA in North Carolina.

Colorado

Clear Creek RV Park

Golden, CO

RVWanderlust:

"There are a few contenders, but our all-around favorite right now is Clear Creek RV Park in beautiful Golden, Co. Golden is the most charming town, and the RV park which is owned by the city is a five-minute walk from the main street. As the name suggests, Clear Creek runs right along the RV park. If you have a water-side site, you go to sleep to the sound of babbling water, and wake up to it the next morning."

Florida

Presnell's Bayside Marina and RV Resort

www.presnells.com

RVegan:

"This place was so beautiful. I stayed for a month last winter, and I loved waking up and seeing the bay and being 20 minutes from the white sand gulf beaches."

Bluewater Key RV Resort

2950 Overseas Highway, Key West, Florida

Steve K:

"Absolutely beautiful luxury RV sites with docks, cabanas, and outdoor kitchens."

Sunshine Key RV Resort and Marina

Florida Keys

Heath and Alyssa:

"Hands down! Beachfront camping at its finest."

North Carolina

KOA

Swannanoa, North Carolina

MilesAwayEveryDay:

"Our favorite campground, hands down. Rhiannon spent her summers there as a child with her grandparents since she was 4 years old so it is a very special place for her. When we set out on our maiden voyage, North Carolina was the easiest decision as our first experience since we both have sentimental connections, as well as friends and family, around there. We returned to that same KOA and the staff was amazing working with us on trying to get us as close to the spot Rhiannon's grandparents had every single year... It's a beautiful campground overall, aside from the sentimental ties. They keep it in great shape, the staff is the best we have ever experienced, there's so much to do there and it's just beautiful. After spending a few days in the old sentimental spot, we were walking the grounds one day and found a spot near a lake and spent a few more days there. Now that is "our" spot" to return to and enjoy in all the years to come."

There's obviously something for everyone! Soon you will get to discover your favorites.

NO MATTER WHAT, JUST KNOW EVERYTHING ALWAYS WORKS OUT

I asked our travelers about the craziest things that have ever happened to them on the road. I wasn't sure what stories I'd get, and I didn't have a pre-designed place to put the stories within this book. I just knew we needed to hear them, and I'd figure out their appropriateness later.

The stories I received mostly had one message: No matter the drama that happens to you, it will work out, and it will make a great tale later. Keep that in perspective and nothing, but nothing, can stand in your way of an amazing adventure.

I'm leaving the travelers to tell their stories here. Remember to laugh, even when you are feeling their pain!

First are the stories of the breakdowns and mechanical mishaps:

RVWanderlust:

"The craziest thing that has happened to us on the road, since we started fulltime RVing in February 2014, was our first breakdown. Actually, it was the only time we have ever actually broken down, to the point that we couldn't move the RV ourselves. We had been traveling for less than five months, when we pulled into a truck stop to get diesel. When we turned on the ignition to leave, nothing

happened. We were on our way to get Eric's elderly mother from the airport, and we had a car full of our kids for their summer vacation. When emergency roadside assistance attempted to go inside to put our rig into neutral for towing, our door handle broke. We ended up having to shove one of our kids through the emergency exit in the bedroom, so he could open the door from the inside. We all rushed to pack all our things from the RV into our Jeep, including emptying our fridge contents into a cooler so they wouldn't spoil. We had to get our bearded dragon out of his terrarium with all of his things. Our Jeep was so full that things were on the roof and on everyone's laps. This was only the beginning of a dramatic week-long adventure that included the prospect of long-term homelessness. It worked out, like it always does."

Steve K:

"I was driving from Pennsylvania to my [RV] dealer in Florida to drop off my motorhome for a few weeks for some maintenance issues. I was flying home, so I didn't tow my car. I also knew I would not want to leave food in my refrigerator for that length of time. I decided I would eat at truck stops on the way down, so I didn't have to throw food out when I got there. As I pulled into the Welcome to North Carolina rest area on a Friday afternoon, a valve in the air ride system failed. The frame of the motorhome rested nicely on top of the front driver's side tire and would not raise back up. Help arrived but could not get the part replaced until Monday. I was stranded! I ate for three days out of the vending machines at the rest area, because I was too embarrassed to tell anyone I didn't have any food in my half-million dollar motorhome!"

TheVanProject:

"Our brakes overheated and stopped working in the mountain roads of Northern California while driving our RV back home from buying it in Washington State. <u>http://thevanproject.co/brake-failure-norcal</u>." [Here's an excerpt from their heart-stopping experience:]

"Amanda and I had an exciting few moments recently while driving West on Highway 299 in Northern California to a friend's house near Humboldt County.

For those of you who haven't driven the mountain roads in NorCal, you might call them treacherous. 299 is characterized by steep grades, sharp curves, and beautiful scenery. As you wind down out of the hills to the coast, you pass through redwood groves on steep hill sides where you have to navigate hairpin turns.

As someone who has driven LOTS of different cars and trucks including semi-sized, fully-loaded production trucks (thanks Burning Man), I am well aware of the hazards of mountain driving with large vehicles. I understand the necessity to keep your brakes cool so that they function when you want to stop. With any vehicle, but ESPECIALLY with older vehicles that have drum brakes, you want to pulse (or pump) the brakes instead of just standing on the pedal all the way down the hills. You also ideally want to downshift instead of constantly braking – it's much easier to let the engine compression modulate your speed and it keeps your brakes cool in case you need more stopping power.

...After what seemed like hours of curving roads (in the pouring rain no-less), Amanda and I were coming close to the end of the steep downhill driving. I had been doing everything correctly, pumping the brakes when I was using them, downshifting and letting the engine do the work to slow me down. But all of this didn't seem to matter. There was just so much downhill driving as we descended from the mountains that [their RV's] brakes started to heat up.

Just as soon as I thought that the brakes were starting to feel a little 'weird', we hit some of the steepest downhill grades of the drive....I had Tez in second gear and was attempting to slow down more, but all of a sudden the brakes went from tired to non-functional. My heart began to race. Amanda asked what was wrong and I was only barely able to say, 'the brakes aren't working!' as we rolled forwards towards the sharp turn. Standing out of my seat against the brake pedal I was able to slow us down just enough to swing through the turn and into a straight section of road with a big enough shoulder to pull off.

I immediately jammed the emergency brake to the floor, still standing on the brake pedal and finally down-shifted to first gear. ...[our RV] slowly lurched to a stop as the combination of the brakes, first gear and the emergency brake was enough to slow her 8000 pounds to the point of stalling. My heart was pounding, but I managed to get her to stop safely on the side of the road after complete brake failure...."

OurVieAdventures:

"Our RV engine literally blew up in the middle of nowhere Canada on our way back down from Alaska. It took over a week to get the right parts shipped in and fixed up (which is actually pretty stinking fast considering where we were). At first we were pretty devastated, but we made really good friends and had a lot of fun in the area, so we can't be that upset about it."

WanderlandTravelers:

"We have an intermittent issue with our gas gauge. While we're driving, we'll hear an alarm sound, and we watch as the gas gauge needle drops to empty. So far, every time it has immediately gone back to normal, but that first time it happened we feared we'd just gotten a major gas leak. The issue has happened nearly a dozen times in the past year. Still not sure what's going on with that!"

There are tales that are too close for comfort:

Jeff and Coffee:

"We were towing our Airstream late one night through the desolate area of Arizona on our way to Canyon de Chelly and battling a very strong crosswind when we entered a very small reservation town. Out of the corner of my eye came a strange object growing from out of the darkness — a large, loose billboard cartwheeled about 25 feet in front of us, as I braked just in time. We were still thinking about that near miss an hour later when we entered the reservation town of Chinle and saw a late model Datsun pickup slowly veer across the two lane highway's divider line. I took our tow vehicle and trailer off onto a nice wide shoulder, and grimaced as I watched the truck in my side mirror, expecting it to swipe the entire length of our trailer. The truck veered back across our lane at the divider at the last instant, just missing our trailer by about a foot. I would say nothing good comes out of traveling late into the night, but we somehow managed to get to bed in one piece."

TravelExploreUncover:

"The craziest thing. Well, we were driving East out of Colorado, while towing our 39-foot toy hauler. The semi-truck in front of us slammed on its brakes and swerved to the right. Because of the dust caused by the semi-truck braking, we weren't able to see the reason he was swerving until it was almost too late. There were two lazy-boy rocking chairs in the MIDDLE of the freeway. Josh quickly started blasting our train horn, thankfully causing the vehicles behind us to slow down, while making a very risky maneuver into another lane to dodge both rocking chairs. It all happened so fast and could have caused major damage to our truck and RV, let alone causing a deadly accident. We immediately called 911, who sent responders out to clear the road."

LivingLifeInBetween:

"The craziest thing we have gone through was a gnarly storm in New Mexico near White Sands National Monument. We hadn't been on the road longer than a month, and it was our first boondocking experience. We had our RV parked on BLM land and we were facing a lake. We knew there was a storm rolling in, but it was supposed to just miss us. We were watching the lightning strikes over the water, thinking "wow that's really beautiful we should record it," so Gerrit went outside and set up our GoPro. Moments later the wind shifted and the storm was coming our way. The lightning was getting closer and it started to rain. The wind picked up to 60 mph gusts that were hitting us broadside. While watching the radar, we pulled up our jacks and put in the slides. Our RV was the tallest thing around, so I don't know how we did not get hit by lightning. However, just as we thought it was starting to die down, we heard a single loud thump on the front windshield. We looked at each other and just said, "hail.".... Golf ball sized hail hammered down on us for 15 minutes. We were so terrified that there would be a lot of damage, but we got lucky. There was some damage to the hood of the Jeep, a few holes in one of our air conditioning covers, a crack on the fan lid and the shower dome. But it was all pretty simple to fix and we came out of it alright."

WanderlandTravelers:

"We got some marble-sized hail in June while in Montana. Luckily we were parked during the storm and amazingly had no damage to the roof or solar panels."

Laura J:

"Scariest was a big storm when I was in Morro Bay, CA. Torrential rain, 50 mph winds. The rig was rocking, the dog and I were huddled in the back, 17 trees fell down at the campground!"

SunnyJunket:

"Dealing with a 35-year old trailer in a Texas downpour! You find out where all your leaks are!"

Jax733:

"We were boondocked in an open area on a reservoir. We watched as a storm started to come towards us. We pulled in our awning, chairs, and anything that was outside. As the storm approached the winds got wilder and wilder. Then the rain came. It was raining sideways, so the rain started to come into our trailer windows at the seams! The wind was rocking the trailer so much, it was worse than any earthquake we'd ever felt in California. Finally it passed... but the next day we discovered the winds had lifted up our trailer to the point that the blocks under the stabilizers had blown down the meadow we were parked in. In addition, the top of the container that houses our propane tanks had blown off, and we almost didn't find it. How the wind got under our trailer to lift it up to that extent still amazes me!"

OurVieAdventures:

"We drove through fire tornados in Tennessee. First, we had been in Gatlinburg at the time of the fires, and we got pushed up north to avoid the smoke. Then, that night a huge storm rolled in and tornados started touching down all

around us! Madison packed the emergency bag, as I drove through the gnarliest hail and wind in the opposite direction of the storm. We were literally looking at the radar on our phones and dodging tornados. Driving a tall RV down the road with gale force winds is not something everyone needs to experience. It was terrifying. I literally thought we were going to get lifted up and blown away. We survived though! And here we are telling what is now a funny (kind of) story.

OurVieAdventures:

"Our cat ran away at a gas station when we were fueling up, and we didn't even notice. We were in the middle of the Utah desert, and the only place to eat was right across the street. We drove across the street and ate and when we got back in the RV we couldn't find the cat. We retraced our path and thought we would never see him again, but he was just sitting waiting for us right by the gas station door. Make sure you always do a roll call before you pull out of any stop!"

There are also just some "this was weird" stories:

WanderlandTravelers:

"We've had a few things that might fall under the category of crazy. We've gotten a knock on our door a few different times, always when boondocking. It's not terribly crazy to have an unexpected visitor, but it can be unnerving depending on the time of day. Once it was 10 p.m.: a woman and her dog were looking for a metal hanger. She had gotten locked out of her car. A different time was at 6 a.m.: it was a construction crew at a rest area that needed us to vacate within a couple hours."

HotSauceHippo:

"We accidentally stopped a high speed car chase with the cops. The story: We were driving on a small two-lane highway in New Hampshire. I noticed a police officer with lights flashing about a mile behind us, fast approaching. About five seconds later, I saw a police car parked perpendicular to the roadway in the middle

of the oncoming traffic. The officer of that vehicle had his gun drawn, pointing his weapon at the traffic traveling in our direction! A school bus directly in front of us pulled over on to the shoulder, and I stopped mostly in the lane of traffic, behind the school bus. Then I realized the cop behind us was chasing a car that was now trying to get by the other cars. The car got stuck behind us and the bus and the perpendicular copy car, which together were blocking the road. The last thing I saw was a man jump out the driver's door of the car and go running into the woods, along the highway. The cop with his gun drawn started screaming, 'go, go, go, go!' to us and the bus so we sped away. Pretty sure they owe us some type of (accidental) [good] Samaritan award."

Vagabroads:

"Taking the wrong route to Semuc Champey in Guatemala, which took eight hours instead of four. Then once we got there, I went tubing and almost died in the Cahabon river."

Jax733:

"We had just left a campground at Priest Lake, Idaho. We had gotten mice in our RV while camping there — there were mice everywhere — and between our cat catching a few and us shooing some out the door, we had gotten rid of four and thought we were done. We were heading to our next destination, on the freeway, going about 65 mph, when a mouse popped out of the hood of our car and started running around over the windshield wipers with its hair blowing in the wind. We couldn't stop since there were no turnouts, and we were towing our trailer. Eventually, he retreated back into the car's engine area. We discovered the little bugger had made a nest out of our battery insulator. No serious damage, though, so we lucked out."

MilesAwayEveryDay:

"We were flushing our black tank, and then we forgot we were flushing our black tank. It started 'raining' — if you want to hear the full story, come find us around a campfire and we will indulge you."

And, before you are convinced this life isn't for you, here's a couple of beautiful stories:

WanderlandTravelers:

"The coolest crazy thing was a full rainbow that hung around for hours while we were in the Anza Borrego desert. It was a stormy day and we watched the rainbow move across the sky over the course of about four hours. It was amazing!"

OurVieAdventures:

"We were sleeping in a pull out in the middle of northern Alaska when I woke up to what felt like a disco in the RV. The outside was lit up all green and purple! I got out and saw the most magnificent display of northern lights EVER. It was like one of those electric balls. Absolutely stunning."

This one has a happy ending, too:

Michael and Brenda:

"We went on an evening hike through a beautiful meadow. It was supposed to be a loop but we took a wrong turn and ended up about two or three miles from our truck. Some friendly hikers gave us a ride. We had visions of being on the trail after dark. Got some wonderful pictures."

While there will certainly be similar challenges that you will experience during your travels, you will find parts of you that (perhaps) you don't yet know exist — a part that is strong and able to tackle any adversity, a part that is fearless, a part that proves that you *love* adventure. A part that is in you now, crying to get out.

FINAL WORDS FROM OUR TRAVELERS

Hopefully by now you are fully inspired to take on a life of full-time travel. Remember *full-time* does not have to mean *forever*. By my definition, it simply means being on the road every day for 365 days or more. If, for some reason, you aren't yet ready, here are some final words from our travelers to you:

Wandrly:

"You can always go back. Maybe not to the same job or same house, but once you hit the road and start exploring and living like this, you realize that anything is possible. Failures happen, you course correct. This is true of living in a house as much as on the road. I feel we have more control over our lives, because we can pack up and move. I make our money, I don't rely on someone paying me a paycheck. It's freeing, really, but it can be scary to take the leap."

OurIncredibleDash:

"Absolutely appreciate each and every moment. Don't be afraid to take a huge scary leap toward making your dreams come true!"

TravelExploreUncover:

"When you seriously start considering this as an option, others around you will tell you it's not possible. But it is! It takes planning, saving, and courage, but it is possible."

Michael and Brenda:

"Follow your dreams and the open road…. Life is never a guarantee. Live it while you can….It's a great life."

WanderlandTravelers:

"Basically, if this is your dream, go for it! It has been one of the best decisions we ever made! You might try renting an RV for a week or weekend to dip your toes in the water! It could help you figure out if the size of the rig is comfortable to drive and to live in."

Steve K:

"Be thankful every day that you have the opportunity of this lifestyle, for the beauty of the country you are seeing, and for the many, many different types of people you will meet in your travels."

HotSauceHippo:

"Don't avoid joining the road life because you think you cannot afford it. The money will come if you want it to and believe it will. I truly believe that every person has a skill or knowledge that can be put to use to make money on the road. You have to find what brings you joy in this world, or it is all for nothing. We weren't put on this planet to sit behind a desk all day and push paper. Go out and live your life. It is only passing you by!"

8Paws1Tail:

"Trust that everything is going to be ok. Go with the flow, don't be afraid to adapt, and always keep learning. Life is about taking chances to chase your dreams and follow your heart. Have a good support system whether it be on or off the road."

Laura J:

"RVers are very diverse. Some go to big RV resorts, park for months and live in luxury. Others live in modest RVs and seek out the most remote, free spots. Others do some type of mixture. No one is having same experience so figure out your own path and embrace it!"

LivingLifeInBetween:

"Just do what is comfortable for you! If boondocking is not your thing don't feel like you have to do it. There are great campgrounds out there and clubs you can join to make them cheaper. You absolutely have to get out of your camper and enjoy nature. That's what this lifestyle is all about, and you can't see it from inside your rig."

RVegan

"You can do as much research as you can...but eventually there comes a point where you just have to make the decision and jump! In my opinion, you can always sell everything and go back to where you were before, if you decide it's not for you."

Jax733:

"It's not the life for everyone, but for people who have chosen it, I have never met anyone who regrets it. It's a special lifestyle for those who value adventure and freedom. Even though there are struggles both mechanically and logistically, working through them is part of self-sufficiency and builds confidence. Things in an RV or trailer are going to break so just expect that. Work together to problem solve."

MilesAwayEveryDay:

"Anything is possible. If you have the ability to work remotely in any fashion, and you want to live this lifestyle, nothing is actually stopping you but yourself. Just do it.… Don't over plan. You can spend all the time in the world trying to get yourself absolutely prepared and ready, and you can always find reasons to prolong it. Just dive in and live. You'll never regret a second of it, but you will regret not doing it sooner."

Steve K:

"I am always amazed when I travel about how many people are actually choosing this lifestyle today! It isn't all about retiring! Younger people are workamping and enjoying the freedom RV gives you to see this beautiful country. Go for it!"

Jeff and Coffee:

"Leave the fog of consumerism behind and the find the clarity of adventure."

Laura J:

"I would encourage folks to take their time. This lifestyle is not a race! If you see something interesting, check it out! Wherever you're headed will be there tomorrow!"

RVWanderlust:

"RV your way. It's good to learn from others, but your journey is your own. Slow down. If you move too quickly, you'll wear yourself out, and you'll miss the hidden gems. We live by this saying: Never get so busy making a living that you forget to make a life. Our work doesn't define us. It's just a means to an end."

Wandrly:

"Stay off the freeway, and take it slow. There's nowhere to go and nowhere to be except wherever you are now and in the moment. Make a few friends along the way, there's no need to check every state or country off as quickly as possible."

TravelExploreUncover:

"It's very possible! Get organized, start saving, become a minimalistic thinker, and plan a route!"

Vagabroads:

"You don't have anything to lose but another day of your life — and how many of those do you waste doing nothing every year?"

TheVanProject:

"You won't know until you try it. As with all things in life, we usually tell people to just go for it — it has mostly worked out for us so far. A lot of success has to do with intention — if you want to be successful at something, you likely can be, but you have to work damn hard."

Jeff and Coffee:

"The process of making the jump, while frustrating and demanding, should be cherished, for that moment of departure is filled with a combination of joy, anxiety, relief, excitement, and even a tinge of fear will never be repeated to the same degree. It is the stuff of adventure."

Vagabroads:

"Anyone can do it, just squash your fears. Stop buying stupid little things that don't matter and put that money in an account for your trip."

Wandrly:

"Spend it all, have a good time, live life!"

Laura J:

"Go for it! If it doesn't work out, you can always go back to a S&B!"
[Note: S&B is slang for a "sticks and bricks" house.]

Heath and Alyssa:

"Don't wait to live your life."

HotSauceHippo:

"There is nothing to be afraid of. Do your due diligence, and research the things that make you most worried (money, dumping fluids, being safe, etc.). Then, once you've made a plan, let go and trust that the universe will put everything where it is supposed to be. We can't control everything, and some of my most enjoyable moments have been when I let life just happen."

OurVieAdventures:

"Go for it. Launching life on the road seems really overwhelming at first. Just like any big project, focus on little bits at a time and before you know it, you will be out there adventuring in no time. You can make it happen!"

Michael and Brenda:

"You have to let go of stuff and build memories."

LivingLifeInBetween:

"Don't hesitate! If you think about it too much you'll never do it. What do you have to lose?"

Jeff and Coffee:

"If you don't go, you will know exactly what and where your future will hold for you. If you do go, your tomorrows are unwritten. One must choose for him or herself as to what makes one happy: routine or adventure."

IF YOU WANT TO TELL ME ABOUT YOU

I've told you bits and pieces about me throughout the book, and I'd love for you to reach out to me and tell me about you! If you are a full-time traveler, fill out my questionnaire and interviews, so that when I revise or update the book, I can include you! (NOTE: If you are reading the paperback version and cannot click on the links below, you will need to type them in exactly the way they show up with the capital letters where indicated. Otherwise, the links won't work.)

Link to Step 1 — Questionnaire: http://bit.ly/RVSurveyStep1

Link to Step 2 — The Interview: http://bit.ly/RVInterviewStep2

Link to Step 3 — The Follow Up: http://bit.ly/RVFollowUpStep3

I will be automatically alerted by email when you have completed any of the above steps. After you finish all three steps, send me a couple of photos (ones of you and/or your family, pets, kids, and rig). Send by email to: pdxadventure2015@gmail.com.

You can also follow me on Instagram @toys.trails.tails or sign up for my blog at www.toystrailsandtails.com. If you want access to great campground and boondocking reviews, those are on my blog, too! If there are products that have been mentioned that you'd like to buy for your travels, check under "Products We Love" and see if it's listed there. Or simply search using our Amazon affiliate link at: www.Bit.ly/ShawtreesAmazon

Finally, if you are not yet on the road, and you want to become a "full-time RV traveler," but have some questions, feel free to reach out to me. I may not answer right away, because I'm either out having too much fun, or I simply don't have cellular coverage, but I will get back to you eventually. Oh, and thanks for understanding!

I really appreciate your interest in RV travel and in my book. Thank you for reading to the end. I hope you enjoyed it!

RICH STORIES —
THE COMPLETE INTERVIEWS

If you have connected with one of our travelers, please read their full interview in the pages that follow. The travelers have given me permission to include their interviews verbatim with minor editing changes where needed for clarity.

INTERVIEW 1:
Lindsey and Gerrit of LivingLifeInBetween

Why did you hit the road? What are your goals, objectives, dreams, hopes?

My husband and I had both just graduated college and we were looking for "big kid" jobs. Gerrit was offered a full time job with the same company he interned with in college, and we were so excited to start living our life as adults. But we truly believe that God had other plans for us. To celebrate our graduation, we took a road trip to Colorado with our two dogs and as much as we could fit in our parent's Jeep Wrangler.

We fell in love with the west during that trip, and the fact that we lived for two weeks with nothing more than the basics. We started thinking about how we could find a way to take more trips out west. Gerrit's dad had always talked about how awesome it would be to travel the country in an RV. So with that in mind we started researching. When we found out that full-timing in an RV was a "thing," we acted fast. Not even six months after our Colorado trip, we sold most of our stuff and bought a motorhome. Our dream is to live life to the fullest and to enjoy every minute of it doing what we love to do, and that is seeing and experiencing this beautiful country.

What have you learned that you wish you knew before you started?

I do wish that we would have remodeled before we moved into it, rather than after. It took us a while to decide that we wanted to make our RV feel more like a home.

What do you miss about your old life? What did you think you'd miss that you don't?

The thing we miss the most is our family. We are all very close, so it can be hard to be away from them for up to six months at a time. For me (Lindsey) I thought I would really miss having a long hot shower every day, but I don't at all. I like the challenge of conserving water when we boondock, which is often.

What do you like best about this life? What do you like least about this life? Describe a "day in your life."

For me (Lindsey) the best part about this life is being with my husband 24 hours a day, seven days a week. He is my best friend, and we have grown so much in the short time we have been on the road. Being with our dogs all day long is awesome too. They are so cute! I also love not just seeing our beautiful country, but experiencing it by rock climbing, hiking, and mountain biking.

The one thing I like least is that my closest friends and family can't be here with us to experience all that we are doing on a daily basis.

A day in our life starts with a cup of coffee for Gerrit, hot chocolate for me (Lindsey) and a whole lot of puppy kisses. While Gerrit works full time 9-to-5, I work on YouTube videos and our blog. When the work day is done we head out and explore where ever we are. We will either go for a hike, rock climbing, off roading, or mountain biking.

How long after deciding to hit the road did it take for you to get your ducks in a row and actually hit the road?

It was quick! Maybe four months. It may sound like we didn't think this through, but if you knew my husband, you'd know that isn't true. He is an over-thinker, but we truly knew that this lifestyle was for us and didn't want to waste a single second more.

How does being a family/couple/single, affect you on the road? What issues do you have and how do you solve them?

It has affected us very positively. It is a lot harder to avoid the other person when your house is only 272 square feet so we talk out our disagreements much quicker and more efficiently now than we did before. The main issue we tend to have is when we arrive somewhere in the dark and we're trying to get settled. We're usually tired and cranky and neither one of us is being very helpful to the other with set up.

If you were a homeowner, did you decide to sell or rent before hitting the road?

We were renting a house at the time and our lease was ending.

If you work, how do you accomplish this while being on the road? What are your challenges? How do you overcome them? What advice do you have for others?

Gerrit is a software developer, he contracts for a tech firm that was built to allow remote work. All he needs is an internet connection, and he's good to go. Sometimes maintaining a stable internet connection can be a challenge, but so far it hasn't been that much of an issue. We have a Verizon unlimited plan that we consume through a Netgear Jetpack. We have a 4G booster, but so far we've only needed it a couple times in six months.

The biggest challenge with working remotely is being self-motivated. If you're going to work remotely when you're parked in Zion National Park, you need a lot of discipline to keep you on track. It's very tempting to just drop everything and go explore. This hasn't been too much of an issue for Gerrit. He simply needs to remind himself that his work is what gives us the opportunity to live this amazing lifestyle. It's also nice when, at the end of the work day, you get to go explore. It's not the simple "work grind" that everyone is used to.

If you have a technical background, it should be pretty simple to find remote work. If not, you'll have to get a little more creative. We know a lot of people with Etsy shops and other businesses.

If you don't work, how do you support yourself on the road? What advice do you have for others?

While Gerrit does most of the real working, I run our blog and YouTube channel which generates a very small income, but it is something we both really enjoy doing.

What rig did you choose? Why? What do you see as its advantages and disadvantages? If you had to do it over, would you pick the same rig? If not, why not and what would you pick?

We chose a 35-foot class A motorhome and tow a Jeep Wrangler. We didn't go looking for a class A, necessarily. We set parameters for ourselves and when we found a rig that met those, within our price range, we pulled the trigger. The advantages we see are that set ups and tear down is very simple. We also get to have our favorite vehicle with us for errands, and adventuring.

We would probably choose the same sort of rig. Ideally we would like a short class A 25-foot or less with a diesel engine that could tow our Jeep. We love having the huge windshield to look out of.

How did you outfit your rig to meet your goals? Storage? Off-grid or On? Work? Play?

In the future we would like to add solar an inverter and better batteries, but as of right now we rely on our generator to boondock.

We did, however, completely renovate the inside of our RV to fit our style and personally. We put in vinyl flooring and painted everything. Not having carpet was a huge deal for us because of our dogs.

How do you manage your relationships back home?

We try to meet up with them whenever possible. We also talk *a lot* through text and Instagram. We really have to make it a point to reach out and call our family and friends. They still think that we're on vacation all the time and don't call us for fear that we're busy all the time. Which is not true.

How do you receive mail back home? How do you manage your bills? How do you receive mail on the road?

As of right now we use our family's address as our own because that is our home base, if you will. All of our bills are online so that's not an issue. We do a lot of general delivery for our mail to the post office if we need something. This lifestyle really helps our online spending habits. It is hard to ship things general delivery for Amazon because they rarely use USPS. We save our Amazon orders for when we are near family and friends and can use their addresses.

Do you have kids with you? If so, how do you manage road schooling them? Any tips?

No kids with us yet and none in the foreseeable future, but if we were to have kids our lifestyle would not change.

If you have pets with you, what tips do you have regarding pet management?

We have two high energy dogs with us: an Aussie and a small cattle dog mix. My main tip for bringing your dogs on the road with you is to have respect for others. There are a lot of people out there that do not like dogs, especially ones that run right up to strangers and bark in delight at a new face. We love dogs, and our dogs love to play with other dogs, but there are some that don't. Just being mindful of how other people may feel about your dog running off leash goes a long way. There are so many hiking trails out there that no longer allow dogs because their humans didn't follow the rules. That's not fair to everyone else who does follow the rules and cleans up after their pup and keeps them on a leash. Other than that, having your dog on the road with you is awesome! Our pups love visiting new places and looking over cliffs as much as we do, and we wouldn't have it any other way.

Do you have any tips regarding money management?

Track your expenses. All of them. You'll want to know how much you are spending on gas and campgrounds and park fees. We like to compare what we spend now to what we spent while living in a house on a regular basis. Usually we spend less while living on the road but that is only because we are stingy. It is very easy to treat this lifestyle like a vacation and spend a lot of money.

What lessons do you have for others? Things to avoid and things to absolutely do?

Just do what is comfortable for you! If boondocking is not your thing don't feel like you have to do it. There are great campgrounds out there and clubs you can join to make them cheaper. You absolutely have to get out of your camper and enjoy nature. That's what this lifestyle is all about and you can't see it from inside your rig.

INTERVIEW 2:
Ashley of RVegan

Why did you hit the road? What are your goals, objectives, dreams, hopes?

I wanted to live more simply, with the goal of saving money and creating financial independence. It's a myth people have that RVing has to be expensive. I work in healthcare as a traveling contractor, and it is far more cost effective to stay in my Fifth Wheel than rent a short term stay traditional option.

What have you learned that you wish you knew before you started?

The only thing I would have done differently is paid cash for a used truck and gotten a professional RV inspection before buying

What do you miss about your old life? What did you think you'd miss that you don't?

Sometimes I miss the large space of a house, and I do miss having my best friends and family close to me.

What do you like best about this life? What do you like least about this life? Describe a "day in your life."

The coolest feeling is the day after moving, waking up with a brand new view. A day in my life is honestly pretty typical, I wake up and go to work in a hospital for eight hours, then come back to the RV. I like to take advantage of whatever town I'm in and find local activities to do after work. I enjoy taking guitar lessons and dance lessons. Every 13 weeks when my contract is up, I either travel and take an RV vacation for one to two weeks or I just jump into my next contract.

How long after deciding to hit the road did it take for you to get your ducks in a row and actually hit the road?

About five months to find my RV, buy my truck, and secure my new job.

How does being a family/couple/single, affect you on the road? What issues do you have and how do you solve them?

I am 25 and single and it is difficult to meet people for dating. I have just been trying to meet people from activities around town — guitar, dancing, etc. It's hard knowing that I won't be in the town for more than 13 weeks. So far I've been on the road for one year and haven't found a partner.

If you were a homeowner, did you decide to sell or rent before hitting the road?

Not a homeowner.

If you work, how do you accomplish this while being on the road? What are your challenges? How do you overcome them? What advice do you have for others?

Traveling healthcare is very well paying, and the job the requirements can range from an associate's degree to a doctorate. The pay is excellent for travel therapy, I bring home around $85,000 per year after taxes. I am trying to transition to starting my own online business selling therapy materials, so I don't have to take four contracts a year and I can take advantage of my RV to travel more!

What rig did you choose? Why? What do you see as its advantages and disadvantages? If you had to do it over, would you pick the same rig? If not, why not and what would you pick?

I have a fifth wheel and Ford F-250. I like that the fifth wheel is like a mini apartment with tons of storage, and 11-foot ceilings make the place feel big. My kitchen is bigger than my old apartment's, and this is the first queen size bed I've ever had! A used fifth wheel is quite cheap, mine was $13,000 so I'm saving a lot in rent. I like being able to take my truck as my daily driver. The truck is a little too big for me in some cities I am in, so if I could do it again I would do a used class C and a small daily driver.

How did you outfit your rig to meet your goals? Storage? Off-grid or On? Work? Play?

I didn't modify anything except new tires. The storage is excellent. I don't like my dinette and my couch is a little small, so in the future I might do a bigger couch and a smaller table. For internet I have a T-Mobile hotspot and an AT&T hotspot. I only stay at RV parks since I have to stay in one place for 13 weeks. On vacation trips, I have occasionally stayed overnight at a Walmart or Cracker Barrel. If I can increase my online business and decrease the number of contracts I take, I would probably travel more outside of RV parks and get a generator to be able to run my high-power electronics.

How do you manage your travel-companion relationships?

I travel alone and I meet people at work! I would like a travel companion someday.

How do you manage your relationships back home?

Social media and phone calls make connecting so easy. I also visit home several times a year.

How do you receive mail back home? How do you manage your bills? How do you receive mail on the road?

My mom handles all my mail. My mom's house is my official address, with my car registration, my voting registration, etc. I pay all my bills online or over the phone.

Do you have kids with you? If so, how do you manage road schooling them? Any tips?

No kids.

If you have pets with you, what tips do you have regarding pet management?

No pets.

Do you have any tips regarding money management?

Buy used and pay cash! Debt is not your friend. I save and invest 60-70% of my income because my current expenses are so low. I plan to be financially independent and not have to work other than for my own passion projects by age 35 (which is 10 years away). My favorite wealth building/debt free gurus are Mr. Money Mustache blog and Dave Ramsey.

What lessons do you have for others? Things to avoid and things to absolutely do?

Avoid dry rot on your camper. Make sure there are no soft spots, push on the walls and make sure you can't see the outside at the seams. If there are any smells at all — walk away and do not buy that rig because there will be an identical rig right down the road in better condition.

INTERVIEW 3:
Cees, Madison and Theo of
OurVieAdventures

Why did you hit the road? What are your goals, objectives, dreams, hopes?

We both love being outside and are stoked on adventure in all of its forms, so I think the trip was born from our passion and love for the earth. We also love to travel, so we thought that we should try to see as much of our own country as possible. We thought, "well maybe we could visit a bunch of the national parks?" Then when we found out that we would graduate during the 100 year anniversary, we thought – why not try and get to **all of them**?! So we went for it!

For ourselves, well, that question is easy – we just want to have fun! We love all activities outside and have an intense desire to travel. We wanted to create an opportunity to get out and discover the beautiful places of America. So a trip to all of the national parks is a dream come true for us!

On a larger, and probably more important, scale – We want to inspire people, as corny as it sounds, to live their dreams! We couldn't care less about convincing people that life on the road is the number one thing… we just wanted to show people that if you are serious about making something happen, *you can*. We had *no idea* how we were going to make it all work… we just went for it. Since we were serious about making it happen, things fell into place and we learned a lot along the way. We want people to realize that no matter what you come up with – writing a book, going to med school, or living in an old RV with the love of your life – it *is* possible. We want to push people to let go of excuses and get out and live your dreams! We want more people to have "I can't believe this is my life right now" moments!

What have you learned that you wish you knew before you started?

How hard that travel blogging actually is. It wouldn't have stopped me from going down that road, *but* it would have helped me set more realistic expectations. Blogging and playing the "social media game" is a lot of work. *But*, it is work that I like, and something that I would be doing anyways... so, why not get paid for it, right?

What do you miss about your old life? What did you think you'd miss that you don't?

Regular showers! It is so nice to have "limitless" hot water. We are always trying to conserve our water and taking super long hot showers is out of the question.

I thought that I would miss my family and friends but have found that because of our mobile lifestyle, we are even more available for the big life events. We make our own schedule, which allows us to be wherever we want whenever we want. It has made moving around to be with our family really easy.

What do you like best about this life? What do you like least about this life? Describe a "day in your life."

I love being able to move anywhere with our home. We don't have to make intense plans or have specific housing reservations made in advance. We can pick up and go and we have everything we need. No planning needed. I also love the simple living that comes with the lifestyle. There isn't room for a bunch of extra crap, so you don't pack it. Sometimes I think that the stuff we "own" can start to own us. Living small and mobile helps combat that.

I don't care for the fact that when we have car problems, we have house problems. it is an all-in-one package. Since we are in an older RV, you can imagine that this happens often. Even though it has taught me a lot about myself, I would still choose not to have to stress about breakdowns. (I have also learned a whole lot about general mechanic work as well... major bonus.)

How long after deciding to hit the road did it take for you to get your ducks in a row and actually hit the road?

About a year-and-a-half. We were finishing school, working a few jobs and saving all we could. Good times for sure. Enjoy the planning stages.

How does being a family/couple/single, affect you on the road? What issues do you have and how do you solve them?

We get asked all the time "how do you live together in such close quarters?" It hasn't bothered us one bit! *But,* that may just be our personalities. I honestly think it has been invaluable for our relationship. We have to work through our problems, because there is nowhere to run and hide. We are always right there together. We are still adjusting to adding the newborn to the mix. So I have a hard time talking about how that has "changed the game." We are excited to show him the world and really learn what it means to be a road family.

If you were a homeowner, did you decide to sell or rent before hitting the road?

Our home on wheels is our first home together!

If you work, how do you accomplish this while being on the road? What are your challenges? How do you overcome them? What advice do you have for others?

Internet is the key. And sometimes, there are places where you just *can't* get a connection. Which is *very, very* frustrating. Half of our battle on the road is finding wifi and/or cell service. I recommend having a few ways to stay connected.

What rig did you choose? Why? What do you see as its advantages and disadvantages? If you had to do it over, would you pick the same rig? If not, why not and what would you pick?

About two years ago now, we saw a little Toyota motorhome driving down the road and we immediately started dreaming of taking a trip in a vehicle like that. Something about a little truck doing big things was appealing. We loved the symbolism.

On top of that, we think that RV's are cool (but, we also think visors, jean shorts, and fanny packs are cool – so take that with a grain of salt!). There is a ton of room, they are set up to live in, and they are way cheaper than a mortgage!

We had a fun time turning our RV into a rolling home that we love. It is our little cabin on wheels!

How did you outfit your rig to meet your goals? Storage? Off-grid or On? Work? Play?

We wanted to stay completely off the grid. We wanted to move around wherever we want, and not be connected to a concrete pad in an RV park. So, we had to make adjustments for internet, water, and power. We have a wifi extender, a cell booster, solar panels, a bigger battery bank, and a power inverter all to accommodate that style of travel. We also had to bring all of our outdoor gear — so that meant *big* storage boxes on the top of the rig along with bike racks.

How do you manage your travel-companion relationships?

We live in a tiny space — you have to work out your problems because there is *nowhere* to go.

How do you manage your relationships back home?

We feel like we are even more available to be "around" when we need to. We decided that we wanted to be there, even if that meant driving long hours to get there. We make a conscious effort to always show up. We have had to jump on cheap flights a few times, which is actually a pretty easy solution as well.

How do you receive mail back home? How do you manage your bills? How do you receive mail on the road?

I hate snail mail but *love* Amazon. We do our best to limit our need of the post, but when we absolutely have to have a real address, I usually use a parent's address.

When we need packages delivered from Amazon or something else, we send them to our "next friend/family" …someone we know who is in the area. We have also done "general delivery" to a post office and picked it up with our ID.

Do you have kids with you? If so, how do you manage road schooling them? Any tips?

We do! The thing is, he is a little tiny guy and is just focusing on learning to hold his huge head up! We show him *everything* though! We love that we are able to be the first to introduce him to all of the amazing places in our country.

If you have pets with you, what tips do you have regarding pet management?

At first, our cat didn't really know what to expect. The first few days he had a hard time walking when the RV was driving. He would just curl up in my lap as I drove. But after a few days, he got his "sea legs" and was able to move freely about the cabin! He runs and jumps and chases the wipers all along the road. He even has learned to use the kitty box at about 60 miles per hour!

Do you have any tips regarding money management?

Live simply.

What lessons do you have for others? Things to avoid and things to absolutely do?

Go for it. Launching life on the road seems really overwhelming at first. Just like any big project, focus on little bits at a time and before you know it, you will be out there adventuring in no time. You can make it happen!

INTERVIEW 4:
Heath and Alyssa

Why did you hit the road? What are your goals, objectives, dreams, hopes?

During the early part of 2014, Alyssa and I came to the realization that our time in Texas was coming to an end. Summers were blistering hot, we didn't love our post-college office jobs, and we desperately wanted to get out and travel. So we quit our jobs, bought an RV and went on a year-long road trip across America, where I worked a job in all 50 states for a documentary we filmed called Hourly America. After a year of living and traveling in an RV, we realized this lifestyle was awesome and we didn't want to give it up. We paid off a bunch of debt, built up our video production business, and continued traveling full-time in an RV.

Our original goal(s): Find a new place to live, enjoy our honeymoon, and do more creative work like film/writing.

Additional goal: After traveling to all fifty states and much of Canada, our plan is to RV in Europe, Australia, and New Zealand in the next two years.

What have you learned that you wish you knew before you started?

The biggest obstacle we had during our first couple years of travel was spending less and making more money.

RVing teaches you to fix things. I hoped I was going to be rich enough to pay a mechanic all the time. That strategy hasn't worked out for me yet, so now I know how to flush my radiator, fix my generator, check gauges, and a lot of other manly stuff I couldn't do before. I even recently outfitted our Honda CR-V for proper towing, Dad would be proud.

What do you miss about your old life? What did you think you'd miss that you don't?

We really miss having a dishwasher and endless hot water. We of course miss our families too, but they have met up with us on the road and it has actually been a really great way to create family memories.

What do you like best about this life? What do you like least about this life? Describe a "day in your life."

1. Our RV has taken us to 49 states across America. My childhood home didn't have wheels.

2. Our RV likes to boast breathtaking views out of his window. In a normal home some of these views would run you a million dollars.

3. RVing across the country makes you not take normal things for granted (i.e., good wifi, nice showers, and a dishwasher).

4. The RV lifestyle promotes being outdoors where as having a big house promotes sitting on the couch, binge-watching Netflix.

5. We have no utility bills.

6. An RV teaches you to be clean. One dish left out is no big deal in a large house, but in a 33-foot RV it's basically going to make the whole place feel like a mess. Clean that up!

7. It takes five minutes to clean the entire house. Six minutes if you vacuum.

8. When you want to move, instead of hiring a moving company you just pull in the awning and unhook from electricity. Plus, you can move every day. Don't like the

weather? Tired of the mountains? Want to live beachfront for the summer? NBD. You can live literally anywhere.

9. It allows you to be nomadic and embrace a lifestyle of whimsy.

10. It teaches you to value experiences over belongings, and relationships over work. At the core of it, this is what our lifestyle is truly about.

A Day in Our Life: Our time is split between travel and work on the road. We spend most days editing videos in the RV, recording new podcast episodes, managing our Facebook group for RVers, and working on my software start up — CampgroundBooking.com.

Or… exploring a beautiful national park. This past summer we ventured up to Banff National Park in Canada and finally got to see Lake Louise in person! One of the most beautiful places we've been so far.

How does being a family/couple/single, affect you on the road? What issues do you have and how do you solve them?

Living in a small space during our first year of marriage forced us to learn how to resolve conflicts.

RVing is like speed dating for friendships. Invite someone over for a cup of coffee and see how long you can stand being with them in a small space.

If you work, how do you accomplish this while being on the road? What are your challenges? How do you overcome them? What advice do you have for others?

During our first year on the road, we filmed Hourly America and made basically zero money. A sponsor company covered our gas on the road, but the lack of income caused us to start our first service-based company. A friend asked for help filming an online course and since he knew about our documentary, he asked us to drive out to California and film for him.

Over the next two years, we took on film clients based on referrals only. Our goal wasn't to make a ton of money, but instead to make enough that we covered our expenses while still having enough free time to enjoy the RV life. This inspired me to start The RV Entrepreneur podcast where I interview other full-time RVers who run their own business on the road. So I have a lot of advice on how to run a business from your RV, all of which you can find on our website.

Currently, Alyssa runs our production company and most of our blog, while I run our podcast, manage our sponsorship relationships, and work on our software startup, CampgroundBooking.com.

The hardest part about working and traveling is just striking the balance. I could work 24/7 and sometimes that leaves Alyssa begging for us to take the kayaks out and enjoy wherever we're camping. But the best part of working from the RV is when I can take an afternoon break and nap in the hammock or hike around a National Park.

A lot of people assume that internet on the road is the biggest hurdle to working from our RV, but this really isn't a big deal. We have an unlimited Verizon plan and a cell booster that give us service almost everywhere. If you want to work from your RV, don't even try it without this!

What rig did you choose? Why? What do you see as its advantages and disadvantages? If you had to do it over, would you pick the same rig? If not, why not and what would you pick?

After living in a renovated 1994 Class C motorhome (named Franklin) for a year and a half, we switched to a Winnebago Brave 31C motorhome. We wanted more work space and a dependable rig to continue traveling. We fell in love with this retro version of the iconic Winnebago Brave and have already put close to 20k miles on it.

INTERVIEW 5:
"Cat" and Family of OurIncredibleDash

Why did you hit the road? What are your goals, objectives, dreams, hopes?

We were tired of the rat race. My husband was military for 12 years and missed the first part of our two oldest children's lives with back-to-back deployments where his life was at risk daily. Ultimately, we just wanted to be together and to not have to worry if he was going to come home alive. Our main focus and goal is to live a fuller life, together. To get back to the basic principles of a close knit family and a simple life.

What have you learned that you wish you knew before you started?

We don't need as much as we have. We still have too much stuff! I wish we'd gotten rid of more before we started but we were under a time crunch, so we have quite a bit still in storage.

What do you miss about your old life? What did you think you'd miss that you don't?

I don't miss it at all!

What do you like best about this life? What do you like least about this life? Describe a "day in your life."

What I like best is that life is less busy and more simple. What I like least is that I can't bring my now widowed father on the road with us — I miss him.

A day in our life might include a day trip to explore the area we are in or it might include just regular life stuff — laundry, school, hanging out at home. It really depends on the day, as each day is never the same.

How long after deciding to hit the road did it take for you to get your ducks in a row and actually hit the road?

About one month. It happened quite suddenly, though we'd thought about it for much longer. We didn't think it was time for it, and suddenly life shifted and it was. We finalized the intent to purchase via phone and I left a week later with our two kids (at the time ages 3 and 1). I drove to AZ where my parents lived, and the RV was located 90 minutes from them. My husband stayed behind to pack our house into storage then flew out to join us 1.5 weeks later. Two days later we drove back to our military base in California with our RV and pulled into the family camp which was our first RV park. All our household goods were in storage by then.

How does being a family/couple/single, affect you on the road? What issues do you have and how do you solve them?

We are so much closer as a family. The only issue we really have are my aging parents. My mom passed last summer, and I took one child and flew back to care for her while my husband continued a "workamping" contract. She passed, and he and the other child flew out right away. By then we had discovered I was pregnant with baby #3. My pregnancies are complicated so we decided to stay near my dad for family support and to aid in his transition. I worry about him being alone as he has cancer. We visit each other frequently.

If you were a homeowner, did you decide to sell or rent before hitting the road?

We rented due to the military moving us too often.

If you work, how do you accomplish this while being on the road? What are your challenges? How do you overcome them? What advice do you have for others?

My husband is former Air Force and receives monthly disability for his injuries. He is also furloughed from the railroad for the last two years. When he is recalled, we will travel from station area to station area as he works. Currently we workamp — only accepting jobs that offer site plus hourly pay for all hours worked.

I do offset some expenses by helping people rid their homes and bodies from toxic chemicals, as well as coaching those who wish to start a travel blog. I blog, and that brings in income for us, and I also do social media work.

Find what works for you. There is a way to make this work for everyone. Be frugal and be determined.

What rig did you choose? Why? What do you see as its advantages and disadvantages? If you had to do it over, would you pick the same rig? If not, why not and what would you pick?

We chose a 35-foot motorhome (Class A) because the timing and price were right. It's not our first choice in an ideal world because we don't want the kids riding in it, so we drive separately. However it has worked well for now, and we own it free and clear, which is important to us. Eventually, we will upgrade to a truck and a fifth wheel, probably a toy hauler.

How did you outfit your rig to meet your goals? Storage? Off-grid or On? Work? Play?

We have completely renovated our rig to make it fit our needs. As our needs change, we make more changes.

How do you manage your relationships back home?

We keep in touch with family via phone, email, our blog, sending packages, and Facebook.

How do you receive mail back home? How do you manage your bills? How do you receive mail on the road?

Paperless bills. Mail goes to a family member's address where we have our residence. He opens and reads it and will scan and email anything he can or mail it to us directly if needed.

Do you have kids with you? If so, how do you manage road schooling them? Any tips?

Three kids. We use Abeka Accredited Academy and have DVD lessons. We mail in the work and receive feedback. We have visited the academy in Florida and met the teachers and love the school! Best tip is to just learn from where you are! The world is your classroom — take advantage of every opportunity as a learning experience!

If you have pets with you, what tips do you have regarding pet management?

We have a yellow lab. He's well behaved. I recommend a kennel at first until your pet is used to the new environment.

Do you have any tips regarding money management?

Strive to have no debt and always have an emergency fund.

What lessons do you have for others? Things to avoid and things to absolutely do?

Absolutely appreciate each and every moment. Don't be afraid to take a huge scary leap toward making your dreams come true!

INTERVIEW 6:
Josh and Laura of TravelExploreUncover

Why did you hit the road? What are your goals, objectives, dreams, hopes?

We hit the road to get away from a traditional 40-hour work week and the expectations of life. We wanted to slow down, get back into nature, and enjoy our lives. During this journey, we hope to find out more about ourselves, create a strong foundation for our relationship, and see our country. After we return from Alaska, we plan to start reaching out to non-profit organizations, to volunteer our time and abilities. We both thrive off of helping others, and want to give back.

What have you learned that you wish you knew before you started?

Patience. As great as this journey is, it takes planning, compromise, and hard work.

What do you miss about your old life? What did you think you'd miss that you don't?

There isn't much. Life on the road is more exciting, enlightening, and free. We miss being close to friends and family, but Skype and regular phone calls keep us connected.

What do you like best about this life? What do you like least about this life? Describe a "day in your life."

Everyday can be new. Every week we have a new backyard. Our least favorite thing is the unexpected problems, such as flat tires, bad suspension, electrical issues, etcetera. Things you normally don't need to be concerned with in a sticks-and-bricks home.

To be honest, our days often look different because we travel at a fast pace. We generally only stay a few days at a time. Our day may include a quick morning workout, a motorcycle ride, kayaking, walking the dogs, and settling in to work on our social media.

How long after deciding to hit the road did it take for you to get your ducks in a row and actually hit the road?

Planning to hit the road took roughly three months. From buying the RV, to selling the house and furniture, to leaving our jobs.

How does being a family/couple/single, affect you on the road? What issues do you have and how do you solve them?

This RV is the first place we've lived together. We both left our separate homes and moved into the rig. This was wonderful, yet also challenging. Communication is key. Luckily, we had a strong foundation of communication, but it's a whole new level when you're together 24/7. When a conflict arises, we address it immediately. Both being very receptive, we offer strategies to improve the situation and implement it quickly. This has been successful for us.

If you were a homeowner, did you decide to sell or rent before hitting the road?

Josh owned a house, which he decided to sell. Laura was renting, and moved out of her apartment. Josh sold his house, rather than renting it out. He didn't want the headache of being on the road and needing to fix problems thousands of miles away. He also didn't want the concern of draining his bank account if issues arose.

If you work, how do you accomplish this while being on the road? What are your challenges? How do you overcome them? What advice do you have for others?

We took the first year off from working. We wanted to see and explore the country without the distractions of timelines. We plan on working next year. Laura is an occupational therapist and can complete short, contract positions all over the country.

If you don't work, how do you support yourself on the road? What advice do you have for others?

While not working, we are supporting ourselves through the money in our savings. The best advice we can give is to save more than you think you'll need. Campground, gas prices, propane, and unexpected expenses can add up very quickly.

What rig did you choose? Why? What do you see as its advantages and disadvantages? If you had to do it over, would you pick the same rig? If not, why not and what would you pick?

We chose a Grand Design Momentum 349M. We chose a toy hauler for a few reasons. It has a large garage area that we can use in a variety of ways, such as a guest bedroom, storage, or a place to let wet dogs dry off. The toy hauler also has a patio/ramp that extends out the back which we love. A disadvantage is while we are towing, we aren't able to get out of seat and be in the rig, as you would in a Class A, B, or C rig. If we did this again, we both agree that we would pick the same exact rig. We were lucky in the sense that we didn't pick a rig that was too small or too big for our needs.

How did you outfit your rig to meet your goals? Storage? Off-grid or On? Work? Play?

We have a solar and lithium battery set-up for off-the-grid. We have a garage that we can use as storage for our two motorcycles, but also as a workplace with a desk and chair.

How do you manage your travel-companion relationships?

We communicate a lot. We continue to have our separate interests and give space when needed. We feel lucky that we continue to grow together in such a small living area.

How do you manage your relationships back home?

Through a mixture of phone calls while driving from one destination to another, to Skype/FaceTime while stationary.

How do you receive mail back home? How do you manage your bills? How do you receive mail on the road?

We have a Traveling Mailbox account. All of our mail is sent there, where the company scans the front of the envelope and emails us the scan. We are then able to choose whether this mail should be opened, shredded, or forwarded to a location that we can pick it up.

Do you have kids with you? If so, how do you manage road schooling them? Any tips?

No kids.

If you have pets with you, what tips do you have regarding pet management?

We have two dogs, one German shepherd and a Labrador mix. We have pet insurance to cover the unexpected scenarios. It's important to be alert when other dogs and dog owners are in the vicinity.

Do you have any tips regarding money management?

As you're traveling around, there will be many restaurant desires! Create a budget from the start and stick to it! If not, this is where money drains quickly.

What lessons do you have for others? Things to avoid and things to absolutely do?

Keep the journey at a slow pace. You can get discounts at campgrounds if you stay a week or more, saving money in the long run. If you travel too fast, you may burn yourself out and not enjoy it as much. Get to know your neighbors, they always have a good story to tell or good tips for fun things to do in the area. If you want to boondock, try to explore the area with your truck or vehicle first before bringing the rig out, as the area may have washed away, or the rig won't fit. Get out in nature! It's refreshing, rejuvenating and beautiful.

Anything I'm forgetting?

When you seriously start considering this as an option, others around you will tell you it's not possible. But it is! It takes planning, saving, and courage, but it is possible.

INTERVIEW 7:
Jessi and Valerie of HappyCamperWives

Why did you hit the road? What are your goals, objectives, dreams, hopes?

We were tired of being sick and sick of being tired. Our goals were to find happiness outside the 9-5 rat race and see if there was more to life than working. Our dreams are to travel the world by car, camp, explore, and to live life to the fullest.

What have you learned that you wish you knew before you started?

That people are more generous than we gave them credit for. People have been unbelievably friendly and kind. We are a lesbian couple, so we wish we would have taken the plunge to travel sooner. It's scary traveling as a minority, and no, it's not always safe. But for us, we are so happy we took the leap of faith.

What do you miss about your old life? What did you think you'd miss that you don't?

We miss a bathtub! We thought we would miss our friends a lot more on the road, but we've been able to meet up with people in every state across the country, so we actually see our friends all the time! And being on the grid makes a phone call super easy.

What do you like best about this life? What do you like least about this life? Describe a "day in your life."

The best thing is being close to nature and seeing a new place every few weeks. The worst part is when your home stops working. Logistically, it can be complicated, especially when you're camping with two dogs and your refrigerator goes out in 100-degree heat.

How long after deciding to hit the road did it take for you to get your ducks in a row and actually hit the road?

One month. We did not plan to live in a RV actually. We were doing summer work in Alaska and the idea just came to us randomly. So we thought, why the heck not — Jessi was already working remotely and we already didn't own "stuff." Then it all came together quickly!

How does being a family/couple/single, affect you on the road? What issues do you have and how do you solve them?

Living in a tight space with your significant other has its challenges, for sure. We've learned communication and still learn to just stop talking if need be. Sometimes it's best to just take a time out even if you're in the same room. Awkward but effective.

If you were a homeowner, did you decide to sell or rent before hitting the road?

We rent out a home we've never lived in. We had plans to move to Florida so bought a house with a renter in it because we were going to Alaska for the summer. When that renter asked to stay longer, we saw it as an opportunity to travel while also having investments.

If you work, how do you accomplish this while being on the road? What are your challenges? How do you overcome them? What advice do you have for others?

Jessi works remotely as a web designer. The hardest part is finding a good internet connection while traveling in the mountains. To get a remote work, you should have experience working in an office first. Then you have credibility when finding clients.

What rig did you choose? Why? What do you see as its advantages and disadvantages? If you had to do it over, would you pick the same rig? If not, why not and what would you pick?

t@b's teardrop because our small truck could pull it and the bathroom/kitchen were located inside. We love the t@b, no regrets, it's perfect for us.

How did you outfit your rig to meet your goals? Storage? Off-grid or On? Work? Play?

It came with mostly everything. Just some dishes and a spice rack, and we were set. We also brought our bikes that we've only used once.

How do you manage your travel-companion relationships?

Talking. A lot.

How do you manage your relationships back home?

Phone calls! We are always chatting with our buddies. Also stalking them and engaging on social media.

How do you receive mail back home? How do you manage your bills? How do you receive mail on the road?

This is the hard one. Valerie's mom manages our mail, and all bills are paid online.

Do you have kids with you? If so, how do you manage road schooling them? Any tips?

No.

If you have pets with you, what tips do you have regarding pet management?

Two dogs. Temperature control is our number one. Make sure to have a good working air conditioner and heater before hitting the road and do regular maintenance.

Do you have any tips regarding money management?

Longer stays at RV parks tend to be cheaper. Other than that it's really what your travel style is.

What lessons do you have for others? Things to avoid and things to absolutely do?

Avoid tourist traps best you can but also listen to recommendations — we've found the best kept secrets from recommendations.

Anything I'm forgetting?

If your front window is glass, change it to acrylic window ASAP. When our window broke it shattered glass throughout the entire home and was a total mess!

INTERVIEW 8:
Amber and Ryan of HotSauceHippo

Why did you hit the road? What are your goals, objectives, dreams, hopes?

We hit the road after having many late night conversations about what was lacking in our lives. Both of us were working 9-to-5 jobs and renting an apartment in Seattle. I really liked the work that I did (assisting survivors of domestic violence navigate the legal field), but something was still missing. I have always had a wanderlust gene in me — I've gone backpacking in dozens of countries in Africa, Southeast Asia, and Europe. The happiest times in both my and Ryan's lives were when we were traveling.

After realizing this, we started trying to figure out how to move our lives to "full time travel." We originally were planning a trip abroad, but one night we decided that neither of us had seen much of the U.S. So, the idea of backpacking through America was born. And what better way to see our country than in an old school RV?

Our main goal was for freedom. We wanted to not feel tied to a desk each day. As we have settled into road life, we have picked up the additional goal of helping others find their freedom, in whatever sense they see best fits their life.

What have you learned that you wish you knew before you started?

Don't put your sink water down the toilet!! There are many places on the internet that suggest you do this to save room in your grey water tank (since the black water tank is larger than the grey). However, we did this, and it caused the worst smell either of us have ever experienced. Seriously, the smell was wretched. After further research, we learned that there is a delicate balance of bacteria that takes place in the sewage tank and putting rotting food, coffee grounds, and toothpaste spit really messes with that balance. It took us weeks, and many gallons of vinegar, to get that balance back. Now, we use a bin in our sink to collect water from washing our hands, washing dishes, or rinsing vegetables, and simply dump it outside to save space in our grey tank. (Note — if you're going to do this, make sure to use an eco-friendly soap and pour it somewhere it is not going to leak into a water stream.)

What do you miss about your old life? What did you think you'd miss that you don't?

I miss having a flushable toilet available at all times. We have a "no #2" rule in our RV because we don't want to have to deal with dumping that type of sewage. So, if the site we're sleeping at does not have toilets you either dig a hole and bury your debris or you hold it until the next gas station. It's not always glamorous, but it is a small price to pay

We also miss the plentiful vegan food and healthy grocery options in Seattle. We've realized that a lot of places in America don't have a lot of healthy options for food. Luckily, we can cook in our RV when passing through these parts.

We thought we would miss our dishwasher. Both of us grew up with dishwashers, so we weren't used to hand-washing dishes, especially when we didn't have an endless water supply. Turns out, we didn't need a dishwasher all along!

What do you like best about this life? What do you like least about this life? Describe a "day in your life."

The best thing about this life is the changing scenery. We lived in a beautiful area of the country, but found ourselves not enjoying its beauty because it became "normal." Now, as we're driving to different spots each week, we get to experience that place's beauty for the first time. The newness, and the knowledge that we won't stay forever, conjures up a true appreciation for a location. We cherish what is right in front of us, because we know we're on to the next beautiful place tomorrow.

The worst part of this life is losing the feeling of "being a local." For example, at the dog park today, I was talking to a woman about her dogs and she began referencing other parks in the area, like I knew the region. I told her I wasn't from the city and she asked why I was visiting. After telling her about living on the road, and answering the typical questions that are asked about our lifestyle, we parted ways and both went on with our lives. A small part of me wished that I could have contributed to the conversation about the nearby locations and maybe created a friendship with the woman through weekly visits to our local dog park.

A typical day in our life — wake up, eat breakfast (usually cereal, oatmeal, or toast – pancakes if we're feeling fancy), discuss the plan for the day (Are we driving at all? Where to? How far? Where are we sleeping tonight? Do we need to dump our sewage or fill up on water? Do we need gas?), make popcorn for a snack while we drive, drive to a park near where we're sleeping for the night, make lunch in the park, hang out in the afternoon (work, write articles, take photos, etc.), drive to where we're sleeping, make dinner, hang out in the evening (work or write some more), enjoy a beer, then go to sleep. Sometimes, if we're exploring a city, instead of the park portion, we will go on a walking tour, see museums, or find local vegan restaurants.

How long after deciding to hit the road did it take for you to get your ducks in a row and actually hit the road?

We decided to hit the road in the beginning of October 2016. We didn't actually take off until late February 2017. During this time we bought an RV, quit our jobs, enjoyed the holidays with family, downsized our lives, and fixed up the RV.

How does being a family/couple/single, affect you on the road? What issues do you have and how do you solve them?

Since life is changing constantly while on the road, stress can be high and challenges often, but being a couple on the road, we tackle these problems together. It's like having a teammate always at your side. We have twice the brainstorming ability and always have another person to bounce ideas off of. It's awesome to always have someone to laugh with, share a new sight with, or discuss weird thoughts with. Just yesterday we had a whole discussion about whether the turn signal always had the ability to stick in the down or up position while your signal is on, or whether that was an invention thought up by someone who was tired of holding the turn signal down or up while waiting to turn.

Our biggest conflicts happen when I'm overheated or hungry. It's usually because I want to get moving in the morning quicker than Ryan wants to. Typically, I'm trying to get a breeze in my face to cool down or lunch in my stomach to quell the overdose of caffeine I drink each morning. We deal with this by making a pre-lunch snack and driving further north as the weather gets warmer.

Ryan and I have lived in no more than 500 square feet for our entire relationship, so space, or lack thereof, is not a problem. If one us is annoyed or grumpy, the other usually opens space by simply not butting in verbally. The silence gives both of us time to think about what the truth is behind our frustration at which point we're able to rationally discuss the real problem or emotional reaction taking place. When your partner truly listens to you, respects what you're saying, and honors your feelings about an issue, then living in small, ever-changing, cramped, sometimes stressful spaces is not a problem.

If you were a homeowner, did you decide to sell or rent before hitting the road?

We were not homeowners.

If you work, how do you accomplish this while being on the road? What are your challenges? How do you overcome them? What advice do you have for others?

I work part-time as a contract attorney. This means I pick up different projects from different clients on an "as-needed" basis. Since I work remotely, the easiest tasks for me to accomplish are contract or letter drafting, summarizing records, and legal research. For internet, I use a hotspot on my phone, or we spend time at a local coffee shop. Documents, or the research assignment, get sent to me by email and I send the completed project back by email as well. Sometimes a phone call is required to ask for supplemental information or to explain my results, but mostly everything can be completed online.

The most difficult part of what I do is balancing work and life. It is very easy for me to get totally enveloped in a project and lose sight of the world around me. This was true prior to us hitting the road, so working on a contract basis, as opposed to a full-time basis, is one way I have overcome this. Also, working remotely has helped to physically remove myself from the case I'm working on. If I want to enjoy life outside of work, I can simply close my computer, whereas when I was in an office, I couldn't just walk away.

My advice for someone looking to work on the road is to not reinvent the wheel. You don't have to go out and look for a "road life job." Take what you're doing right now, or what you know you're already good at, and turn that into a job. Finding a job on the road is not difficult, you just have to change your mindset that it is possible, and the opportunities will present themselves.

If you don't work, how do you support yourself on the road? What advice do you have for others?

I am answering both of these questions, because my part-time work is not the only monetary source we use to support ourselves. Ryan and I saved a lot of money prior to starting this adventure, knowing that neither of us wanted to work full-time while on the road. We lived frugally while we both had 9-5 jobs, so we could save as much money as possible. Things we did to save money, that other people can adopt, included cutting down how often we ate out at restaurants, living in a smaller home (rent for a studio was far cheaper than a one-bedroom), reviewing our spending each month so we were always aware of places we could cut back, using the bus system instead of taking an Uber for convenience, and maximizing our credit card rewards. Now we can live off our savings for a long time, if we choose.

What rig did you choose? Why? What do you see as its advantages and disadvantages? If you had to do it over, would you pick the same rig? If not, why not and what would you pick?

We chose a 22-foot 1988 Lazy Daze RV, which sits on a Ford E350 chassis. We chose this rig because we wanted a single-unit, all-inclusive rig (as opposed to a truck and travel trailer combo) and we wanted something under $10,000 with less than 100,000 miles on it. We contemplated buying a Class B or van, but after touring a couple rigs, we realized that we liked to be able to stand up in our home and have a living area that was separate from the bed area.

The advantages of our RV are the size and maneuverability that a truck and travel trailer combo, Class A, or larger Class C wouldn't have. We can drive through most cities and park on the street (although sometimes we have to feed two meters). We feel that we are at the maximum size capable of doing this, and anything larger wouldn't fit. The disadvantage of our rig is that once we are parked, leveled, and hooked up for the night, we feel a bit stuck. If we had a truck and trailer combo we could unhook the truck and take it to dinner or grocery shopping, instead of having to take our entire RV along with us.

I would buy our same RV again because the advantages of our rig fit our lifestyle significantly more than the disadvantages. We aren't hooked up very often, and we move locations most nights. We do very little city driving, and we fit in the areas we want to explore. If we were to park for longer periods of time or want to explore large cities, having a separate vehicle from the living quarters might be a better way to go.

How did you outfit your rig to meet your goals? Storage? Off-grid or On? Work? Play?

The two things we did to the rig to fit our lifestyle were removing the microwave for more storage space in the kitchen and removing the air conditioner for more head room in the main living space. To use these appliances, we needed to be plugged into electricity and we knew we were primarily going to be boondocking. So, removing them for the extra space and discarded weight was the way to go for us. We also bought two solar panels (not attached to the rig) for off-grid electricity and bought a gym membership for off-grid showering.

How do you manage your travel-companion relationships?

My travel companions are Ryan (my husband) and our two dogs (Nelson and Gizmo). I manage these relationships just as I would if we were not living on the road — I spend quality time with each of them, make sure I focus on their needs, and we respect each other's space. Ryan and I share responsibilities related to our rig and life in general. We switch off driving, cooking, cleaning dishes, cleaning the bathroom, etc. Ryan primarily is in charge of dumping our sewage (because chivalry isn't dead) and I make our bed each morning (because Ryan can't quite fit in the overhead space without just laying down). We each have our role and respect the other person's roles. Chores aren't necessarily 50-50 because we believe that keeping "count" or "track" of what each person does just leads to a tally that can cause resentment or frustration. If one person feels they are doing more than the other, we simply discuss this and shift responsibilities around until if feels right for us. Our relationship is about love, mutual respect, and not taking anything too seriously.

How do you manage your relationships back home?

The phone and the internet are key to keeping in contact with loved ones back home. I am horrible at calling my friends, but through text, emails, and social media, I stay in touch and keep updated on everyone's lives. We call our moms regularly, mostly for advice, help on the road, or to let them know we are still alive. We both have lived far away from family in the past, so staying in touch while we are long-distance on the road hasn't been a challenge.

How do you receive mail back home? How do you manage your bills? How do you receive mail on the road?

We receive mail at my mom's house back in Washington. It is still technically our "permanent address" for purposes of our IDs, credit cards, and other important documents. If you don't have a family member that will help you with this, I believe you can get a UPS box that has an actual address (not a P.O. Box) associated with it. You can put this on documents and have this mail forwarded to a different UPS where you're located for a fee. We receive mail on the road by either purchasing items through Amazon and having the item delivered to an Amazon locker nearby or having mail delivered to a UPS nearby for pick up.

All of our bills — credit cards, insurance, and car payment — are on auto-payment that are paid electronically.

Do you have kids with you? If so, how do you manage road schooling them? Any tips?

No kids with us (unless you count our two furry ones).

If you have pets with you, what tips do you have regarding pet management?

We have two small dogs with us – Nelson and Gizmo. I would recommend finding a vet that has multiple locations throughout the United States so you can easily find a vet if your animals get sick or injured. We use Banfield Pet Hospital (they are located inside of most PetsMart stores). This has saved us the hassle of transferring our dogs' records from one vet to another each time we take them in. It has also saved us from having to research local vets and compare prices. All Banfields are the same price whether you're in Vermont or Texas.

We also recommend finding activities for your pet to be included, so they're not stuck in your vehicle all day. Take them hiking, sit outside of a restaurant so they can join you, or hang out by the water with your companions. Make sure to bring water for your pet wherever you take them, make sure the ground is not too hot for their paws, and make sure they are allowed on any trails you plan on hiking. It would be ideal if they could be strapped in while driving (they make specific dog seat belts that attach to the human's seat belt), but at a minimum make sure they are not in a spot where they can walk around and get injured or distract the driver.

Do you have any tips regarding money management?

My biggest tip for money management is to actually look into what you're spending each month. Ryan and I use an Excel worksheet where we type in every purchase for that month, the amount of the purchase, and the category of that purchase (e.g. household, dining out, groceries, vehicle, etc.). Then we look at each category and see where we're spending the most, where we can cut back, and where we're hitting our goals. There are programs that will go into your banking statements and created these breakdowns for you, but we think that the process of actually typing in each purchase makes you really digest what you are spending your money on.

Other tips we use for money management are using credit cards that provide the best rewards for your lifestyle, don't eat out at restaurants too frequently, use apps like Gas Buddy to find the cheapest gas or Sanidumps to find the cheapest dump stations, and use websites that show you free places to park (e.g. freecampsites.net).

What lessons do you have for others? Things to avoid and things to absolutely do?

Be ok with not knowing all of the answers in the beginning. Be willing to make mistakes and learn from those along the way. There are a million lessons we've learned along the road, mostly things that someone couldn't have taught us by simply telling us the answer.

Don't avoid joining the road life because you think you cannot afford it. The money will come if you want it to and believe it will. I truly believe that every person has a skill or knowledge that can be put to use to make money on the road.

You have to find what brings you joy in this world or it is all for nothing. We weren't put on this planet to sit behind a desk all day and push paper. Go out and live your life. It is only passing you by!

INTERVIEW 9:
David, Madison, Graham, and Margaret of TheAmericanfieldTrip

Why did you hit the road? What are your goals, objectives, dreams, hopes?

Living on the road and traveling full-time have always been goals of ours. We wanted to travel more in the U.S. and specifically, to see all the national parks, and we knew driving was the best way to do that. As we were talking about our goals last year, we decided that the timing would never be perfect to leave our lives and move onto the road, and that we didn't want to put this dream off. Our goals have evolved over time; after the election, we wanted to do something that would help us understand better the current moment in the U.S., and we wanted to try to document different cultures and people within our country. We have also learned much more about public land issues since we started, and are working to educate other people about the current issues and legislation surrounding the public land in the U.S.

What have you learned that you wish you knew before you started?

We converted our shuttle bus to live in, so there are a million skills we wish we'd had before embarking on that project! But in terms of actually living on the road, I wish we'd known how busy we'd be. We are much busier than we were at home! A lot of that busy-ness is doing fun stuff: hiking, visiting national parks and other places we're interested it. But a lot of it is related to the lifestyle and the logistics of road life. A lot of things take longer or are more complicated in a small space. And because we have kids, we spend a lot more time entertaining than we did at home, when there was more space for them to play in.

What do you miss about your old life? What did you think you'd miss that you don't?

We lived in New York City before, and there are a lot of things we miss about being in a city. It's nice to be able to get anything you need from a local store; now when we need things, we frequently have to find them online. We also really miss our friends and neighborhood. We knew we'd miss these things, but we didn't anticipate how much!

What do you like best about this life? What do you like least about this life? Describe a "day in your life."

We love traveling, and especially seeing all the "in-between" places that we wouldn't experience if we traveled another way. The money part is stressful. Even though we're working, it's freelance work, so we don't have the security of a full-time job.

A day in our life: we usually get a slow start in the morning. Our bedroom area is super cozy so it's hard to leave! We make and eat breakfast, then usually have a little driving to do to get to our next activity. Usually we're exploring a national park, so we'll go to the ranger station, attend a ranger talk, and do a short hike. After lunch, we usually set out on a longer hike. We try to get to a camping spot early in the evening so we have time to make a good dinner and let the kids run around, but often we're hiking until later and don't make it back to the bus until bedtime.

How long after deciding to hit the road did it take for you to get your ducks in a row and actually hit the road?

About six months from the time we started seriously considering it. We were second-guessing ourselves up until the moment we bought our bus.

How does being a family/couple/single, affect you on the road? What issues do you have and how do you solve them?

We're traveling at a pretty fast pace in order to visit all 59 national parks, so we spend quite a bit of time driving. The kids do really well in the car, but we have moments where we all get cabin fever. We listen to a lot of music, play a lot of road games, and try to have a sense of humor about things.

If you were a homeowner, did you decide to sell or rent before hitting the road?

We own our apartment in New York and are renting it while we're on the road. The rental income helps with our expenses.

If you work, how do you accomplish this while being on the road? What are your challenges? How do you overcome them? What advice do you have for others?

David sells prints of his photography online and does a little graphic design freelance work. He spends a lot of time editing photos. We also spend time working on our website and social media in order to get sponsorships for our trip. We mostly work at night, after the kids go to bed; the hardest part is making enough time for work, since one of our primary goals was to spend more time together as a family.

What rig did you choose? Why? What do you see as its advantages and disadvantages? If you had to do it over, would you pick the same rig? If not, why not and what would you pick?

We chose a 25-foot 2007 Ford E-450 shuttle bus. We're really happy with our choice and would pick it again. We liked designing a layout that met our needs and building the bus ourselves. We also liked the safety of a bus. The size of the shuttle bus was perfect for us, too.

How did you outfit your rig to meet your goals? Storage? Off-grid or On? Work? Play?

We built our bus with a separate "garage" and office space in the back. We have a desk back there, along with a pegboard where we store most of our gear. Having a separate space for work makes it much easier for one person to get things done, while the other hangs out with the kids in the main part of the bus. In the bedroom, we built bunk cubbies for the kids next to our full-size bed, and the big bed lifts up so we have a lot more storage underneath. Our kitchen has a full-size counter, so there is plenty of workspace, and a huge apron-front sink, which has been really functional for us and makes the space feel like a real kitchen. The whole rig runs off 600 W of solar power, a small propane tank, and a 40-gallon freshwater tank (stored under our bed). We have a self-contained toilet for emergencies (we haven't had to use it yet), and an outdoor shower that runs off a propane tankless water heater.

How do you manage your travel-companion relationships?

Living in the bus actually hasn't felt much different from living in our apartment, in terms of our family relationships. Maybe because we've always lived in small spaces, maybe because, having kids, we're used to not having much alone time, we really haven't experienced an adjustment. Kindness, consideration, and a sense of humor are key. We also know our limits as parents; if one of us needs some time, the other makes it happen.

How do you manage your relationships back home?

Lots of phone calls, FaceTime and postcards!

How do you receive mail back home? How do you manage your bills? How do you receive mail on the road?

Our mail is all sent to David's parents, who travel a lot and are able to see us occasionally. We manage all bills online.

Do you have kids with you? If so, how do you manage road schooling them? Any tips?

Our kids are 4 years old and 19 months, so they're not officially school-age yet. But we do love the opportunities our lifestyle gives us to learn about all kinds of things. Our 4-year-old loves the junior ranger program from the National Park Service and learns a lot from the booklets they give him at each park to fill out. We also practice his reading and writing while we're driving. Mostly we follow the kids' lead—if they are interested in something, we use whatever resources we have to learn more about it.

Do you have any tips regarding money management?

We very rarely pay to camp; instead we find free campgrounds or dispersed camping on the AllStays app or online. We also save money by cooking all our own meals and avoiding processed food.

INTERVIEW 10:
Becky and Steve of GowiththeFlowandCo

Why did you hit the road? What are your goals, objectives, dreams, hopes?

Steve and I decided to make this life change because that is exactly what wasn't happening — change. Our lives were good, but, we wanted more out of it (maybe it's because we hit the 30 + mark). We went to work, came home, ate dinner, went to sleep — repeat. We were also getting tired of "living for the weekend" and the "daily grind" eating away at our mental and physical health. Ok, also, we just love traveling and have always wanted to have our dogs with us on our journeys! We hope to keep up the traveling lifestyle, whether it's in a fifth wheel, truck camper, boat, or apartments! We would also love to inspire others to step outdoors every once in a while to see more, do more, and live more.

What have you learned that you wish you knew before you started?

Wow — *so much*! We did a lot of research before hitting the road, but, we have had to "go with the flow" quite a few times. We've learned 1,000,000 things pertaining to the RV lifestyle, but, also a lot of things about ourselves. We've learned that we like everything in moderation — even each other — haha! We've learned that we prefer getting to new spots on weekdays. We've learned that we *love* boondocking, but on the other hand, we *love* full hookups — haha. So, now we will start learning about a solar set up and a few holding tank arrangements that will get us to the next level!

What do you miss about your old life? What did you think you'd miss that you don't?

My friends. My family. But, we've met a ton of people that are new friends and have made us feel "at home." I don't miss the stuff, the house, the mortgage payments.

What do you like best about this life? What do you like least about this life? Describe a "day in your life."

The best thing about this lifestyle is the mobility and flexibility. If you don't like a location, *move!* Haha! We've never really not liked a neighbor, but if you don't...beep beep! It's also great to experience the different weather in such extremely different locations — from the dry heat of the desert, to the damp, tree covered coast line...I love it! Also, we are very active and always walking the dogs in new environments — it's so enjoyable to always have something new to look at or experience! My least favorite thing is...Wow, still thinking about it...I guess it would have to be missing my friends!

How long after deciding to hit the road did it take for you to get your ducks in a row and actually hit the road?

We decided in May 2016 and rented out our house in September 2016. We still had to complete a renovation project and line up some work stuff before we left at the end of November 2016.

How does being a family/couple/single, affect you on the road? What issues do you have and how do you solve them?

It is just Steve and me, our 12-year-old golden retriever (Lenny), and our yellow lab (Maybel). So, we definitely see *a lot* of each other, but luckily we like each other! But, like I said earlier — everything in moderation! It's important for us to have time away from the pups —

and they do a good job staying in the RV when we go into national parks or out for a happy hour drink. Also, we run errands separately sometimes and work on different projects or activities for our "alone time." Sometimes we get a tad bit annoyed by each other, so we occasionally argue, then love each other the next second — so messed up haha! Usually, if I'm well fed, and Steve has cell phone reception, all is good in life.

If you were a homeowner, did you decide to sell or rent before hitting the road?

We rented it out.

If you work, how do you accomplish this while being on the road? What are your challenges? How do you overcome them? What advice do you have for others?

Along with our home that we rented out, we have a total of six rental properties. We manage them all from the road, and (fingers crossed) we have been successful at being on top of it! We had two leases ending (luckily at the same time), and we were able to complete most of the process from the road, but Steve did end up flying back to check on them as well as a project house that we were "flipping." We have a work partner who does the construction while we're away, and we will go back to Ohio for the summer to work on the construction, as well. Then — back on the road!

If you don't work, how do you support yourself on the road? What advice do you have for others?

Ahhhhhhh…Someday.

What rig did you choose? Why? What do you see as its advantages and disadvantages? If you had to do it over, would you pick the same rig? If not, why not and what would you pick?

We chose a fifth wheel. We probably could have chosen anything and been happy with it — we think about other rigs daily, but *love* ours. The under belly storage is lovely, it tows wonderfully. We love that we have a 4x4 truck along with it — it makes getting through tough terrain much easier and allows us to get to some amazing boondocking spots. If we do it again (which, we will haha), we would definitely pay more attention to the tank sizes because it is only 40 gallons and sometimes we run out of fresh water. We also think we may get a toy hauler to get some fun little scooters or off-road motorcycles to explore with (to keep miles off the truck and cut down on diesel costs — and it'd be so fun)!

How did you outfit your rig to meet your goals? Storage? Off-grid or On? Work? Play?

We bought it new, so we did very little alterations. We do have plans for a larger battery bank, inverter, and possibly a composting toilet so that we can have more grey tank or fresh water capacity. Our fresh water tank is 40 gallons, so we did purchase a drill pump and external water tanks, which we *love*.

How do you manage your travel-companion relationships?

Thank God for wifi!

How do you manage your relationships back home?

We write a travel blog that family and friends can read, send postcards, and make a lot of phone calls and text messages to stay in touch.

How do you receive mail back home? How do you manage your bills? How do you receive mail on the road?

Thank God for Steve's mom! Every so often she ships all of our mail to a nearby post office, but most of the time we are able to pay any bills or take care of mail online.

Do you have kids with you? If so, how do you manage road schooling them? Any tips?

We would love to! This will also be a "go with the flow" learning experience!

If you have pets with you, what tips do you have regarding pet management?

Before we hit the road, we got all of their annual shots and heart worm medicine taken care of, BAM! Good to go! Our dogs love car rides, walks, and people — so we're pretty lucky! We also always try to exercise them a lot before we leave them, so that if they have any anxiety, they're too tired to notice — haha! Pets on the road *rules*!

Do you have any tips regarding money management?

We write down our spendings *everyday* in our planner and *try* to stick to our daily and monthly budget.

What lessons do you have for others? Things to avoid and things to absolutely do?

Large holding tanks! We wish we had them.

Visit national parks on weekdays!

Enjoy everything! (Even when your sweating profusely while dumping your black tank and gagging) because, come on! You could be back in the daily grind, in a building from 8-5.

INTERVIEW 11:
Matt and Amanda of TheVanProject

Why did you hit the road? What are your goals, objectives, dreams, hopes?

A big part of getting on the road was living a less expensive lifestyle that gives us more freedom and time to pursue the things we love to do. Because we save so much money not paying rent, we can afford to work fewer hours for others allowing us to spend more time on our own creative endeavors. Some of our goals are to write more, take more photos, make our website better (and monotone it), and start a podcast. We also want to start a vlog.

What have you learned that you wish you knew before you started?

Learning as we went has been part of what we enjoy about the process. We wish we had known how long our renovation was going to take us — it took roughly twice as long as anticipated.

What do you miss about your old life? What did you think you'd miss that you don't?

The thing we miss the most is having reliable internet. It makes it very difficult to work on the website or any other project online. We thought we would miss showering a bit more (we don't mind going a week between showers now).

What do you like best about this life? What do you like least about this life? Describe a "day in your life."

The best part of living in our RV has been the freedom it affords us. The thing we like the least is how quickly things become disorganized if you don't put them in their place.

Right now a day in our life consists of waking up doing some light exercise, preparing food for the day, and going to work. We have been working for a friend in a mobile gear shop that is run out of an airstream trailer. We usually finish work between five and seven which gives us a little bit of time to go for a jog or do some climbing before making dinner, then we usually read a bit and then go to bed.

How long after deciding to hit the road did it take for you to get your ducks in a row and actually hit the road?

It took us roughly eight months from the time we decided we wanted to try this to the point of finishing our van renovations and getting on the road.

How does being a family/ couple/ single, affect you on the road? What issues do you have and how do you solve them?

Living in such close quarters means you're in each other's faces all the time. For us, if we ever have any disagreements or conflicts, we deal with them right away.

If you were a homeowner, did you decide to sell or rent before hitting the road?

We were renters in San Francisco before hitting the road.

If you work, how do you accomplish this while being on the road? What are your challenges? How do you overcome them? What advice do you have for others?

Amanda and I do as much remote work as possible via the internet. Unfortunately, a lot of the places we like to travel through have poor internet connection. To overcome the problem of poor internet connection, we try to get as much work done as possible when the connectivity is good. Sometimes this means staying in one place for a little longer than we want. It's not a bad trade-off.

The best advice we can offer is to diversify yourself. Give yourself lots of options for earning income, especially passive income, if possible. Be prepared to take on unconventional work too.

What rig did you choose? Why? What do you see as its advantages and disadvantages? If you had to do it over, would you pick the same rig? If not, why not and what would you pick?

We chose a 1964 Clark Cortez. It's limited in terms of the terrain that we can take it on, but it has way more character than any sprinter. It has a fully functioning toilet and an on-demand hot water heater. There is ample storage and we fit a queen size bed in it. We also have a two burner propane range and added to it a basin sink.

Based on our experience so far I think I would choose a four-wheel-drive vehicle next time.

How did you outfit your rig to meet your goals? Storage? Off-grid or On? Work? Play?

We added a lot more storage than our Cortez originally had. We also added a queen size bed which has been quite luxurious. We have three solar panels that are powerful enough to power a refrigerator, LED lighting, and to charge all of our electronics.

How do you manage your travel-companion relationships?

Amanda and I have traveled a lot together including multiple months on the road in South America. We've had enough experiences that we know how to deal with conflicts when they arise.

How do you manage your relationships back home?

We call our families and friends frequently to stay in touch, but they also follow along on our adventures via our Instagram and Facebook accounts. We also have a website where we write about our experiences.

How do you receive mail back home? How do you manage your bills? How do you receive mail on the road?

We have mail sent to our former roommates or family members. We don't have many bills, and the ones that we do have we can pay online.

Do you have kids with you? If so, how do you manage road schooling them? Any tips?

No kids.

If you have pets with you, what tips do you have regarding pet management?

No pets.

Do you have any tips regarding money management?

Amanda and I have had good self-control when it comes to spending money. Because we are so limited on space we don't feel the need to buy stuff, mostly we spend our money on food. We don't do a budget, but this hasn't been a problem so far.

INTERVIEW 12:
Gabi, Stephan and Kali the K9 of 8Paws1Tail

Why did you hit the road? What are your goals, objectives, dreams, hopes?

We were tired of living in the hamster wheel life that the city was giving us. Feeling over worked, we knew we wanted more in life. We love the outdoors and wanted to pursue our passion of exploring. Our motto is "adventure is life," and the world had so much to offer and so much to see. Being stuck in an office-type of career was not where we saw us living the rest of our lives.

We hope to continue this full-time RV lifestyle as long as possible, getting to see much of the states and hopefully venture out to Alaska. We have many dreams, one of them being to own our own campground and maybe eventually build our cabin in the woods when we find a home base.

What have you learned that you wish you knew before you started?

We wish we would have done more research and been better prepared prior to our departure about living off the grid, or that we'd gotten setup with solar panels and had known more about boondocking options. We found the Campendium site — which is a great tool for that — midway into our travels. Our next run will be to save more money and to use RV parks less of the time.

What do you miss about your old life? What did you think you'd miss that you don't?

We miss long showers. Right now we're in a primitive site and taking a long hot shower without thinking about it would feel oh so good! A nice hot bath wouldn't be too bad either.

We thought we'd miss the vast space we had in our old home but really living in around 300 square feet has not affected us at all.

What do you like best about this life? What do you like least about this life? Describe a "day in your life."

We love the freedom and being in nature. We also love that we are together a lot more. When in the city, I (Gabi) worked extremely long hours, and it felt like Steph and I were sometimes two ships passing in the night. Now we're exploring together, working together and love discovering the world together. With our dog, we're a happy little family of three.

What do we like least...nothing really. I mean it's a more leisurely lifestyle, but at the same time it is a lot harder, if that makes sense? People think camping or RV life is easy but it's work...setting up, planning your destinations constantly, running into weather issues, road conditions and overall being safe while on the road. I think people don't realize how much work it can be moving your home all the time. We've definitely worked a system, and it really isn't like we're bothered by it, because in the end getting to the next destination and seeing beauty makes it all worth it. But you're constantly moving, ya know?

Day in the life of 8Paws1Tail: When we were traveling it would be having our morning coffee together, taking our pup on a quick morning walk, then planning out our adventures. Checking on points of interest in the area or sometimes just driving and being spontaneous to see what we can discover. Taking photos along the way.

We report our adventures on Instagram to keep friends and family connected. Right now our days are mostly taken by working as Camp Hosts for the US Forest Service. We get to meet a lot of campers and then explore the Tahoe National Forest when we have some free time.

How long after deciding to hit the road did it take for you to get your ducks in a row and actually hit the road?

It took us about four months. Putting our house on the market, selling and downsizing everything, purchasing our RV, and finally finishing our careers. In between all that, we did research and put a general itinerary together.

How does being a family/couple/single, affect you on the road? What issues do you have and how do you solve them?

We really haven't had any issues as a couple on the road. We're both pretty calm and know when the other needs extra space or time out.

If you were a homeowner, did you decide to sell or rent before hitting the road?

We debated both. We ended up choosing to sell our home. We knew that we no longer wanted to live in California and wouldn't be coming back to our previous home. We also wanted the money to help fund our travels and purchase our RV.

If you work, how do you accomplish this while being on the road? What are your challenges? How do you overcome them? What advice do you have for others?

The challenge for us is finding work on the road. We've started the Camp Host workamping and will be trying it out for the summer season. Hoping to find other means of making money and traveling more is a goal. The challenge is balancing the time of wanting to explore and still getting internet connection to be able to work on our blog.

Making sure you have the knowledge and have done your homework will allow you to complete more tasks. And make sure you have good internet connection. Or at least know of wifi locations around you.

If you don't work, how do you support yourself on the road? What advice do you have for others?

We just started working, prior to that it was just money management and working off our savings.

You can start this RV Life by just working off a savings. You'll see so much, and you won't regret taking that vacation of a lifetime. Life is about taking chances, and if you're resilient you can survive. Ideas change along the way, and sometimes destiny has a different plan for you.

What rig did you choose? Why? What do you see as its advantages and disadvantages? If you had to do it over, would you pick the same rig? If not, why not and what would you pick?

We bought a 37-foot 2007 Winnebago Voyage. We purchased a used model, because it was within our budget. We knew that we personally no longer wanted to tow our home. We've had trailers and fifth wheels, and I think we also just wanted something different. We are Jeep people and enjoy off-roading so felt that an RV and tow would be a better setup for the lifestyle we wanted.

Advantages: Comfort, easy leveling system, luxury residential amenities.

Disadvantages: fuel economy, two motors so more maintenance, bigger rig means unable to get into more rural locations.

Yes, we love Winnebago but would probably go with a newer model.

How did you outfit your rig to meet your goals? Storage? Off-grid or On? Work? Play?

We did purchase a 100-Watt panel and inverter for energy to be off-grid.

For play we bought two kayaks for some better exploring and fun in the water. We are usually always parked by a body of water.

For work: we are working on purchasing a better internet connection spot system.

How do you manage your travel-companion relationships?

Knowing how to respect and trust each other is first and foremost. Communication is key, and knowing to give yourselves time for enjoying each other's enjoyments, as well as your own.

How do you manage your relationships back home?

We stay connected with Instagram, Facebook and YouTube. We use these social media platforms to share our adventures. Then of course it's a phone call to say hello.

How do you receive mail back home? How do you manage your bills? How do you receive mail on the road?

We've had our mail forwarded to Steph's parents who live in South Lake Tahoe. We aren't too far from them, so it's easy to receive mail when we head down to their area. We have automatic withdrawals on our fixed expenses i.e., phone bills, insurance and some storage fees.

Do you have kids with you? If so, how do you manage road schooling them? Any tips?

No kids.

If you have pets with you, what tips do you have regarding pet management?

Yes, we have one dog. A 2-year-old German Shepherd. Our dog has been a great companion, she loves hiking and exploring as much as we do. We found that when traveling, you should make sure you know the nearest vet in case of an emergency. Also, we had her previous vet records emailed to us so we have them on hand at all times.

Also, make sure that you are able to get their specific food regularly. We have two 10-pound storage bins for her dry food. We make sure that where we are going next has a store that sells her food. We ran into an instance being in a small town that didn't have her food, and we had to pay a high price for some other type of kibble. We make sure her pads don't dry out with all the hiking by using utter butter. She's protected with Frontline for ticks, dry shampoo for those non-easy clean days, and a comfy bed to rest her tired bones. During hot days we make sure the RV has plenty of ventilation, and we keep the fan on if she has to stay in the RV. We have her on a lead at camp so she doesn't stray but give her plenty of freedom playtime.

Do you have any tips regarding money management?

Maintaining a budget as much as you can will save a lot. We are not big going-out eaters, so we cook a lot of home meals to save on costs. We enjoy being outdoors, and most outdoor exploring doesn't require spending a cent. Hiking, kayaking, packing a lunch spending time outside is free. That doesn't mean you shouldn't treat yourself. Allow a couple of treats once or twice a month, so you don't feel the urge to splurge.

What lessons do you have for others? Things to avoid and things to absolutely do?

Trust that everything is going to be ok. Go with the flow, don't be afraid to adapt and always keep learning. Life is about taking a chance to chase your dreams and follow your heart. Have a good support system whether it be on or off the road.

INTERVIEW 13:
Brad and Maggie of WanderlandTravelers

Why did you hit the road? What are your goals, objectives, dreams, hopes?

Brad had a nomadic lifestyle in mind over 15 years ago, when he was choosing his college major. He went with Computer Science, thinking that someday this might lend itself to working from anywhere. I was a bit more skeptical about being a nomad. I was feeling quite comfortable in my job and loved our life and community in Oregon. It seemed far-fetched to sell the house we'd only owned for a few years and being a nomad was just kind of an abstract idea.

Brad really won me over when he said he wanted to take me on a Grand Adventure! We actually started out talking about moving onto a sailboat. We were thinking about buying a boat in Florida, and we would have needed to cross the country to do that. So we started talking about those logistics and thinking about what would be our home base as we boat shopped; we didn't want to rush into buying something. An RV started to make a lot of sense (as opposed to renting an apartment or tent camping while we boat shopped), and then we started talking about "not rushing" across country and enjoying the drive. The more we talked about RVing the more excited we got about all the places we wanted to visit, and suddenly our vision changed to full-time RVing.

Maybe someday we'll do the sailboat, but for now, we just feel like there is still *so* much to see and do on land, and we truly love this lifestyle.

We've made ourselves a road trip bucket-list, things like: stand-up paddle-board in Glacier National Park, hike Angels Landing in Zion, catch sunset at Horseshoe Bend...we love being connected with other travelers on social media, and learning about new places to add to our list. I (Maggie) am a nature photographer and this lifestyle has really been a dream come true. Our goals are fairly simple: stay in scenic places, camp for free as often as possible, visit national parks, see old friends, make new ones, and go on adventures in every place we visit.

What have you learned that you wish you knew before you started?

We learned that our 33-foot long RV is bigger than we need and can really be a hindrance, due to size limitations at campgrounds or boondocking sites.

We've learned that we really have the ability to control our cost of living, much more so than when we lived in a house. Our biggest costs are gas and camping fees and those are really within our control. We try to stay in places that have national forest or BLM land that allows free camping, and if you drive fewer miles between destinations, or stay in one place for a longer period of time, you'll spend less on gas than if you're hopping around every few days. You can even control your "utilities" cost by layering up instead of blasting heat when you're in cooler areas, and finding free dump and water fill stations.

Our RVing experience so far has been in the western half of the United States and the opportunities for free camping, and free dump stations, are quite plentiful.

Another lesson we've learned is that we are far more adaptable than we give ourselves credit for! With RV living, you'll be in a smaller space, have a much smaller shower, and if you're boondocking a lot, it becomes very important to be much more conservative about water and power usage, but these are pretty inconsequential when you consider the richness you gain in this new lifestyle. Those things that we thought would be difficult adjustments (navy showers, less frequent showers, limited energy to power our devices, limited fridge space) just became our "new normal," and we just moved forward and accepted it for the reality that it is. We wake up every day excited about our life, the places we're in and the places we're going.

There will always be difficulties, bumps in the road, breakdowns and costly repairs, but having an open mind, patience, humor, and a willingness to try to fix things yourself will go an exceptionally long way.

What do you miss about your old life? What did you think you'd miss that you don't?

Brad misses the spacious garage with all his tools, toys, and half finished mad scientist projects. We both miss getting together with friends on a moment's notice, going to our favorite restaurants and breweries, and just our community of people in general.

We thought we'd really miss long hot spacious showers, but as we stated before, that was a surprisingly easy transition.

What do you like best about this life? What do you like least about this life? Describe a "day in your life."

We love the constant variety and changing landscapes. We love getting to experience places that we never would have thought to visit in our previous life. Some of our most favorite spots are those that we just happened upon when looking for a place to camp along our route. There is immeasurable beauty in the desert and mountain landscapes of eastern California, Utah, and Arizona.

Our least favorite thing about the life would have to be engine trouble. We do our best to avoid it by keeping up with maintenance, but random breakages are unavoidable, so we try to face it with stoic determination. Troubleshooting online has been pretty helpful as well and has given us confidence to do a lot of repairs or parts replacement ourselves.

I'll describe three days. Weekdays typically have me doing photography and video editing for our YouTube channel Wanderland Travelers — we share weekly episodes of our adventures. Brad works his job from 8 to 5, Monday through Friday. After 5, we try to find something fun to do in the area like a hike or a brewery to visit, or if we need to we'll use that time to get some chores done. Saturday is most often a travel day. We find somewhere to dump the tanks in the morning and do the first part of the drive before lunch. After lunch, we do the second part of the drive, find a place to fill our fresh water tank and get settled at a camp site. We usually do some grocery provisioning on Saturday as well, either at the lunch stop or at our end point. Sunday is our day to play. We switch spots once a week usually, so Sunday is Brad's one full free day. We try to find a bigger adventure to do on that day, like a longer hike or a day trip to somewhere nearby that's a bit of a drive.

How long after deciding to hit the road did it take for you to get your ducks in a row and actually hit the road?

In the fall of 2015 we started getting really inspired by some YouTube channels of people that were living nomadic lifestyles. It really helped us visualize what that life could be like. By the winter we started telling our friends and family that we had plans to hit the road and we decided that spring would be the best time to sell the house. We purchased our Class A motorhome in February 2016 and started doing a lot of work to get the house looking its best. We put it on the market in late March and about a month later we had finalized the sale and were moving onboard!

How does being a family/couple/single, affect you on the road? What issues do you have and how do you solve them?

Traveling as a couple, we've fallen into our different roles and we each have certain duties or chores. Brad handles the outside of the rig while I tend to things inside. We both work on trip planning: how many miles we want to travel and whether there's free camping at the destination, figuring out dump stations along our route, and researching hikes or activities to do once we're there. Any issue that might arise between us can usually be solved by being a better listener and not letting emotions flare. If at least one of you can keep calm, it helps to bring the other one back down. I'd say that's the same as life before. It's just so important to be respectful and be sincere.

If you were a homeowner, did you decide to sell or rent before hitting the road?

We sold our house. For us, we didn't want to worry about any possible home repairs, yard maintenance, or even just keeping it rented. And we knew we'd be on the road for several years at a minimum and we figured if and when we got another house, we'd go with something smaller and we didn't want to keep a storage unit with all the furniture, etc. We just got rid of pretty much everything! It was quite liberating.

If you work, how do you accomplish this while being on the road? What are your challenges? How do you overcome them? What advice do you have for others?

Brad works as a web developer at a small company where all employees have been working remotely for a couple years now. He worked remotely out of our house for almost a year when we started taking the idea of going nomadic seriously. Once we had made up our mind, Brad let his manager know our plans and she was really supportive and excited for us. He was accustomed to a stand up desk in the house, and it was important for him to keep using a stand up desk, so he spent some time retrofitting the TV area over the dash to have a drawer that pulls out into a desk where he can work standing up.

The biggest challenge is having good internet. Brad needs to have a pretty strong internet connection (most public wifi won't do) for his daily video conferences with coworkers. We use our cell phone hotspots for most of our internet needs, supplementing with wifi when feasible. We have a mobile booster for when the mobile signal is too weak, and a wifi booster for when the wifi signal is weak. Both have come in handy innumerable times. We use the unlimited plans on Verizon and AT&T and have never run out of data, though we occasionally have spotty connections, even with the booster. The best advice we can give is to use boosters, they help a lot!

If you don't work, how do you support yourself on the road? What advice do you have for others?

We do have a steady income, but still have some advice for saving money. As we mentioned, the two biggest costs in our life are gas and campground fees. You can save a significant amount of money by spending more time in each spot, keep the distance between each spot short, and try make each spot free (BLM, National Forest Service land, etc.). We have a couple of campground memberships (Good Sam and Passport America) so that if we do stay at one, we can usually get a discounted rate.

Another benefit of the reduced driving of course is reduced maintenance costs. Before we hit the road, we also made sure to have a savings account set aside just for repairs — that can really help ease the stress when you have to get into a mechanic.

What rig did you choose? Why? What do you see as its advantages and disadvantages? If you had to do it over, would you pick the same rig? If not, why not and what would you pick?

We ended up with a 2003 Fleetwood Bounder 32W. It's a 33-foot Class A motorhome. There were many factors influencing our decision. We needed something that could propel itself because we didn't own a vehicle that could tow, so that ruled out trailers and fifth wheels. We liked the giant front windows and the spacious rooftop space and bays of Class A style motorhomes. One big disadvantage is the long length, which prevents us from staying at many state park campgrounds, as well as some boondocking sites which have narrow roads or small sites.

If we could do it over, we would get a smaller rig with four wheel drive; we're currently drooling over Sportsmobiles. Thirty-three feet is a lot bigger than we need, and it's a gas hog. A smaller 4x4 rig would enable us to camp almost anywhere as well as being a little stealth if necessary.

How did you outfit your rig to meet your goals? Storage? Off-grid or On? Work? Play?

We made sure to get a rig that already had some solar set up, and bought a couple extra panels to get more watts (we have 535 watts). We also installed a larger inverter (4000 watts) and set it up so that we can plug in our shore power cable to it to power all the outlets in the RV. We wanted to be as self sufficient as we could so we could comfortably boondock and save money on campsites, as well as enjoy the more peaceful solitude that we find in our great country's public lands. We spent 200 days dry camping over the last year and it was mostly pretty comfortable.

Brad installed the stand up desk and set up a curtain that he can close behind himself to section off the area and make it more like an office. He also replaced the old box TV in the front of the RV with a flat screen on an adjustable arm. I painted the walls white and used chalk paint to color the couch, dinette, and window valences. Both of those made a huge difference in how the interior looks, and it made it feel so much more like our space.

We also installed a tire pressure monitoring system (TPMS) so we're immediately aware of leaks. That has come in handy more than we might have expected.

How do you manage your travel-companion relationships?

We each have our roles and duties, and this works quite well when getting the rig ready to move, keeping our home clean, and taking care of our pets. Brad is the driver of the rig, basically because he's so much more comfortable behind the wheel than I am, so I'm the navigator and DJ, and I capture video along the drive for our episodes.

How do you manage your relationships back home?

Social media is a pretty amazing tool to stay connected with friends and family and feel like you're not so far apart. We like to text with people and that's a fun way to get real-time interactions or get updates. We've actually seen more of our families since we started traveling! We lived in different states before, but now we have the freedom to spend a month with each side of our family. That's been really amazing. We've also met up in some of the different locations we've been. Another bonus has been visiting old friends that are now spread across the country, and that's been really special.

How do you receive mail back home? How do you manage your bills? How do you receive mail on the road?

We use one of many mail forwarding services called Anytime Mailbox (anytimemailbox.com). They partner with mail collecting services throughout the country, and they happened to have a partner in our home state of Oregon, so we went with them. We pay all our bills online. About once a month, we'll have our mail collector forward our mail to our current location. If we are near a friend or family, we'll have it shipped there, or if we're at a campsite we'll ship it there. If neither of those are an option, we'll use USPS General Delivery, a wonderful option that we didn't discover until halfway through our first year.

Do you have kids with you? If so, how do you manage road schooling them? Any tips?

We don't have kids, and no plans to have any.

If you have pets with you, what tips do you have regarding pet management?

We have two sweet Chihuahua/terrier rescues who are way too pampered, hehe. I suppose our main tip is if you leave them alone in the RV, be thoughtful about what the weather is doing and make arrangements (open windows, run A/C, etc.) to make sure they will be comfortable until you return. If you can't make sure they will be comfortable, then either take them with you or don't leave the RV.

A tip for those with a dinette, don't leave any food on the dinette. It is much more accessible to them than a table in a stationary house. In the same vein, if your pets have access to your recycle bin, make sure there is no food waste left on your recyclables (this is requested by recycle centers anyway). If you are recycling something particularly pungent and desirable to the pets (like tuna cans), you will need to keep it out of reach of the pets or they will get into it.

Another good idea is to get copies of the pet medical records from your vet. This can be helpful and more efficient when you need to see a new vet on the road.

Do you have any tips regarding money management?

Use software, like Mint, to chart expenses/income over time. You can categorize expenditures so you know what you spent each month on gas, groceries, etc. It's a handy way to reference spending history and see your net income each month.

What lessons do you have for others? Things to avoid and things to absolutely do?

Get a smaller rig than you think you need. You'll thank yourself later when you have a larger pool of campgrounds to choose from when searching for a place to stay.

Bring bikes. It's great exercise, and it's one of our favorite ways to explore a new (or old) town.

Drop into the local tourism office for maps and local tips on some of the best things to see and do in a location.

It wasn't talked about at the dealerships we visited, but make sure you're getting a rig that has enough carrying capacity for being a full-timer. Once you start adding up the weight of gas, passengers, food, gear, clothes, books, tools, water...it can add up quickly and it's so dangerous to be overloaded. Of course it's best to travel with empty holding tanks as often as possible.

Take your time and think things through while dumping so you don't make mistakes! One tiny mistake can result in crap in your face (not kidding).

Be aware of the age of the tires when buying a rig — we learned the typical lifespan is 6-7 years and we ended up replacing our tires within our first year...that was a big expense!

INTERVIEW 14:
Nathan, Renée, Tristan, Winter & Wylder of Wandrly

Why did you hit the road? What are your goals, objectives, dreams, hopes?

Well, I'd started up this successful little freelance web design gig for myself after spending a winter in England, and then the next on in Portland, working out of coffee shops in the town I lived in then, Pittsburgh, PA. I really wanted to travel more, and more often, and one day it just sort of dawned on me that if I could work out of any coffee shop, I could work just about anywhere.

This was back in 2008, and there weren't a ton of people doing this, but I did see a couple on the road and figured if they could do it, I could, too. So, I packed my then 8-year-old son into an RV, and we hit the road.

The only goal was to adventure and explore. Check!

What have you learned that you wish you knew before you started?

That RVs are cumbersome, and vans make life easy. That buying old and cheap means spending a lot of your travel time working on your rig instead of exploring. Everything is a trade off (vans are kind of a bummer when it rains, for example, and the newer your ride, the more you've got to work to pay for it), but I'd say those are about the only two things that have really frustrated us over the years.

What do you miss about your old life? What did you think you'd miss that you don't?

Absolutely nothing. I lost a few friends over this, but anyone who doesn't support our life's decisions probably isn't a great friend anyway. And we actually get to see friends more often, because we can drive around and visit these people who've scattered all over the US...old, really good friends we wouldn't have seen for years, maybe decades, if we weren't moving around like this.

What do you like best about this life? What do you like least about this life? Describe a "day in your life."

I love the amount of time I get to spend with my family. I sit outside at campgrounds and work the early part of the day away designing websites or writing articles. I see my kids scoot by on their bikes or skateboards. I taught them to do both, heard their first words, saw their first steps, taught them to swim in Cenotes in Mexico and just more or less am not missing everything because I'm off at some job.

No offense to those who do that, or to the public school system, I understand that everyone has a different life and wants and needs...but for me, for us, not shuffling them off to let the village raise them in lieu of the parents means the world to me, and I am so grateful we've figured it out.

A day in the life though? Well, it's wildly different every day but a more typical one would be...

The boys stir all too early in the morning. Either Renée (my wife) or I say something like, "Hey, not until the sun comes up!"

As soon as it does, they inform us of this fact. We make coffee on a Coleman stove. Renée sits down at a picnic table and tries to convince Winter that learning to read is fun. He's already good enough at it to get by, and so tries to convince her that, no, riding bikes and making swords out of sticks and shields out of last night's pizza box, that is fun. Reading is school. Meanwhile, his brother puts together a puzzle or makes something out of Play Doh. They ask to watch the iPad too much and eat ridiculous amounts of oranges, bananas and yogurt drinks.

Then I finish work, usually between 1 to 3 p.m. or so. We go do whatever our day has planned, which could be anything from hiking Mount Rainier to checking out a restaurant and walking some small town's Main Street, or even just regular old stuff like going to the movies.

When that gets old, we head back to camp, crack some IPAs and make a fire. I tell ghost stories that are probably inappropriate for a four year old and instead his older brother (6) gets spooked. Renée gets frustrated because putting them to sleep is now going to take an hour instead of five minutes.

"If you tell them stories like that, you're putting them to bed."

She and I get up to whatever adult fun we can, and then it's off to bed to see if we should do that — or something entirely different — all over again tomorrow!

P.S. There are also breakdowns and being in crappy places and more breakdowns and even worse places and sometimes it's too hot or too cold or it rains for a week straight. It's not all fun and games, and don't get me started on bathrooms...

How long after deciding to hit the road did it take for you to get your ducks in a row and actually hit the road?

About six months.

How does being a family/couple/single, affect you on the road? What issues do you have and how do you solve them?

Well, our biggest "issue" right now is that our teenager wants to live a more stationary life, so we're figuring out what that's going to look like. He's got about two years left of high school, and we think we can make it work for everyone.

But with our younger ones, both of whom were born on the road, there is nothing different or special or weird or "needs adjusting to" for them. This is the only life they've known and it's as natural as anything, more natural I think because having five people in a van forces you to live outside, to accept hot days and find a swimming hole or go for a bike ride to cool off, rainy days where you play in a tent with your brothers and have to learn to get along or get wet, and cold days where we make lunch at some place with a heater last for three hours.

Things like breaking down and the kids occasionally needing stitches or whatever we've faced, we've learned it's all just a process. Problems seem insurmountable until you just sit down and make a list of what needs done with a reasonable outcome...things somehow do always work out in the end.

It all depends on how far away the end is though. :)

If you work, how do you accomplish this while being on the road? What are your challenges? How do you overcome them? What advice do you have for others?

My biggest challenge is keeping the sun out of my eyes when I'm at a picnic table.

We have a solar setup, often stay at state parks where there's an electrical hookup, and are connected to the web via our phones. T-mobile in Mexico and AT&T in the U.S., and that works well for me.

The best advice I have for others who want to live a traveling life is to have some type of an income...because you just may get addicted and that whole "sold my house to travel for a year" thing, well, a year can go by really quickly.

Aside from my web design work we're starting to get into AirBNBing out property, hopefully for more of a passive income.

What rig did you choose? Why? What do you see as its advantages and disadvantages? If you had to do it over, would you pick the same rig? If not, why not and what would you pick?

We started in a Class C RV. It was too big and bulky. The bed was very comfortable.

After a year, I ditched it for a 1978 VW Bus. I also convinced my college sweetheart to move into it with me at the same time. We chugged along happily in that for years, making two more babies in it before we decided to "upgrade" to a 1976 Airstream, which we lived in for three years before finally admitting that we loved space less than convenience, and so ditched that Airstream to climb back into our Volkswagen.

Unfortunately, due to a terrible human being of a bad mechanic who completely destroyed our engine instead of just swapping out our exhaust system, that VW is not running right now so we're literally moving into a Ford E350 as I write this…

How did you outfit your rig to meet your goals? Storage? Off-grid or On? Work? Play?

100 watts of solar, wooden floors (carpeting is a terrible way to lose your hair while living in a van), a custom bed, 12 volt fans and on or off grid depending on where we are or what we want to be doing.

How do you manage your travel-companion relationships?

With lots of sex and hugging and poems and beer and patience and remembering that we are the primary example to our children, if there's one thing we need to do it's slow our roll when things get heated, step back and wait until we can make that example work in their favor.

How do you manage your relationships back home?

I call my mom and dad about once a week. Some of our family is very supportive of us. All of the grandparents miss these boys immensely and jokingly — or not so much — inform us of that. They are wonderful people. For some other family members who aren't quite as supportive, well, my favorite musician has a line that says, "If I judge the judgmental than what am I?" and I'll just leave it at that.

How do you receive mail back home? How do you manage your bills? How do you receive mail on the road?

Escapees.com, it'll change your life with mail on the road. All of your mail goes there, you technically become a Texan (which means no state income tax), and you just shoot those guys an email and they'll forward it wherever you are, which for us usually means a General Delivery address, which basically just means they send it to the local post office where we are. In Mexico or further south, we just don't get mail. We spent 16 months there and aside from needing to order some parts, we never saw our mail for the entire time, and yet somehow the earth kept on a-spinning. :)

Bills are all online these days.

Do you have kids with you? If so, how do you manage road schooling them? Any tips?

We have done everything from paying a teacher to come up with curriculum for us (first year on the road, I see that as silly now) to unschooling (basically just "not doing school" and letting the world's influences teach your child). For us, the right balance is a couple of hours a day focusing on subjects the kids actually enjoy. Everyone learns more that way.

Our teenager has gone to public school a couple of times, when we were cooking our other youngsters, and he has absolutely destroyed any notions I have had that a public schooling setting can ever fully meet the needs of most children. They're either going to be "too smart," intellectually I guess, and so be held back by those children who don't get stuff as quickly, or they'll need a different approach to learning than this factory life, sit-down-at-a-desk-all-day-and-absorb-largely-pointless-facts. Some kids just don't work that way. Those are the best kids, in my opinion, but I digress.

I am simply a huge fan of any parents who make the big, tough decision to teach their children on their own.

If you have pets with you, what tips do you have regarding pet management?

We used to have a lovely old chocolate lab named Annabelle. My best suggestion is not to have pets, especially if you're going to live in a van (with no AC) or ever want to go to national parks (where pets are often not welcome). It just makes things really tough, but I know some people absolutely love their pets and plenty of folks (including us, previously) make it work!

Do you have any tips regarding money management?

Spend it all, have a good time, live life!

What lessons do you have for others? Things to avoid and things to absolutely do?

Avoid private RV parks. Learn to boondock, go to national forests and state parks. They are better, and usually much cheaper, too.

Stay off the freeway and take it slow. There's nowhere to go and nowhere to be except wherever you are now and in the moment. Make a few friends along the way, there's no need to check every state or country off as quickly as possible.

INTERVIEW 15:
Laura J

Why did you hit the road? What are your goals, objectives, dreams, hopes?

I hit the road for a number of reasons: I was laid off from my job and couldn't face the prospect of looking for a new one; I was renting a place in the Bay Area and the cost of living is very expensive there, and I wasn't getting much for it. I don't mean in terms of the townhouse I was living in, but rather in terms of paying to be in the Bay Area. I'd always dreamed about traveling around in an RV.

My goals, etc., are to see as much of the country as I can by meandering the back roads, not zooming down the interstate, to stay on the road as long as I can, to see how cheaply I can live, and to not get a blowout!

What have you learned that you wish you knew before you started?

I've learned lots of things by experience; I'm not sure you would necessarily learn them ahead of time. If pressed, I would say that I have been surprised by how much my travel has been influenced by the weather! Get some good weather apps, bookmark the NOAA severe weather page and learn how to use it!

What do you miss about your old life? What did you think you'd miss that you don't?

I miss knowing my way around town and puttering in the garden. I didn't think about what I might miss, and I don't miss anything.

What do you like best about this life? What do you like least about this life? Describe a "day in your life."

I like being in control of where I am, where I'm going next, when I go.... not being tied down to others expectations or schedules (like work, school, etc). What I like least is paying a lot of money to park in a parking lot with hookups and nothing else and with unpredictable connectivity.

A typical day involves reading/listening to the news, walking/hiking/exploring with the dog, tidying up/sweeping, making meals, planning where I'm going next, watching downloaded Netflix.

How long after deciding to hit the road did it take for you to get your ducks in a row and actually hit the road?

Six months.

How does being a family/couple/single, affect you on the road? What issues do you have and how do you solve them?

I'm a solo traveler, so the biggest impact is that I have to know how to drive, set up, attend to the systems, and troubleshoot the vehicle.

There have been a few times when I haven't done something because I didn't want to leave the dog alone in the vehicle. If I was traveling with someone, one of us could stay with him and the other one could explore. I'm checking out various devices to ensure that he is comfortable if I want to leave the vehicle.

If you don't work, how do you support yourself on the road? What advice do you have for others?

I'm supporting myself with my savings. I could work remotely, but there would be impacts of that that I don't want right now: I'd need to be connected more consistently, I'd need to have more of a schedule/availability to others; that's what I'm enjoying being away from!

I also try to be pretty frugal: boondocking as much as I can, preparing my own food (not eating out much).

My advice for others is to live in a way that is most comfortable and feasible for them and don't feel like you have to live how someone else thinks you should.

What rig did you choose? Why? What do you see as its advantages and disadvantages? If you had to do it over, would you pick the same rig? If not, why not and what would you pick?

I have a 2016 Minnie Winnie 22R, and I don't tow anything. I have a bicycle for supplemental transportation. I originally wanted a class B van like a Roadtrek but I just couldn't afford it. At the end of the day, I think the Class C is better for a full-timer in that it has more room, and you don't have to make the bed to eat dinner and then clear off the table to go to bed! If I did it over again, I might not pick the same rig because driving this is a bit cumbersome. There are some vehicles that are a bit bigger than a B but smaller than a C which I might investigate, but I know I don't want to tow a travel trailer or a fifth wheel.

How did you outfit your rig to meet your goals? Storage? Off-grid or On? Work? Play?

I haven't made any changes. I'm not very creative or handy! I did bring regular plates, glasses and cutlery, because I hate eating and drinking from paper, plastic or Styrofoam. I have acquired plastic storage totes to replace cardboard boxes. I'm making adjustments as I go. I've considered adding solar panels but have been able to camp off-grid successfully without them so far.

How do you manage your travel-companion relationships?

My travel companion is my dog. I could not do this without him! I always look for dog-friendly places for us to camp at and visit.

How do you manage your relationships back home?

I am in regular (almost daily) contact with my mother; my sister and a friend have me on the Find Friends app, so they can see where I am as long as I have cell service. I have a group of about six family and friends who I inform whenever I arrive somewhere new. I also have a blog so friends can follow my adventures (www.splashesalongtheway.com).

How do you receive mail back home? How do you manage your bills? How do you receive mail on the road?

I have a UPS mailbox for receiving mail since I don't have a sticks-and-bricks anymore. They will send my mail to me whenever I want. I pay bills online. I have a lot fewer bills now!

If you have pets with you, what tips do you have regarding pet management?

Pets like routine. My guy is always crated when we're on the road. I always have distilled or bottled water for him. No campground water. We try and go on a good length walk every day so he can stretch his legs. The biggest adjustment has been his diet which previously was raw food. I've had to find new food sources, and now we do more freeze dried or dehydrated. He is also very protective of me and the rig, so he is never off leash when we're outside. He's adjusting pretty well!

Do you have any tips regarding money management?

Unless money is no object, keep track of your expenses so you can make decisions and prioritize how you spend your money.

What lessons do you have for others? Things to avoid and things to absolutely do?

I would encourage folks to take their time. This lifestyle is not a race! If you see something interesting, check it out! Wherever you're headed will be there tomorrow!

Anything I'm forgetting?

RVers are very diverse. Some go to big RV resorts, park for months and live in luxury. Others live in modest RVs and seek out the most remote, free spots. Others do some type of mixture. No one is having same experience so figure out your own path and embrace it!

INTERVIEW 16:
Jax and Michelle of Jax733

Why did you hit the road? What are your goals, objectives, dreams, hopes?

We both love to travel, and the older we've gotten the more we have valued experiences over things. The more things we accumulated, the less fulfilled we were. We initially downsized to a smaller house and really enjoyed living in a city environment, but we also really love access to nature around us.

We were doing a lot of camping and no matter how long we were gone we never seemed to want to go back home, even though home was a fun and enjoyable place to be. We liked waking up in nature and having the flexibility to do whatever we wanted to do that day.

One day at a campground, we were on a walk and saw a trailer and said, "Why don't we buy one of those and hit the road." The more we thought about it, the more we realized we should at least give it a try. It seemed more feasible and easy that we thought.

Now that we are on the road, we want to see and explore the United States and Canada. Our intention is to live simpler and more thoughtfully. We want to spend time in nature and explore the less traveled parts of the country. We want to be flexible and plot a course based on weather, intuition, and random chance. We want to be open to what the road brings us, both in terms of people and of places.

What have you learned that you wish you knew before you started?

That a fifth wheel is easier to drive than a bumper pull! It may have been worth the extra expense.

What do you miss about your old life? What did you think you'd miss that you don't?

I miss the easy availability to get together with good friends, often, and without a lot of planning. I thought I'd miss dining out at good restaurants frequently, but I don't miss it.

What do you like best about this life? What do you like least about this life? Describe a "day in your life."

Best: The open-ended adventure of it and being able to wake up in a different place and explore different options.

Least: Moving days! And I really don't like it when it's cluttered.

Day in our life: coffee, breakfast, admiring the view, a hike or a bike ride, hopefully some paddle boarding or kayaking when the weather cooperates, reading or playing cards, exploring little towns or local trails, cocktail or "mocktail" hour, dinner, fire and reading or TV.

How long after deciding to hit the road did it take for you to get your ducks in a row and actually hit the road?

Four months.

How does being a family/couple/single, affect you on the road? What issues do you have and how do you solve them?

Lack of alone time/space. We do things separately occasionally. We have our defined tasks that we've gotten good at. We divide and conquer errands and chores. Give each other space.

If you were a homeowner, did you decide to sell or rent before hitting the road?

We have two houses that we rent out.

If you work, how do you accomplish this while being on the road? What are your challenges? How do you overcome them? What advice do you have for others?

We don't work.

If you don't work, how do you support yourself on the road? What advice do you have for others?

We live off of our rental income and savings. There certainly are downsides to renting out your home (or maintaining other rentals for income), but for us the pros out-weigh the cons. We've been pretty lucky with tenants. We've had to hire people to make some repairs, but our tenants have been very cooperative and have helped make it a smooth process.

My advice is that if your life and days are filled with beauty and adventure, you need less stuff to make you happy. Putting ourselves on a limited budget has made me appreciate things more and think through purchases more carefully. It feels good not to be as much of a consumer. I take more pleasure in the smaller things in life like a beautiful campfire, a frosty drink on a hot day, and feeling more in tune with nature and the natural rhythms of the seasons.

What rig did you choose? Why? What do you see as its advantages and disadvantages? If you had to do it over, would you pick the same rig? If not, why not and what would you pick?

We have a travel trailer toy hauler: Eclipse Attitude 27SAG.

Cons: It's supposedly harder to drive than pretty much anything else from what we've been told. Even though it's not huge, its size still limits us to what parks we can go to and small, windy roads are stressful.

Pros: We have the ability to detach, and if our vehicle breaks down we still have a house. For a not-huge rig, it has a lot of storage space and the ability to carry our "toys." It was affordable and doesn't have a motor to break down. It's rugged enough we can go to boondocking spots and be "off grid."

Because of our budget I'd pick the same rig. I think the only other thing I'd consider would be a fifth wheel version of this, but I'm not sure we could justify the extra expense.

How did you outfit your rig to meet your goals? Storage? Off-grid or On? Work? Play?

We use crates to organize everything: jars in one, canned goods in another, and we store those in our "garage" area in the back of the toy hauler.

In our overhead cupboards, we use crates for our pots and pans, dishes, extra glasses, etc. Crates are invaluable.

We use our bunk beds in the garage area to store our camp chairs and off-season clothes.

For off-grid camping, we outfitted our trailer with a composting toilet, strong solar system, generator, inverter, and extra batteries.

How do you manage your travel-companion relationships?

We've found ways to have time alone. We have quiet time with each other, yet not interacting. We sometimes will take turns playing outside with the dog. Occasionally, we'll do separate bike rides or walks.

How do you manage your relationships back home?

Texts. Instagram. FaceTime.

How do you receive mail back home? How do you manage your bills? How do you receive mail on the road?

We have some really close friends who receive our mail and open and sort it. We pay them a nominal amount to do this. They deposit rent checks and any other checks into our bank accounts. They alert us to any urgent mail. Anything else they send to us when we are somewhere that we can easily receive mail. We pay all of our bills online. When we are near a big city, we take delivery of packages and letters at local UPS stores.

Do you have kids with you? If so, how do you manage road schooling them? Any tips?

No.

If you have pets with you, what tips do you have regarding pet management?

Get pet insurance! We use HealthyPaws which is super easy. When we get the bill at the vet, we open the app, take a photo and press send. Then a check arrives about a week later (to our friends' house who receive our mail), with whatever reimbursement we are owed. It has been a lifesaver.

We have needed vets a number of times on the road. Get your medical records from your vet back home in a digital format so you can give these to vets on the road and scan the "road vet's" reports (we use the Scanner Pro app) to have an ongoing record of your pet's care.

If you are planning on using doggy day care when you hike in national parks (dogs usually aren't allowed on the trails), then vaccination records in a digital format are invaluable, as these businesses will ask for proof of rabies shot and other required vaccinations.

Our dog has lots of allergies and our cat has had crystals in his urine, so both of them are on special diets. We've learned to plan ahead and order their special food from Chewy (which has an app and a website) and have it delivered to a UPS or Mailing Store in a larger town we are headed to. Chewy shipping is free at a certain dollar amount (which we always exceed), and it's fast, too (FedEx). But they don't deliver on Saturday, Sunday, or Monday so plan ahead!

Do you have any tips regarding money management?

Set up a budget and keep track of how closely you stick to it. Avoid collecting more "stuff." Prepare your meals and avoid eating out. Budget for emergencies because they will happen!

What lessons do you have for others? Things to avoid and things to absolutely do?

Lessons: Don't be afraid of visiting colder places off-season. Some of the national parks are amazing with snow on them.

Buy a Mr. Buddy propane heater. It is super efficient, affordable, and effective.

Be flexible in your travels and don't map out every step if you don't have to. Be open to staying longer at certain places if you want to. Pick areas where there is a lot to do and stay in one place and explore.

Reach out to other people through social media who live this life. Most are very friendly and helpful.

Really pare down your life and bring as little as possible: you need less than you think.

Change campsites on weekdays, Tuesday through Thursday.

Unless you are a really social person and want to be surrounded by people, don't solely do the typical snow bird areas of the southwest and Florida all fall and winter.

Watch the weather carefully!

If you decide to be a landlord while on the road, plan for unexpected expenses and hassles.

Anything I'm forgetting?

It's not the life for everyone, but for people who have chosen it, I have never met anyone who regrets it. It's a special lifestyle for those who value adventure and freedom. Even though there are struggles both mechanically and logistically, working through them is part of self-sufficiency and builds confidence. Things in an RV or trailer are going to break so just expect that. Work together to problem solve.

INTERVIEW 17:
James and Rhiannon of MilesAwayEveryday

Why did you hit the road? What are your goals, objectives, dreams, hopes?

The idea came to us towards the end of June 2016, in what we would call our hell week — really the absolute worst week we've ever had. Rhiannon had three grandparents fall gravely ill with hospice. Fortunately, by an absolute miracle, two survived, but she lost her first grandparent that week — one of her grandfathers. Needless to say, these three particular people have always been a huge part of her life, and she has a bond with them that's impossible to put into words — but amazing to witness — so it was a lot for her to process.

James was still working as Creative Director for a company in Orlando in the midst of us running our own businesses, and he had to lay off a chunk of people and cut salaries and bonuses for the rest. It was the hardest week for him, because he knew he didn't want to continue working for someone who didn't care enough about their business and their team.

Rhiannon asked him if the worst were to happen, what would we do. We needed to come up with back-up plans, just in case. James paused, and said that he didn't care if we just hooked a trailer to the truck and drove off, we would figure it out and be better off. Without hesitation, Rhiannon agreed and suggested we research the idea. Turns out that not only was it feasible, but people were doing it. It simply proved to us that we could work remotely, run our businesses and still thrive. Hell, thrive more than we imagined.

We've been big on setting goals for ourselves before, but this one was definitely the biggest and we dove right in and tackled our goal list quickly. A lot faster than we thought we would too.

We knew we wanted to be happier, healthier and live our daily lives that way.

We absolutely love travel and this was an ultimate way to do that.

Major collaboration of work, travel, living, fulfilling goals for everything and being completely happy with our choices and achievements.

We set a lot of dreams and goals for ourselves, and we work so well together to make them happen and have no fear doing it. We would rather attempt and live, than dream and never take a chance.

What have you learned that you wish you knew before you started?

This sounds hilarious and ridiculous, but this question was a tough one for us. We did *so* much research and learned from others mistakes and challenges before we hit the road, *but* we figured it out.

Travel days are exhausting — for both of us. We did *not* see that coming. James has always loved driving and could drive for hours and hours on end. However, when you're cruising along in our Class A on travel days, it wipes us out, and the distance doesn't matter.

What do you miss about your old life? What did you think you'd miss that you don't?

We miss having certain comforts, such as a cozy couch we can both stretch out on and a better place to sit for meals and working. We do plan on replacing our couch and dinette in the future, though, to remedy that.

We thought we would miss long hot showers, which we used to take daily and sometimes more than once a day. We actually enjoy the quick showers and saving loads of water.

What do you like best about this life? What do you like least about this life? Describe a "day in your life."

We love the freedom and that we never feel stagnant or stuck with this new life. We also really love that we have the ability to chase the good weather and move on when it's bad.

We find it to be quite a struggle to think of something we don't like about this life. We thought about it, but there's nothing!

How long after deciding to hit the road did it take for you to get your ducks in a row and actually hit the road?

Well the idea came to us the week of June 23rd, 2016. We purchased our Class A less than two months later and sold everything we owned.

We did have two other family members pass away, unfortunately, before the end of 2016 — Rhiannon's two grandparents that fell ill when her grandfather passed in June. They were constantly in and out of the hospital, having surgeries, fighting pneumonia and countless other challenges. Then another one of her grandparents ended up in the hospital, so we spent a lot of time helping and caring for him, putting our plans on hold a bit — priorities!

We took our RV out on its maiden voyage in October and November 2016. One of Rhiannon's grandfathers, who brought her on road trips and camping throughout her childhood, loved receiving our phone calls every day on where we were and what we were doing; it put him in much better spirits.

We returned to Florida to take care of family, enjoy the holidays and wrap up the rest of our lives before finally leaving Orlando on January 31st, 2017.

How does being a family/couple/single, affect you on the road? What issues do you have and how do you solve them?

Time is our biggest challenge, more so when we want to get up really early to enjoy a play day. It takes some time for Rhiannon to get up and move super early, but she's tried different things to prepare both of us in order to be more time efficient, and it has helped a lot.

We used to take a lot longer to get ready when packing up and in, so we could move to another location. We've really come together well with that, and now it takes us very little time to get everything ready inside and outside of the RV and to hook up our tow car. We get excited and high five each other when we are all done, and again when we are rolling down the road.

You have to allow yourself the time and patience to acclimate to this new life and when you start to, it's a great feeling.

We made a great team before this. When we started, we allowed ourselves the time to acclimate, and we helped each other, and we found news ways to accomplish things. That's really important. No matter the change or challenge, you just have to help each other and keep that teamwork going. Anything that comes our way, throws us a curve ball or tries to slow us down, is simply a temporary challenge.

If you were a homeowner, did you decide to sell or rent before hitting the road?

We leased our home we shared together in Lake Nona, Florida when this whole plan came to fruition.

We were originally planning on building a home or two there, with the intention of moving within a year or two and leaving Florida altogether.

We look back now and are really happy we didn't do that. Rhiannon had worked in real estate before, managing HOAs and rental properties, and we didn't want any of that stress with us on the road. It would have felt like more of a burden for us, and it simply wasn't worth it.

If you work, how do you accomplish this while being on the road? What are your challenges? How do you overcome them? What advice do you have for others?

We definitely work! Hahaha. We have often been asked, since we are younger than the typical RVer, if we are independently wealthy, hit the lottery, are trust fund babies, or just have wealthy parents footing the bill. All you can do is laugh it off, tell them they guessed incorrectly and explain that we have done this all on our own, and we continue to work really hard to make this life possible. Our main company provides all elements of branding for your business, as well as web applications, and more. We love that we are so fortunate to work remotely.

We schedule out our weeks with play days, work days and travel days. We find that we get far more work done in less time than when we were slaving away behind a desk in an office building — or even at home every day.

The only challenge we really have is we must have cell signal wherever we plan to stay.

We research as much as possible when planning our routes and potential places to stay. When we arrive somewhere, we scout the area for a spot that works for us. We've only had an issue once where there was absolutely no signal. We had to leave after one day, because we had client meetings we needed to conduct and files that needed to be sent. Other than that, we've been really lucky.

We have gone off grid before for days at a time, but only when we know we have nothing scheduled and time sensitive. There's plenty of work that can still be done offline.

We had lightning fast service out in the middle of a forest once, that was the most surprising for us yet. So you never know what you're going to get, and plenty of times we've been pleasantly surprised.

Advice: Research! There's no such thing as too much research. Anything is possible. If you have the ability to work remotely in any fashion, and you want to live this lifestyle, nothing is actually stopping you but yourself. Just do it.

What rig did you choose? Why? What do you see as its advantages and disadvantages? If you had to do it over, would you pick the same rig? If not, why not and what would you pick?

After *tons* of online and onsite research, our dream home on wheels was a 31-foot Class A and we love it.

When we first started, we thought the only option that would fit our needs was a fifth wheel, and we could not have been more wrong. We looked at, and walked through, every type and size option of RV out there.

When we actually decided to walk through the Class A options, we realized how well it would work and fit our needs. We knew we didn't want to go too big, because national parks tend to have size limits, and we knew we didn't need a ton of space. In fact, anything we looked at that was larger than 31, we would both exclaim that it was just too much room and would walk right out. We would have gone for 27 feet, but it would have involved a lot of renovations that we just didn't have time for with everything going on. We were able to get everything we needed, without renovations, when we saw ours at the dealership.

We love the huge windshield; it is amazing when you're driving, and it's even better when you camp somewhere with a gorgeous view. Our rig is gas, which we like as well. We can have the perfect tow car for us, which is a Jeep instead of having to drive around in a huge truck that tows an even bigger fifth wheel. With our Jeep, we can go anywhere.

Class Cs weren't an option as soon as James tried to sit in the cab of one. There's just no room and the view isn't there. When you have our view while driving, it helps us in more ways than one to ensure we are safe on the road.

The set up time when we stop somewhere is minimal compared to something you have to tow as well.

We wouldn't pick anything else. We are oftentimes reminded in different ways and situations as to why this was the perfect choice.

How did you outfit your rig to meet your goals? Storage? Off-grid or On? Work? Play?

The only big customization we've done to our rig was have a custom install of a washer/dryer combo done as soon as we signed the papers. We had originally planned to do some renovations inside for the walls and the bedroom. We even purchased new flooring, but when family health challenges kept happening, we put all other renovations on the back burner. We know that sometime after our first year, we will renovate the main living area and replace the couch and dinette — turn it into a far more functional spot — and bring in a real couch that we can both enjoy.

How do you manage your travel-companion relationships?

We do all of the same things we did before RV life.

We have date nights out and date nights in. We love to cook together, and we come together for the regular day-to-day stuff like washing vehicles and cleaning the house, and we make it fun.

We schedule play days throughout the week so that we can go experience and explore new things together.

We love food, music and countless other things, so if we are in an area that has great food, we will try it! If there's live music, we are all ears. Golf course, let's at least hit some balls. Museums, zoos — it doesn't matter, we just make time for each other.

We still do nights in where we veg out and just talk; communication is a huge piece of the puzzle. We love campfires. We would say we do movie nights in, but the beauty of this new life is that we so rarely watch anything anymore. We've only had one movie night, but it was great! We curled up in bed at a rest stop after a long day of driving and watched Tombstone — after we stayed in Tombstone — because it makes sense to watch it afterwards and before. Haha.

How do you manage your relationships back home?

Lots of phone calls, texts messages, FaceTime, and even snail mail!

Thank goodness for technology, we can talk to our family and friends all over the world and give them updates on everything we are doing.

We also utilize social media accounts, so they can keep up on our journey, and they *love* that. We can't keep up with their demand of more photos and to update posts, hahaha. We've heard a lot of our photos have been printed and hung on the wall already, and our journey has just begun!

We do send postcards like crazy though. Every park we go to in every state — and any other postcard we come across that looks like a winner or is perfect for a specific person — we will send them out all the time. Our friends and family have really enjoyed receiving those too, because it's just another form of communication that is even more personal and thoughtful. Who doesn't love receiving fun mail?!

How do you receive mail back home? How do you manage your bills? How do you receive mail on the road?

We have our mail sent to a family member. If it's worth keeping, they will either send us a digital copy or send us a package of mail to a particular stop somewhere on our route — whether it's another family member or a UPS store of some kind. We haven't had any challenges with it.

All of our bills are digital. It saves paper and again, technology is amazing. Autopay is a beautiful thing.

Do you have kids with you? If so, how do you manage road schooling them? Any tips?

No kiddos, just us and our fur baby!

If you have pets with you, what tips do you have regarding pet management?

We have a rescue dog who just turned 16 on June 9th. Her name is Chloe. She's a Jack Russell/Beagle mix, and she's been an amazing addition for all these years. Rhiannon adopted her early on, before we got together. She spent a lot of time working with her — since she was abused before — to make her feel comfortable and able to do normal dog stuff like car rides and walks around the park.

When we chose this new lifestyle, there was definitely a transition period for Chloe. Not just because it was a new home, but occasionally the house moves and that's a lot to process.

Chloe was not only abused by her breeders as a puppy, but they actually threw her out of the window from their moving van into a ditch on an interstate. She's overcome a lot in her years because of Rhiannon's commitment and love for her. Now we both continue that process with her whenever she gets anxious — which is less and less — since we've been on the road.

It's one of those things that you simply need to be patient with.

When Chloe steps outside at new places, she can get confused, and there's sensory overload. We work with her to make her feel comfortable and remind her that we are all still here. We try to play with her as much as we can, if she has the energy in her old age. Most spots she loves. She hated Tombstone, haha — too much rock and dirt beneath her feet and not enough grass.

Do you have any tips regarding money management?

Budget and spreadsheets! Rhiannon loves spreadsheets and paperwork, etc. even though she's also quite creative herself. She's wonderful at keeping us organized and maintaining structure all across the board. She's really great at it.

It's so important, especially when traveling full time, to keep up on every expense. Sometimes you travel more often in a month, or you do more activities in certain areas. If you're somewhere visiting family or friends, you can safely assume a higher expense report. Managing your money is crucial.

Sit down and discuss all of it and come up with a very realistic budget. Then add more to each category, just to play it safe. Rhiannon makes time to update everything multiple times a week. That may sound like too much, but when you are in this lifestyle, you can easily lose track quickly. Your schedule is always full of work or play. If you get distracted at a national park for days on end, and you don't make the time to update everything, it just adds more work and second guessing. A receipt may get lost, you forget you paid a bill, or you forget about that bear spray you had to buy. Especially since there's two of us, it's just another element in our relationship where communication is huge. So we have gotten really good at that.

What lessons do you have for others? Things to avoid and things to absolutely do?

Just do it. Don't over plan. You can spend all the time in the world trying to get yourself absolutely prepared and ready, and you can always find reasons to prolong it. Just dive in and live. You'll never regret a second of it, but you will regret not doing it sooner.

Do enough research and watch enough videos to prepare yourself for anything — to help you learn what rig is best for you and your needs — especially, so you don't end up buying multiple rigs before you find what really works. Research tow cars, if you go that route. Learn about things that could go wrong on the road, and how to avoid them or fix them.

Things to avoid: Cities. Hahaha.

We learned early on that we love spending the majority of our time outside of cities. Maybe that's because we spent *so* much time living in cities ourselves, but you get to see and experience more when you leave the city.

INTERVIEW 18:
Brittany and Eric of RVWanderlust

Why did you hit the road? What are your goals, objectives, dreams, hopes?

For us, it became a "why not?" We both love to travel, and RVing seemed the most cost-effective and practical way to do it full-time.

We'd love to eventually hit all 48 continental states, but we're in no hurry. We've spent at least one night in 22 states so far. If we don't spend a night, then we don't count the state!

What have you learned that you wish you knew before you started?

We did a ton of research before we started, so our expectations were fairly in line with reality. Like pretty much everyone else, we were overeager to cover a lot of miles when we first started. That burned us out quickly. We went from traveling every Saturday, to moving every other Saturday. That gave us more time to relax, live "real life," and see each area. It really is not sustainable to play tourist all the time.

What do you miss about your old life? What did you think you'd miss that you don't?

We miss having a stable community, especially at our local church. I personally miss Austin a lot, our "home base" where we started our travels. From time to time, I also miss having a bathtub.

What do you like best about this life? What do you like least about this life? Describe a "day in your life."

In my opinion, the only downsides to full-time RVing are insignificant. It can be annoying to go into a grocery store and have no idea where things are.

There's hardly anything I don't love. Every day is an adventure when I step out my front door. When I step back in, it's home. I have everything I need here: the food I like in my fridge, my pillows, my books, my family. It's the best of both worlds.

We work every day from 7 a.m. to about noon. When Caspian, our baby, is awake, I take care of him and play with him. The afternoon is for exploring or running errands. Caspian goes to bed early, so we haven't been doing a lot at night since he was born, but that will change as he gets older.

How long after deciding to hit the road did it take for you to get your ducks in a row and actually hit the road?

We probably talked about RVing for a couple of years before we bought our RV and started traveling. We spent that time researching — reading online forums and blogs — and walking through tons of RVs to figure out what we wanted.

How does being a family/couple/single, affect you on the road? What issues do you have and how do you solve them?

Caspian has always lived in an RV! Because Eric and I had been living the RV life for three years, adding a baby was pretty seamless. We knew what to expect and planned accordingly. We've been very minimalistic when it comes to baby items and clothing.

The biggest issue is juggling his sleep schedule. When he naps in the bedroom during the day, we can't go in there. When it's time for him to move to his crib in the living room at night, we have to retire to the bedroom. It took some figuring out, but we have a good rhythm now.

If you were a homeowner, did you decide to sell or rent before hitting the road?

We purposely rented, because we knew this is what we wanted to do. We actually cancelled our lease before we even had an RV! We had to scramble to avoid homelessness, but we sort of did it on purpose. We knew we would be forced to make the lifestyle switch happen.

If you work, how do you accomplish this while being on the road? What are your challenges? How do you overcome them? What advice do you have for others?

We own a boutique online marketing company and work with small businesses. We started our company in January 2011, and built it up before we started RVing. Our long-term clients had learned to trust us, so they didn't have any issue with our travels. As long as we have an internet signal, we can do our work. We plan all of our stops ahead of time, to ensure we'll have connectivity. Eric is also retired military (he spent 20 years in the United States Coast Guard).

Full-time RVers Heath and Alyssa Padgett have developed some fabulous resources for working RVers. The RV Entrepreneur Podcast showcases people who are living and working on the road. Xscapers is also my top recommended membership program for working RVers. It's an arm of Escapees.

What rig did you choose? Why? What do you see as its advantages and disadvantages? If you had to do it over, would you pick the same rig? If not, why not and what would you pick?

We chose a used Class A diesel, and we would do it again if we could go back in time! Diesels are built for full-time travel. The heavy duty chassis can support the weight of possessions and sturdier building materials, like real tile and real wood. Gas models and trailers are typically full of flimsy material that can't withstand the wear and tear of full-time travel.

The downside to diesel is that it's most expensive to repair. But we plan ahead and it's not a huge deal.

How did you outfit your rig to meet your goals? Storage? Off-grid or On? Work? Play?

We haven't put a huge emphasis on being able to wild camp (also known as dry camping or boondocking), because our work schedule requires a lot of stability. Since it isn't a priority right now, we don't have solar and we haven't upgraded our batteries. Maybe we will with our next RV!

How do you manage your travel-companion relationships?

Eric and I are best friends and we genuinely never get sick of each other's company. We do things on our own from time to time. Eric loves off-roading with his Jeep, and I enjoy quiet reading time at local coffee shops. But we mostly do everything together, and prefer it that way.

How do you manage your relationships back home?

It does take work to maintain friendships when we're away. For our friends who have shown a desire to stay in touch, we love to do so. It takes two to make and keep a friendship, so we can only do our part.

Though we have had friendships quietly fade away since we've started traveling, we've also been able to reignite friendships by meeting up with old friends on the road, who we never would've been able to see otherwise.

How do you receive mail back home? How do you manage your bills? How do you receive mail on the road?

We have a box at a UPS Store in downtown Austin that we use for business and personal mail. They forward our mail to us whenever we ask them to. All of our regular bills are managed online.

Do you have kids with you? If so, how do you manage road schooling them? Any tips?

Eric and I have five kids together. Two are now grown, two are in high school in California, and Caspian is with us all the time. Caspian will be home schooled when he's old enough. I home schooled all the way through high school before attending The University of Texas at Austin, so I'm very comfortable with how it works and what to expect. There's also a huge community of families on the road now, and I look forward to building friendships with other parents and learning from them.

If you have pets with you, what tips do you have regarding pet management?

Until last year, we had two pets with us: a bearded dragon, and a feral cat who we rescued as a kitten in rural Kentucky. The bearded dragon passed away last year from old age. Rhythm, our cat, is easy to travel with. She hides under the sofa as soon as the RV engine comes on, and we don't see her again until the engine goes off! We are very careful about her getting out of the RV. Since we're always going to new places, she may have a hard time finding her way back to the RV if she ever gets lost.

Do you have any tips regarding money management?

One of the things we love about this lifestyle is how flexible our budget items are. If we ever had emergency expenses or lost a client, our spending on food, fuel, and lodging (campground fees) could all be scaled back. We chose not to get an extended warranty for our used diesel RV. Instead, we keep $5,000 in an emergency fund. We also have redundant roadside emergency memberships, with AAA and Good Sam. If we were to ever break down in the middle of nowhere, the towing costs could be exorbitant without these services.

What lessons do you have for others? Things to avoid and things to absolutely do?

RV your way. It's good to learn from others, but your journey is your own.

Slow down. If you move too quickly, you'll wear yourself out, and you'll miss the hidden gems.

We live by this saying: Never get so busy making a living that you forget to make a life. Our work doesn't define us. It's just a means to an end.

INTERVIEW 19:
Sunny and Karin of the Vagabroads

Why did you hit the road? What are your goals, objectives, dreams, hopes?

I decided to hit the road because we only live once. There is *so* much to see, and it is all so different than you can imagine sitting at home on the couch. I originally wanted to travel and find a place to settle down, but now after traveling this way, I just want to explore more. I don't know if I'll ever be content just being in one place.

What have you learned that you wish you knew before you started?

Everything. I've learned to not take a lot of clothes...it's better to buy them along the way. Also clothing will not last because things get torn, shrunk, stretched out, lost, etc. Also I've learned that you can go at your own pace, but if you like a place, be prepared to spend more time than you thought there.

What do you miss about your old life? What did you think you'd miss that you don't?

I miss consistently hot showers, my own washer and dryer, knowing where to get everything, Amazon, my friends, my family, having a consistent income, having space to relax.

What do you like best about this life? What do you like least about this life? Describe a "day in your life."

I love the adventure of getting to a new place and figuring things out. I also loathe having to always figure things out. It really all depends on how the day is going and if I like the place or not. I have loved having all the tropical fruit that is available everywhere. I love the markets and the randomness that comes with them.

A typical day on the road consists of waking up, fixing a papaya boat (papaya with mango, passion fruit and banana... Yum!), sometimes going to a gym in town, usually finding a market for more fruit and veggies, making sure we have enough clean water and if not then getting that, looking up a recipe for dinner and buying those ingredients, spending a few hours exploring and seeing the local sights, looking online for work, updating the website, working on whatever project I might be involved in (currently writing a book), and then cooking dinner. Usually there are drinks with new friends/"overlanders" once a week or so.

How long after deciding to hit the road did it take for you to get your ducks in a row and actually hit the road?

Six months.

How does being a family/couple/single, affect you on the road? What issues do you have and how do you solve them?

I get along with my partner really well. I am surprised that we haven't fought more, but we've both learned what is and isn't actually important on this trip, so that has helped a lot. Typically when we do fight, we just need a little bit of space from each other for a little while. Sometimes I will stay down in the car or go to the beach, and she will stay in the tent or vise versa. Knowing that space is a good thing on occasion is key. It helps to be around other people — friends, public places, human contact — to focus on outside of just the two of us.

If you were a homeowner, did you decide to sell or rent before hitting the road?

We decided to sell but looking back, we should've kept our house and rented it out. It was nice to have the money up front, but in the long run the investment in the house would've made more sense. I can say this mostly because our property value went up a lot while we were on the road...I might not feel the same way if that were not the case.

If you work, how do you accomplish this while being on the road? What are your challenges? How do you overcome them? What advice do you have for others?

Sunny:

I maintained my law firm back home where I am able to complete a small bit of remote work — document preparation, etc. The biggest challenges have been our "road schedule" — not having one, really, but being dictated by safe times to travel, weather, wifi. I try to get as much done as I can while in comfortable places. That may mean working 16 hours in one day, so that I don't need to worry for the next 3. My advice would be to schedule your work time and stick to it as closely as you can. It's okay to stay at a campsite for an extra day for the peace of mind of getting something accomplished or to get an Airbnb or hostel bed for a few days to ensure good wifi. The more money you make, the more sustainable this way of life becomes — it's about priorities.

Karen:

I think consistent internet would be somewhat of a problem if I could find some online work. Finding something that you could do while offline would be better...then you could upload your work when you do have good internet.

If you don't work, how do you support yourself on the road? What advice do you have for others?

We saved and used that money, plus the money from selling the house to support ourselves. I would recommend putting the money in a high-interest account before you go so you can make a little money on your money just sitting there.

What rig did you choose? Why? What do you see as its advantages and disadvantages? If you had to do it over, would you pick the same rig? If not, why not and what would you pick?

We chose a 1997 Toyota Landcruiser because it has solid axles and lockers. My main goal was to be able to get out of any situation if needed, and also not to break down. We had the top end of our engine rebuilt before we left the states just to make sure everything was tip top. I would pick our rig again, however, I wouldn't go with a rooftop tent. I miss having "indoor space." It would be nice to be able to cook, etc. inside versus in the tent if it's raining, etc. Even with our awning, it's still a task being outside all the time.

How did you outfit your rig to meet your goals? Storage? Off-grid or On? Work? Play?

It's about organization — you can never add enough compartments, drawers, shelves, to your rig. Open storage space is messy storage space. We took out the backseats and had a steel locking storage box built in its place. We have an ARB drawer system for our kitchen and clothing, a locking storage box with several compartments — oh, and packing cubes are the best thing ever. We have a refrigerator and two Duralast Platinum 31M batteries to power everything. We have a two-and-a-half lift, winch, Slee back gate, ARB front bumper, etc. You can see more on our website at vagabroads.com/our-build.

How do you manage your travel-companion relationships?

We do far better than we expected to do. We have to listen more closely to each other's needs, spoken and unspoken. The biggest gift we have is time with other people as well. Any time things are getting rocky, it really helps to hang out with others — break things up a bit.

How do you manage your relationships back home?

It's very difficult to do, but I find the more I update social media accounts, the more people at home feel connected to what we are doing. I try to talk to them as much as possible on Facebook or through text.

How do you receive mail back home? How do you manage your bills? How do you receive mail on the road?

I have mail sent to my old address, because my partner's mom bought our house. I pay all of my bills online.

Do you have kids with you? If so, how do you manage road schooling them? Any tips?

No.

If you have pets with you, what tips do you have regarding pet management?

We did a lot of planning and research as it relates to our dog but overall, it was easy. We just tried to keep in mind that the car would become a huge part of my dog's world — we made it as comfortable inside for her as possible — we gave her the things she would have had at home — nice bed, blanket, toys, good food whenever possible. And we planned a lot for weather contingencies. We put a remote starter on our car so that we could let the air conditioner run when we went places she could not go. We got her a heated mattress pad for cold nights. She is part of our team and needed to be treated as such.

Take plenty of flea meds and heart worm meds. Make sure you are aware of a good vet in each town, and don't forget that the expat Facebook pages are a great resource.

Do you have any tips regarding money management?

We have a variety of banks and credit cards. We transfer a small amount from a bigger account into the account that we have a card for. It has worked so far. Have some backup cards hidden somewhere. I think setting a daily budget is great and especially in the very beginning, sticking to it. Build up a surplus of your daily budget by going under, and then you can begin to just live your daily life more normally — including things like eating out and having some mojitos.

What lessons do you have for others? Things to avoid and things to absolutely do?

Familiarize yourself with the local laws...like seatbelt laws (if there are any), how to properly pay a ticket, etc. That way, if you get pulled over, then you will know what the right thing to do is.

Things to do...just try to say "yes" to every opportunity. This has been most rewarding for us.

Anything I'm forgetting?

Know that you can get most things on the road that you will need. However, if there is that favorite lip gloss, great pair of boots, perfect facial cleanser, etc. then bring a couple of them with you. We have a stock box that holds spares of things for when we run out. Don't listen to anyone that has not traveled by land to places you are going. Avoid being a jerk — say hi to everyone, stop being afraid of people around you, try to let go of expectations and roll with the day. Never turn down invitations — the best experiences come from them.

INTERVIEW 20:
Jeff and Coffee Fujita

Why did you hit the road? What are your goals, objectives, dreams, hopes?

Two things that really pushed and enabled us to hit the road: quadruple bypass heart surgery for me and an inheritance left by my parents upon their passing. The former made us realize our window of opportunity was closing and the latter allowed us to jump through the window. Life in Southern California was a soulless one, filled with constant obligations to the 40-hour plus work week and a sense of being lost in what I called "the fog of consumerism."...and to what end? A series of adventure documentaries, (Mile...Mile and a Half, 180 Degrees South, Long Way 'Round and Long Way Down) and one tailing behind a travel trailer, in a short time turned on the light bulb...and with that a newfound energy and purpose: to live a life of adventure. It took us only two months from the time we visited an Airstream dealer lot to driving out of our old neighborhood one last time — every day and night researching the internet to learn the basics of life on the road. Our goal was to exchange the paradigm that is formerly known as The American Dream (go to college, work a life-long career, buy a house) for a simpler, untethered life. We chose to accumulate experiences over material things...and full-timing in a travel trailer helps one discard the unnecessary.

What have you learned that you wish you knew before you started?

Nothing. The process of making the jump, while frustrating and demanding, should be cherished for that moment of departure is filled with a combination of joy, anxiety, relief, excitement, and even a tinge of fear that will never be repeated to the same degree. It is the stuff of adventure.

(Oh, one learned condition: We thought we could make it on $1,200/month by really living minimally. It could be done but for a couple to live a simple life comfortably with insurance, eating healthily, and a bit of traveling, it requires about $2,300/month.)

What do you miss about your old life? What did you think you'd miss that you don't?

Our friends and family...and that's it. We don't miss a schedule, a deadline, suburbia, materialism, congestion, industry, noise, and a blocked horizon.

What do you like best about this life? What do you like least about this life? Describe a "day in your life."

The freedom to choose when to work, where to work, and then the same with travel. I was college-educated but wanted to try the common-man jobs. So far we have worked as line cooks, motel maids, camp hosts, a tiny bit of carpentry, and a convenience store clerk. However, we must say the BEST thing we have experienced is making new friends, many of them who live outside our realm of experience...conservative, liberal, young, old, well-to-do, poor, hiker, hunter.

We have been very fortunate the last 2.5 years. The first year we stumbled into a camp hosting stint: 20 hours work in exchange for a beautiful site with full-hookups in a southern Utah state park for three months. The remainder of that year was spent traveling the western states, boondocking 75% of the time. The next year, we decided to remain in one our newfound favorite areas: Escalante and The Grand Staircase National Monument in southern Utah. The typical day of the first-year nomad was either total relaxation or exploration; every day was something new. The second year we spent seven months in a small town of 800 to really feel that small town life. The biggest realization of life on the road is that each new day's events are unwritten.

How long after deciding to hit the road did it take for you to get your ducks in a row and actually hit the road?

Two months of studying the internet, purchasing a used travel trailer and used tow vehicle, giving notice to employer, and saying good-bye.

How does being a family/couple/single, affect you on the road? What issues do you have and how do you solve them?

We learned early that the two truest pieces of advice for a couple was that each partner needed to be invested close to 50-50; any great skew of that percentage would eventually lead to failure; and that one of the partners would need to know how to cook. Photographs can lie on Instagram or Facebook; life together as couple 24/7 definitely has its challenges — there are bound to be arguments. Our dealer was very wise when he advised us to get our older 28-foot trailer over a newer 19-foot trailer...if we wanted to stay married. But square footage doesn't necessarily solve differences...it's the realization that we both needed each other, and that always came to both of us within a half a day.

If you were a homeowner, did you decide to sell or rent before hitting the road?

We inherited my parents' home and first we thought we should sell it to start our journey, but later, deciding to rent it, immediately paid dividends. A very reliable and experienced property manager led to a dream tenant, and that person unknowingly has been paying for our adventure. Definitely a win-win situation.

If you work, how do you accomplish this while being on the road? What are your challenges? How do you overcome them? What advice do you have for others?

We have camp hosted three winters in southern Utah at a state park; the area also is our medical base. It provides us with electricity, water, and sewage, and a relatively mild winter in exchange for 20 hours per week of cleaning camp sites. We get to work together, and it's relatively easy work, while enjoying being outside among red canyon walls. We have stumbled onto the other temporary jobs by talking with locals and staying long enough in an area to better know the community. There are plenty of online sources to find work, either the traditional minimum wage jobs or camp hosting in national parks. Even the most tedious jobs are manageable with the right attitude in trying something new and knowing one can move on at any time.

If you don't work, how do you support yourself on the road? What advice do you have for others?

Rent your property for passive income. Find a trustworthy property manager to deal with the headaches, such as repairs, and look for the electronic deposit each month. We find work to replace any extra expenditures and then move on with the seasons.

What rig did you choose? Why? What do you see as its advantages and disadvantages? If you had to do it over, would you pick the same rig? If not, why not and what would you pick?

We like to hike and fish, and after seeing the RV, trailer, and 5th wheel setups, we chose a 28-foot Airstream that was nine years old when purchased, and a two year old Toyota Tundra 4WD for the tow vehicle. We can explore much more with our 4WD truck but still have all the comforts of a tiny house with our Airstream. We are not big people and lived the apartment life our entire adult lives, so the move into a trailer was more lateral than say, a couple used to a large house. We have no regrets and would do it all over again with no changes. The size of our trailer has proved to be not too small and not too big.

How did you outfit your rig to meet your goals? Storage? Off-grid or On? Work? Play?

One of our first purchases was a 2000-watt Honda generator, which supplies all our needs, specifically our television monitor and LED interior lighting. We wanted 4WD for mountain roads. We purchased four freshwater containers and two gasoline containers. We hope to install solar panels some day, but we really haven't needed it since we boondock most of the time and our generator doesn't bother anyone in isolated areas. We only have hiking and fishing gear.

How do you manage your travel-companion relationships?

We listen to a lot of music, enjoy whole foods, and just know deep down, we really need each other. We go through the whole gamut of the couple relationship: shared laughter, very hard arguments, and the constant realization of just how lucky we are.

How do you manage your relationships back home?

Facebook, email, and phone calls.

How do you receive mail back home? How do you manage your bills? How do you receive mail on the road?

We made friends with our winter-location postman, and he forwards our mail as needed with our pre-paid envelopes. Bills? What bills? Okay, exaggerating there but bills are paid online.

Do you have kids with you? If so, how do you manage road schooling them? Any tips?

No.

If you have pets with you, what tips do you have regarding pet management?

None.

Do you have any tips regarding money management?

I do not micromanage our expenses and accounts, never did, and maybe that's perhaps why I never was a better saver. But life on the road is much more simple: fuel, propane, food, search for water, and the cell phone/data bucket bill.

What lessons do you have for others? Things to avoid and things to absolutely do?

The best lessons are the ones learned yourself. Full-timers are different in what they want out of their life on the road. Some want the company of others and others want the seclusion. Some want to stick to asphalt, others follow the dirt roads. I would say the best advice is to know one's limitations...but also to push them a bit. That's adventure.

Anything I'm forgetting?

The wallet. Always the wallet.

INTERVIEW 21:
Michael and Brenda

Why did you hit the road? What are your goals, objectives, dreams, hopes?

To see this beautiful country that I spent 22 years defending. Our goals are to see all 48 continental states, make lots of memories and friends.

What have you learned that you wish you knew before you started?

Should have started sooner. Living on the road is a never ending learning experience.

What do you miss about your old life? What did you think you'd miss that you don't?

Nothing is missed about the old life. There is less stress on the road. You live by your own schedule not someone else's.

What do you like best about this life? What do you like least about this life? Describe a "day in your life."

What I like the best is that I make my own schedule. I go when and where I want with no issues.

What I like the least is missing my friends and family back at our home-base. But we go back whenever we want.

How long after deciding to hit the road did it take for you to get your ducks in a row and actually hit the road?

About a year. The last six months was the most stressful and crazy. Trying to sell *everything;* deciding what to keep and not.

How does being a family/couple/single, affect you on the road? What issues do you have and how do you solve them?

It's my wife and me only. We are best friends and complement each other.

There are no issues yet, and I don't see any in the future.

If you were a homeowner, did you decide to sell or rent before hitting the road?

We sold. We plan to buy again when we have done all we want with the open-road lifestyle. We should know then, as well, the best places to settle back into a sticks and bricks home.

If you work, how do you accomplish this while being on the road? What are your challenges? How do you overcome them? What advice do you have for others?

I'm retired.

If you don't work, how do you support yourself on the road? What advice do you have for others?

I have retirement income, 401, social security, and disability income.

What rig did you choose? Why? What do you see as its advantages and disadvantages? If you had to do it over, would you pick the same rig? If not, why not and what would you pick?

We have a 2015 Winnebago Tour 42HD. We bought the Winnebago because of the quality of the product, affordability and class of layouts and detail.

We decided if we were going to do this, either go big or go home.

How did you outfit your rig to meet your goals? Storage? Off-grid or On? Work? Play?

Took factory installed pictures down and put up our own to give it a family touch.

It is a 42-foot tag axle RV with all the comforts of our old home.

How do you manage your travel-companion relationships?

It's no different than living in a house.

How do you manage your relationships back home?

We FaceTime with our daughters and grandkids on a regular basis.

How do you receive mail back home? How do you manage your bills? How do you receive mail on the road?

We have a P.O. Box for mail and have it forwarded to an upcoming stop while we're there.

Our bills are handled through online bill pay through our bank. Banking is done online and direct deposit, so money is just a click away.

Do you have kids with you? If so, how do you manage road schooling them? Any tips?

No kids — all grown and married.

If you have pets with you, what tips do you have regarding pet management?

One small service dog; well trained, very quiet and never leaves my side.

Do you have any tips regarding money management?

Build a budget and try to stick with it. Unexpected situations will occur. Just handle them when they arise and figure out your recovery plan afterwards. If it means boondocking for awhile — that doesn't cost you anything. Or staying longer where you're at until next payday. It's all workable and can easily be done.

What lessons do you have for others? Things to avoid and things to absolutely do?

Follow your dreams and the open road. Take advantage of any discounts or programs you can. Life is never a guarantee. Live it while you can.

Get to know your neighbors when you're in a RV park. Chances are pretty good you will run into them again down the road.

Living on the road is made up of extraverts who are always looking for more friends. It's a great life.

INTERVIEW 22:
Leslie and Eric of SunnyJunket

Why did you hit the road? What are your goals, objectives, dreams, hopes?

We hit the road for a simpler life and to get out from under mortgages and/or rent and to take on the challenge while enjoying our passion for travel.

What have you learned that you wish you knew before you started?

It has been a bit more difficult and stressful than anticipated.

What do you miss about your old life? What did you think you'd miss that you don't?

We lived close to our oldest son and we recently found out that we will be grandparents in the next seven months. I don't want to be far away from them!

What do you like best about this life? What do you like least about this life? Describe a "day in your life."

We love our lower cost of living! We don't have a typical day yet (this is our 2nd month). Eric just got a full-time job that will coordinate with our travels, but he does have to work "9-5" so we are adjusting to that. As much as we want to be completely carefree, we still need to make money but this life style will enable us to save more money.

How long after deciding to hit the road did it take for you to get your ducks in a row and actually hit the road?

Five to six months.

How does being a family/couple/single, affect you on the road? What issues do you have and how do you solve them?

We have our moments where we get mad at each other but we've been married over 32 years, so we know each other pretty well.

If you were a homeowner, did you decide to sell or rent before hitting the road?

We were renting. There was a time prior to 2008 when we owned two homes, and then we had a financial disaster which is part of our long story that ultimately led to this point!

If you work, how do you accomplish this while being on the road? What are your challenges? How do you overcome them? What advice do you have for others?

Eric recently, miraculously, got a full-time travel job. We are just learning about our challenges such as not going exactly where we want to go!

What rig did you choose? Why? What do you see as its advantages and disadvantages? If you had to do it over, would you pick the same rig? If not, why not and what would you pick?

We have an 18-foot vintage 1982 trailer. We wanted a small trailer so we can boondock and be more flexible than in a large rig. With a trailer we can leave it parked and we can go places in our car.

How did you outfit your rig to meet your goals? Storage? Off-grid or On? Work? Play?

We have been renovating to make it cute (very important!).

We are putting in a composting toilet. We also just purchased Mobley for internet in the car...not sure how that is going to work out.

How do you receive mail back home? How do you manage your bills? How do you receive mail on the road?

We will be using Eric's parent's address for some mail. Other bills are set up through email and paid online.

How do you manage your relationships back home?

Phone, text.

INTERVIEW 23:
Dawn L

Why did you hit the road? What are your goals, objectives, dreams, hopes?

I'm retired and wanted to see the country. I'm a hospice nurse and noted that what people regret the most is what they didn't do; I wanted to not have that regret.

What do you like best about this life? What do you like least about this life? Describe a "day in your life."

Totally enjoy the freedom and the meeting of other people. At present don't have a lot of dislikes. It's all pretty new.

How long after deciding to hit the road did it take for you to get your ducks in a row and actually hit the road?

About six months.

How does being a family/couple/single, affect you on the road? What issues do you have and how do you solve them?

We started in a travel trailer. We found it was just a tad too much togetherness. The fifth wheel is just right.

If you don't work, how do you support yourself on the road? What advice do you have for others?

We both get social security. My husband has a Navy pension and this helps. We actually stay on a lot of bases, the campgrounds are beautiful, and they are usually very nice.

What rig did you choose? Why? What do you see as its advantages and disadvantages? If you had to do it over, would you pick the same rig? If not, why not and what would you pick?

We have a 2001 Montana fifth wheel. We love it. I sometimes wish we went with a Class A or C but think I really like the room we get in the fifth wheel.

How did you outfit your rig to meet your goals? Storage? Off-grid or On? Work? Play?

We have two batteries and two generators.

How do you manage your travel-companion relationships?

Same way we have for the past 45 years.

How do you manage your relationships back home?

Same way we have for the past 45 years.

Do you have any tips regarding money management?

Boondock, eat in when possible, spend time with family.

What lessons do you have for others? Things to avoid and things to absolutely do?

Know you will make mistakes; learn from them.

INTERVIEW 24:
Michael and Loida

Why did you hit the road? What are your goals, objectives, dreams, hopes?

My first wife died, and I decided that rather than maintain a house, I would buy an RV and travel. My work as a software designer allows me to work remotely. I hoped to see more of this country. Then I met my current wife, who always dreamed of traveling.

What have you learned that you wish you knew before you started?

RV maintenance requires more money than I thought. I might have liked a tow vehicle that seats more than two people. In any case, I highly recommend a tow vehicle.

What do you miss about your old life? What did you think you'd miss that you don't?

I miss friends from my old community. That's what I thought [I'd miss]; people are more important than places. I didn't expect much, and I now have a new wife and traveling companion. We enjoy parks and mission work together.

What do you like best about this life? What do you like least about this life? Describe a "day in your life."

The ability to travel and move about as I want. It can be a hassle to find an affordable parking location. On the road, we try to get out and explore nature, state and national parks. Some days I spend working in the RV on a computer. Loida, my wife, brings a sewing machine and looks for new projects when I work.

How long after deciding to hit the road did it take for you to get your ducks in a row and actually hit the road?

About four months to move into the RV, then another five months to sell the house. Loida took five months to consolidate her house and have one of her sons move in. We now have a bedroom at the house when we need it.

How does being a family/couple/single, affect you on the road? What issues do you have and how do you solve them?

We travel well together. We're conflicted about being near family, especially around holidays, and the desire to travel. My new wife has young grandchildren; I have elderly parents. We are learning to balance our time.

If you were a homeowner, did you decide to sell or rent before hitting the road?

I decided to sell; I couldn't support the RV and a house. I would rather travel while I can.

If you work, how do you accomplish this while being on the road? What are your challenges? How do you overcome them? What advice do you have for others?

I work remotely on web-based software. The challenge is keeping a reliable connection to the internet. I have used services from SinglePoint but am on the lookout for more bandwidth at a better price.

If you don't work, how do you support yourself on the road? What advice do you have for others?

I am semi-retired, so social security helps. My wife took social security early when she retired, so we could travel. We are looking at other options to supplement our income.

What rig did you choose? Why? What do you see as its advantages and disadvantages? If you had to do it over, would you pick the same rig? If not, why not and what would you pick?

It is a Class A motor home by Tiffin, 35-foot-long front engine diesel. It's almost nine years old, so we don't have all the latest technical gadgets. It is a good size for two people. The price was right.

How did you outfit your rig to meet your goals? Storage? Off-grid or On? Work? Play?

The biggest need was the internet. Storage is pretty good; in fact, we probably have too much and need to remove some things to better control weight.

How do you manage your travel-companion relationships?

In general, we travel well together. We have been married for a year and two months. We traveled a good bit in the RV and made four overseas trips. Three were faith-based mission trips. The other was a honeymoon cruise. Our faith brought us together, so we turn to God to help us through the rough spots.

How do you manage your relationships back home?

We call, text, post pictures on Facebook and send post cards. This is important for the grand kids. Our immediate families are all in the same metro area, so visits can be managed.

How do you receive mail back home? How do you manage your bills? How do you receive mail on the road?

My mail goes to a PMB in South Dakota. My wife's son lives in the family home, so she still gets mail there. All the bills are handled on the

Internet. A few magazines go to family members, who get to read them first.

Do you have kids with you? If so, how do you manage road schooling them? Any tips?

None that travel with us. All our kids are over 21, someday we might bring the grand kids on a trip.

If you have pets with you, what tips do you have regarding pet management?

No pets for us. I never had any so I don't miss them.

Do you have any tips regarding money management?

Try to eat in whenever possible. Keep a budget but allow for splurges. Travel while you have your health and can enjoy it.

What lessons do you have for others? Things to avoid and things to absolutely do?

Travel often, get out even for short trips and enjoy the world around you. Don't be shy about parking at Walmart, most are welcoming.

Anything I'm forgetting?

We have disconnected from most TV, just couldn't justify the cost for the latest technology. Do use cable service at parks from time to time. Take good care of the waste and water tanks.

Note: I asked Michael this personal question, and here is the question and answer. Question: "I've heard people use the excuse of not wanting to leave their congregation as a reason for not pursuing this lifestyle. How do you and Loida address that in your lives?"

That is a consideration for sure. Very much like leaving family behind. In this day and age, there are ways to stay in touch. There are also opportunities to serve in a town or on the road. Two of our three mission trips have been with our former congregations. We are welcomed at my church outside Atlanta and at Loida's in Baytown. When we are in town, we attend services and volunteer as we can. On the road, we look for local churches to drop in on. If you want consistency, then local ties are strong and hard to break. When the desire to travel is strong enough, then you are ready to make the change. For us, it was the desire to travel and see the country that won. The stronger pull than the church is her grandchildren.

INTERVIEW 25:
Mandy J

Why did you hit the road? What are your goals, objectives, dreams, hopes?

I love to travel. My significant other and I have Harley motorcycles, and we love to explore new places.

What have you learned that you wish you knew before you started?

Wish we had a better idea of what we needed in RV — a checklist is a necessity!

What do you miss about your old life? What did you think you'd miss that you don't?

I miss routine and my home.

What do you like best about this life? What do you like least about this life? Describe a "day in your life."

I like the freedom and the ability to see new places and make new friends.

I dislike the confinement of a camper and the closeness of RVs in a park.

Day in my life: Morning coffee outside if possible, catch up on news, decide where to ride to, take a long motorcycle ride with lunch, clean and take care of bikes, read, grill supper outside, visit with neighbors, watch TV, then go to bed.

How long after deciding to hit the road did it take for you to get your ducks in a row and actually hit the road?

Not long.

How does being a family/couple/single, affect you on the road? What issues do you have and how do you solve them?

We are a couple and share the work. I don't think we have any issues.

If you were a homeowner, did you decide to sell or rent before hitting the road?

Still have home.

If you work, how do you accomplish this while being on the road? What are your challenges? How do you overcome them? What advice do you have for others?

I work very part time, all through online. The challenge is to set aside time and schedule work time. My advice is to set up work area to suit your needs, and try it out before going on road.

If you don't work, how do you support yourself on the road? What advice do you have for others?

Retired.

What rig did you choose? Why? What do you see as its advantages and disadvantages? If you had to do it over, would you pick the same rig? If not, why not and what would you pick?

We have a fifth wheel toy hauler (40 feet). The advantage is it can haul bikes, and there is more room when bikes are unloaded.

I probably would not pick this one, but I got too good a deal from friends to pass it up. Once you have had an extended stay in a camper, you realize more what you need.

How did you outfit your rig to meet your goals? Storage? Off-grid or On? Work? Play?

We have a portable computer set up that can be put away when not in use. We turned the overhead loft bed into storage. We replaced the fold out bed in living area with a reclining love seat.

How do you manage your travel-companion relationships?

Patience and good communication.

How do you manage your relationships back home?

Facebook. Messaging. Facetime.

How do you receive mail back home? How do you manage your bills? How do you receive mail on the road?

We have a family member pick up mail and forward what is necessary to where ever we are.

All bills are online.

Do you have any tips regarding money management?

Budget, budget, budget and stick to it.

What lessons do you have for others? Things to avoid and things to absolutely do?

Be flexible.

Maintain your rig.

Use surge protectors.

Have fun, and don't sweat the small stuff!

INTERVIEW 26:
Steve K

Why did you hit the road? What are your goals, objectives, dreams, hopes?

I'm not on the road full-time yet but working toward it. I have dreamed of full-timing since I was a child. My parents loved camping and could never afford more than a tent, but we always had wonderful vacations. As soon as I could afford an RV, I was off with my parents. I have tried every new and larger RV, wishing my father was still here to see the new motorhome. There is so much of the country to see, and RV people are the "kind" of people I find myself wanting to be around. My goal is to be commitment free and financially stable to choose my travels and destinations. It feels good to be getting closer.

What have you learned that you wish you knew before you started?

The more money you spend on an RV does NOT mean you will have any less maintenance issues — and maybe even more — than a smaller, less expensive RV. The new coaches have so much more technology and gadgets and so many more chances for things to go wrong. I always laughed that they were "money pits," and you had to be prepared for that, but in reality it can get really frustrating. I have spent the last two years in a high-end RV and spent a great deal of time listening to fellow high-end coach owners tell their stories of maintenance nightmares. You need to be prepared to spend down time while repairs are being made and have a contingency plan in place.

What do you miss about your old life? What did you think you'd miss that you don't?

I always thought I would miss my family and friends more as I traveled more often, but I don't. You make new friends on the road, and you have more things to talk about with your friends and family when you visit them.

I think I *will* miss the stability of a traditional home. I think I will need a small "home base" somewhere where I will have an option to be out of the RV for a period of time.

What do you like best about this life? What do you like least about this life? Describe a "day in your life."

Best part of the RV life for me is the "my" things when traveling. I'm still using *my* bathroom, sleeping in *my* bed, having *my* coffee — just in a different location all the time. I hate packing suitcases, and even though I still need to fly a great deal, I'm beginning to dislike airports. The RV travel to me is so much less complicated and I love being on *my* schedule — not an airline or housekeeping/check-in/check-out schedule.

The only thing I can think of that I like least about RV travel is the other people on the road!

My favorite days are waking up to sunshine, a palm tree, and water. A nice relaxed morning having coffee, reading an online newspaper, Facebooking, and emails and then a slow bike ride around the campground. Finding new restaurants and shopping in the afternoon, and a relaxed evening by a campfire, are high on my list.

How long after deciding to hit the road did it take for you to get your ducks in a row and actually hit the road?

56 years — seriously — I'm still working on it!

I would not want to enter into this lifestyle in a hurry. It has taken my whole life to learn from experienced RVers. I have had four RVS (each one a little bigger and better) since the age of 30 and am still working with financial advisors to plan a healthy retirement.

Workamping is always an option, but I would prefer that to be an option, not a necessity.

How does being a family/ couple/ single, affect you on the road? What issues do you have and how do you solve them?

I am so fortunate that my partner (husband in six weeks) has taken to the lifestyle with me. We have been together 12 years, and some of our favorite times together have been in our RV. He asked me to marry him in front of the coach on the water in the Florida Keys at one of our favorite RV resorts. We are actually amazed how much we still enjoy being together in a smaller place and even spend time in the RV when we are home. Issues are: he isn't comfortable driving a 45-foot coach towing a car down the highway, so I need to do almost all the driving. He is also younger than me, and at the height of his career, so not ready to full-time yet.

One of my fears was always that I wouldn't be able to find someone that appreciates this lifestyle as much as I do.

I have friends that bought a motorhome with the thought of full-timing in retirement, and when they got to that point, she just didn't like it — he was heartbroken.

If you were a homeowner, did you decide to sell or rent before hitting the road?

Still own our home, a log home on 10 acres. We have just begun discussing future plans for the house when we are on the road longer. It is difficult to try to maintain both, especially of this size. I think I will still always need a home somewhere, or a rented condo space, and we will probably sell this home.

If you work, how do you accomplish this while being on the road? What are your challenges? How do you overcome them? What advice do you have for others?

I am an Administrator of a family-owned medical practice. With today's technology and electronic medical record systems, I am able to mange my office from anywhere in the world where I have internet access and have done this for the last three years. The challenge is just having to plan very well in advance, and nothing is guaranteed to be smooth. You must have a good support team behind you.

If you don't work, how do you support yourself on the road? What advice do you have for others?

I have always thought I would work through Workamper or some similar service if I had to make money on the road. Every RV resort needs help and many rely on full- or part-time RVers to fill those needs. Amazon now even has a huge RVer workforce for temporary help at different times of the year.

What rig did you choose? Why? What do you see as its advantages and disadvantages? If you had to do it over, would you pick the same rig? If not, why not and what would you pick?

Our current RV is a 2015 Entegra Coach Anthem 45-foot. Other than an awful lot of maintenance issues we absolutely love it. We chose this particular coach for its floor plan and power. We tailgate at sporting events and this was an ideal coach for entertaining and dry camping for an extended period of time. The ride and handling is exceptional. The engine is one of the quietest on the market. It is a joy to drive.

How did you outfit your rig to meet your goals? Storage? Off-grid or On? Work? Play?

We added more electrical outlets and more circuits to the outside entertaining area for catering. We had power slide trays installed in the storage bays. We bought NuWave induction cooking units to add to the outdoor cooking options.

How do you manage your travel-companion relationships?

Patience, understanding, and lots of communication! Spend time traveling to places of interest that you both like and take turns suggesting the next destination.

How do you manage your relationships back home?

Texting, emails, and whatsapp.

How do you receive mail back home? How do you manage your bills? How do you receive mail on the road?

Most bills and banking can be managed online. Regular publications can be subscribed to online. Most postal service mail can be minimized to junk mail. Our post office will hold mail for 30 days. Have not used an mail forwarding service yet.

Do you have kids with you? If so, how do you manage road schooling them? Any tips?

No children.

If you have pets with you, what tips do you have regarding pet management?

No current pets, however we have traveled with dogs and cats in the past. My biggest worry was always a power loss when we wouldn't be in the coach and then there wouldn't be air conditioning; however, many of the newer coaches have a "smart" electrical system that will automatically turn on the generator if the power is out for any period of time. I have to admit — as much as I loved my pets — it is so much easier traveling without them.

Do you have any tips regarding money management?

Set a realistic budget based on your financial abilities. Sometimes I just enjoy staying in a Flying J truck stop while we are traveling — it's free. Not every campground has to have a resort-type environment. Save the money for special destinations.

What lessons do you have for others? Things to avoid and things to absolutely do?

Talk to every full-time RVer you can find and *listen* to their advice and experiences. Fellow RVers are the best source of information and usually more than willing to spend time telling you of their adventures. Find a reputable RV dealer that stands behind their product. Find the factory location of your RV and visit the facility on one of your trips. Look for ways to deal with the stress that *will* happen when your RV breaks down or anything goes wrong. Accept the fact that it is *going to* happen. Enjoy being flexible because you have thought of a plan in advance.

Anything I'm forgetting?

Be thankful every day that you have the opportunity of this lifestyle, for the beauty of the country you are seeing, and for the many, many different types of people you will meet in your travels.

360-424-
1320

Made in the USA
Middletown, DE
10 March 2018